The Dissenting Feminist Academy

American University Studies

Series XI
Anthropology and Sociology

Vol. 9

PETER LANG
New York · Bern · Frankfurt am Main · Paris

The Age of Global Transformations:
the Human Dimension

INSTITUTE FOR WORLD ECONOMICS

The Age of Global Transformations: the Human Dimension

by Mihály Simai

AKADÉMIAI KIADÓ, BUDAPEST

Published by Akadémiai Kiadó
P. O. Box 245, H-1519 Budapest, Hungary
www.akkrt.hu

ISBN 963 05 7818 2

Printed in Hungary

CONTENTS

FOREWORD

This book is the result of a research project in the frame of the Institute for World Economics on the different aspects of gloablisation. The volume is focussing on the human dimensions of transformation in the early years of the 21st century. In every couple of centuries of human history, at least of the Western world, there was a comprehensive radical socio-economic change characterised as transformation with profound influence on political, economic and social structures. New interests and values emerged, institutions were replaced, relations rearranged. Much has been written over the years on transformations. At the beginning of the 21st century there is however a rare coincidence of profound transformations in a number of areas, in population dynamics, in human settlements in science and technology, economics, social structures, in the role and functions of the states and in the global power structure. These processes are interrelated and have a major influence on people, on the different countries and on international relations. In my research work, I drew the attention already during the 1970s to the fact that epoch-making changes started in the global system, with far-reaching consequences. My book on the "Future of Global Governance" published in 1994 offered a comprehensive analysis of those changes (Simai, 1994). The ongoing research programme of the Institute for World Economics of the Hungarian Academy of Sciences on globalisation is a continuation of that study. It places the transformations in a broad interdisciplinary context in a world, which is more like a great Tower of Babel than a global village. Political, economic and social conditions vary immensely throughout the world, influenced by the size, natural endowments, development level, economic structure, political and institutional patterns, and competitiveness of countries. Among the external factors the global (or regional) regulatory framework influencing the relationships between the participants in the act of exchange, the degree of competitiveness, the role of oligopoly or monopoly, the degree and the character of the fusion or interconnectedness of the markets for goods, capital, services and labour, are some of the most important. These factors are not constant, and their variations (fluctuations) reflect the diversity of the market system on the one hand, and on the other transforming place and role of the countries in the global markets as price takers or price markers. The impact of the external political and economic environment may contain favourable and hostile factors for every country.

There are enormous differences among countries and regions also in the human dimension of changes, with major divisions between the developing and developed countries of the world's population that has doubled since 1960, to 6.1 billion, most of that growth occurring in developing countries. Since 1970, consumption has doubled, 86 per cent of which realised in the developed world. Human beings collectively consume six times as much water as did 70 years ago, dangerously depleting local aquifers. Deforestation, pollution and emissions of carbon dioxide have reached unprecedented levels, altering the global climate. The "ecological footprints" of human beings on the earth are heavier than ever before.

The systemic transformation of the former Socialist countries is an important component of the ongoing changes. It is influenced by them and influencing them. The systemic changes represented the first case when a democratic, political, and market-based capitatlist economic system has to be built from "above" by political initiatives and instruments in a large group of countries. The role of the state had to be transformed. They had to initiate profound structural changes in income distribution. New administrative structures had to be built within some countries, which were the successors of disintegrated states. The tasks had to be implemented rapidly, and at the same time they had to initiate measures related to their participation in the global markets as market economies. They had to start large-scale ecological rehabilitation.

The book is analysing the different dimensions of transformations in an interdependent and interdisciplinary framework, looking at their political, sociological and economic aspects. Its conclusions emphasise the fact that the institutional capacity of countries to collectively apprehend and manage factors of risks to the environment, economic development, trade, capital flows, and of poverty is outdated and needs to be adjusted to respond to new global realities in the interest of sustainable human development. In some particular areas, however, like in the case of environmental dangers, the complex nature of the tasks is better understood, and the interests, values, and goals more clearly articulated. Consequently, international mechanisms are being reviewed in a more realistic way for problem identification and management, with the aim of improving the odds for their solution. In the longer run much depends on whether the outcome of co-operation is satisfying the needs and interests of the states and improving the welfare of their people. Historical comparisons of transformations from the perspectives of the countries proved that "success stories" were dependent on a number of factors including long-term policies (for example, the development of human capabilities, infrastructure building, etc.), short-term components, including luck and sound macroeconomic management, and the favourable international sources of growth, including efficient international co-operation. There have been also many specific factors involved in the failures; a politically divided population, mismanagement, weak institutions, a hostile global environment, and disintegrating governments.

I express my thanks to Prof. Dan Puchala, Roger Coat of the University of South Carolina, prof. Thomas Weiss of New York City University, to Prof. Takashi Inoguchi of Tokyo University, to Mr. Jerome Glenn, Director of the United Nations University Millennium programme for their critical remarks and suggestions, and to the Hungarian Academy of Sciences for supporting the research programme on Global Transformations and Sustainable Development. I am also grateful for the help provided by the linguistic editor, Mr. Brian McLean.

INTRODUCTION
THE ERA OF TRANSITIONS AND TRANSFORMATIONS

Scholars, particularly social scientists, usually agree that terms such as the turn of the century or the new millennium make artificial milestones, but they are strongly tempted to use them when presenting the changing trends. The end of the 20th century and the beginning of the 21st (at least according to the Christian calendar) have brought a rare coincidence of changes. The beginning of the Third Millennium has given inspiration not only to the usual professional clairvoyants and pundits, but to the leaders of major states, of the Christian churches, the academic community and the UN system. However, the calendar was not the only factor behind this. Some important changes have been evolving in a number of areas of global development, including population trends, politics, economics, technology and the environment. The world has entered an era of various transitions and transformations. It is too early to formulate a scientifically sound answer to the question of how the combined, cumulative influence of these changes will transform the globe. Different forces, hierarchies and interdependencies influence and shape the changes in an extremely complex global system and set of subsystems. They are rooted in the economic, social, political and cultural heritage of the 20th century and are interconnected with the evolving new regulating forces. Some of the historians suggested that the 19th century ended in 1914 or even later in the 20th century. The past century will be also with the world for some time. Its legacy will be present in many processes and problems. Changes unprecedented in former human history were condensed in the 20th century, which transformed the globe. It was an era of violent nationalism and of internationalism, presented under different banners. It witnessed the worst dictatorships in human history and some unprecedented accretions to freedom and democracy.[1]

---

[1] In 1900 democracy was scarce. Only in six countries out of the 50, recognised as sovereign state, had something similar and even there the suffrage was limited. Discrimination based on gender or on other factors was more or less general even in these countries. The real democratic transformation started after 1945.

The course of the 20th century was punctuated by revolutions and counter-revolutions, world wars, wars of national liberation and ethnic conflicts. About 170 million people were killed during the century in these wars and by government actions. Some of the great political changes of the 20th century included the end of colonialism and legally sanctioned racism, the progress of political, social and economic rights for women. Cultural changes influenced politics, technology, law, institutions and values. Outstanding statesmen, people of goodwill and vision, contributors to civil society who preached human solidarity and compassion, alongside bigoted fundamentalists and merciless dictators, terrorists and organised criminals were the main actors on the stage of the past century. Nine-tenths of the scholars and scientists who lived and worked in human history were concentrated in the past century. They helped to shape and develop the rapid progress of science and technology, embodied in new products, processes, consumer goods and ghastly weapon systems. Throughout the century "brain power" replaced gradually "material power". In 1900 agriculture, forestry and fishing occupied a large place even in the industrial countries both in output and employment. By the end of the century mechanised farming and new agricultural technology were spreading even in the less developed parts of the world industry. New branches emerged and industrial service blocks dominate the "post-industrial" age. The past hundred years saw on the one hand the raise and decline of the welfare state, radical improvements in the quality of life, and on the other, mass poverty and misery. Mass consumption stimulated by mass advertising through mass communication by radio, television and the Internet. It embodied both expectations and disillusionment and despair. The ecosystem and the ecological conditions of development deteriorated, but if the population of the globe, which more than trebled produced and consumed goods in the same way as in 1900 or 50 years later, the world would be much more toxic and dangerous place to live in.

The focus of this study is the human dimension of transformations in the global system and its political, economic, and ecological subsystems and the different outcomes: the major global trends and changes shaping the world order and the new "human condition" of the world in the 1990s and in the early part of the 21st century. In the global system, change takes many forms: regular and irregular, predictable and unpredictable, evolutionary and unsteady, linear and non-linear, cyclical and non-cyclical. On the global level, change is always multifaceted. The global system also contains elements of progress, decline, and retrogression that affect not only states but also groups of states, corporations, and international organisations. Some of these actors have been more astute than others, in adapting themselves to a dynamic environment. But, when actors adapt to their institutions as required by systemic change, does the old order simply vanish?

Transitional periods in the past have engendered uncertainty and tension; in those regions of the world most adversely affected by change, wars have erupted and nations have strategically realigned. Not surprisingly, patterns of transition differ according to the diversity of historical actors and forces.

To what extent have the global changes, which have occurred especially at the end of the 1980s and the 1990s, paralleled earlier historical patterns, and what are the distinguishing features of these changes?

From among the main differences compared to the past, the most important is the depth and multifaceted character of change.

A key political element of this change has been the collapse of the Soviet Union, the last great empire of the modern age. The decline of the great empires of the last half millennium has been protracted. It began with the collapse of the Spanish Empire, which was followed by the successive disintegration of the Ottoman, Austro-Hungarian, and German empires. After World War II, all other great empires disappeared except for the Russian empire, the greatest continental empire of modern history. Although the Russian empire had transformed itself into the Union of Soviet Socialist Republics with the declared aim of creating an international community based on political and economic equity, the Soviet state simply revitalised the geo-strategic structure and goals of the Russian empire. Ultimately, this empire was liquidated by internal forces – by nationalism, anti-communism, and popular dissatisfaction with the state's inability to solve the basic needs and problems of the Soviet Union.

One result of imperial collapse has been an increase in the number of sovereign states, all of them patterned more or less along the lines of the European state structure. The current number of states is greater by far than at any other time in modern history, and it is still increasing. Between 1816 and 1946, 52 states were created and 23 destroyed. At the turn of the century, there were 50 states in the world, with only 26 of these being represented at the 1899 Hague Peace Conference. At the second Hague Peace Conference in 1907, 44 states were represented. Following World War I, 10 to 12 new states were either established or had their frontiers redefined. By the end of 1945, there were 63 states in the world. With the disintegration of the British, French, Belgian, Dutch, and Portuguese empires in the post-World War II period, 80 new states came to existence. The dissolution of the Soviet Union further enlarged the ranks of independent states. By the end of the 21st century, the number of states may be much greater.

The disintegration of the Soviet Union has also ended an era of political and military bipolarity, closing the book on Cold War alliances, proxy wars, and the magnitude of the nuclear threat known in the period of mutually assured destruction. At the same time, this disintegration has brought about the partial collapse of Europe's political structure as established by the Allies at Yalta and Potsdam in 1945. The central element of this structural break-down has been the unification of Germany. There have also been changes – most notably, the fragmentation of Yugoslavia and Czechoslovakia – in the peace regime established by the Versailles treaties after World War I. These changes and the multiplicity of ethnic and small-state conflicts they bring in their wake pose new challenges not only for European security but also for the global security system as established within the framework of the United Nations.

The transitions from the imperial order of the 19th and 20th centuries to the era of U.S. economic hegemony and U.S.–Soviet bipolarism is significantly different from the present post-Cold War transition to hierarchical multipolarity. At the top of the hierarchy is the United States. The other major powers occupying various ascendant positions in one or another area are Western Europe, Japan, Russia, and China. Although some experts presume certain similarities in the transition processes from one power structure to another, the present transition period will likely exhibit more dissimilarities with other such periods.

Professor Ralph Buultjens suggested the following cyclical sequence for the 20th century:

First: Serious disputes between the major powers lead to a large and prolonged conflict, which destroys a large number of people.

Second: After an intense and costly struggle, the conflict is won by the power and powers which espouse values of freedom and liberty. This arouses high expectations that a new era of democracy has dawned. The victors establish or revive international peace-keeping institutions to prevent another catastrophe.

Third: Victory also results in the creation or redefinition of several small and medium states – entities which proclaim their commitment to sustain freedom and often embrace democracy.

Fourth: Despite initial efforts, these states are unable to maintain democracy and many soon lapse into types of authoritarianism. International peace-keeping structures prove ineffective.

Finally: The new states develop internal conflicts, engage in conflicts between themselves, or become adjuncts in big, fresh conflicts between major powers.[2]

---

[2] Ralph Buultjens, "The Destiny of Freedom: Political Cycles in the Twentieth Century". *Ethics & International Affairs*, vol. 6 (1992), p. 58.

This sequence expresses a widely shared pessimistic view about the present. Even though nothing can be completely excluded regarding patterns of post-Cold War events, Buultjen's cyclical scenario is much less probable now than earlier in this century. Buultjen's scenario assumes major powers challenging the status quo and preparing to engage in succession wars, which is not the case in this era.

The multidimensional complexity of the transitional phase is of critical interest to social science. This is the uncertain period between the old and new systems, during which factors of each intermingle and compete, eventually producing change in the global order. Here, there is an interplay of a wide range of factors – geo-strategic, environmental, anthropological, political, economic, social, technical, and organisational. A study dealing with the human dimensions of global transformations must cover a great variety of problems but cannot be equally comprehensive in all issue areas. Hence, the focus of this book is on those problems which are critically important and require or influence collective actions. A "non-conventional" systems theory framework is employed because it seems the most relevant of competing theories for the analysis and synthesis of the interactions among the primary global actors and of important processes and their anticipated outcomes.

A system can be defined as the entirety of interactions and interdependencies among groups or items within a specified structure or framework. Naturally, different structures can be characterised as systems, and different theories seek to explain, describe, or quantify the intensity and nature of interactions, sources of change, and consequences of transformations within specific systems. Analysts of specific systems usually try to insulate a part of the empirical world against the randomness of the rest of that world. General system theory (or theories) deals with those problems that characterise all systems: equilibria and disequilibria, regularities and irregularities, sources and consequences of turbulence, and so forth. The systems have been created, influenced and transformed by human beings. They are exposed to the turbulence and conflicts in the systems as winners, losers or by-standers.

The global system encompasses the entirety of relationships among those actors that influence processes and changes beyond national frontiers. Operating in a structure characterised by the existence of states, these actors inevitably include the states themselves. Other important actors are inter-governmental organisations assigned of the responsibility of managing destabilising forces and risks, as well as certain non-governmental institutions and organisations, like transnational corporations. A great number of relations have developed among these different actors in a wide variety of fields. Some of these relations are integrative; others can lead to disintegration and fragmentation.[3] Both have major influence on people and their communities.

Further, the global system is, by its nature, embedded with social, ideological, and cultural structures. The role of social formations in systemic processes is especially important, because it influences virtually all of the system's components. In economic terms, social formations are defined as the structures of property, motivation, information, and institutions – all structures through which power is concentrated, diffused, and transferred.

For political, economic, and ideological reasons, nation-states have developed according to different societal formations. Freedom, democracy, particular moral principles, and pragmatic optimism, together with certain elements of social-Darwinism, were key to forming the societal structure of the United States. The tsarist institutional heritage of Russia, combined with a utopian communist ideology, in a semi-developed economic environment, had a major impact on the early social formation of the Soviet Union. China developed on the basis of cultural and social traditions over thousands of years, interwoven with major experiments in modernisation, either ideological, administrative, or economic. The process of social formation and transformation manifests great variety, flexibility, and adaptability, and represents a dynamic factor in the global system.

While the global system is constantly undergoing change, the amount and rate of change within its subsystems varies. The international political system, the world economic system, and the ecosystem form the global system with its curious dynamics, synergies, and integration and disintegration processes. A "subsystem" is an autonomous system having unique attributes that determine a certain logic to be followed by the actors and regulating forces within its parameters. However, all subsystems – political, economic, and ecological – have a few important common characteristics, like the mul-

---

[3] There are many different understandings of the "global," "world," or "international," system. For instance, Wallerstein has posited its foundation in the capitalist world economy, whereas Ougaard has emphasised the system's connection to social formations. See George Sorensen, "A Revised Paradigm for International Relations: The 'Old' Images and the Postmodernist Challenge." *Cooperation and Conflict* 26 (1991), pp. 85–116.

A more comprehensive definition is offered by Stanley Hoffman: The world system today is … a complex game played at three levels: a world economy that creates its own rewards and punishments and provides both opportunities and constraints for the players (not all of whom are states); the states themselves; and increasingly, the peoples who intervene insofar as they are unhappy with the effects, inequalities and inefficiencies of the world market, or with the inadequacy of established borders or with the nature of their governments.

See Stanley Hoffman, "Balance, Concert, Anarchy, or None of the Above." In Gregory F. Treverton (ed.) *The Shape of the New Europe* (New York: Council on Foreign Relations, 1991), p. 196.

tiplicity of the actors, the complex character of their interdependence and interactions and the often contrasting nature of individual and common interests. Another common feature is that change and disequilibrium determine their processes. The quantity and rate of change in subsystems may become a world-wide source of conflict, especially when reacted to differently by the world's various regions.

The international political system is a multilevel structure. At its base it represents the totality of relations among states. These relations are characterised by power politics, interdependence, and diplomatic and military relations in peace and war.

Relations between states and the non-state actors of the system are conditioned by several factors. Among these, domestic political motivations play a crucial role. Indeed, the international political system is broadly inclusive of domestic political structures, processes, and institutions, in addition to various relations between states and non-state actors. After all, domestic factors define the quantity of national resources that can be devoted to international issues. They also define national objectives in international relations and discriminate among the different partners and forms of co-operation. National objectives include strengthening national security, increasing national wealth and welfare, advocating certain values and ideas, improving the national reputation, and pursuing national self-interest in other issue areas. States do not exist in vacuums, nor do domestic factors. Both are interactive components of the international system.

The leading part in international affairs is played by a handful of powers – the "price makers" of the system. Even these countries, however, must adjust their policies to accommodate one another's actions. Adjustment, of course, is the permanent requirement for the smaller states – the "price takers" in the system. It is as states adjust to each other, or to price makers, that political ideologies are generated by domestic actors. Although change is a constant characteristic of the international political system, major, epoch-making changes are produced by global crises that result from global wars, hegemonic decline, or large-scale and long-lasting economic contractions or depressions.

It has been suggested that the use of systemic model in the political subsystem tends to minimise the importance of political ideologies, notwithstanding the ideological justifications given for the actions of states. One American scholar has argued:

This de-emphasis on ideology, then, suggests that the analyst of world politics need pay little attention to what policymakers say about their policies. Clearly, they will say whatever will make their actions look good. They will talk about freedom, national self-determination, liberating people from Communist or capitalist slavery, and bringing about world peace, law, order and justice. But such concepts should not be confused with the concrete interests that are the real, underlying reasons for the state's behaviour.[4]

In fact, political ideologies are more than window dressing for national policies. They express interests, values, attitudes, and culture in international relations, and they often reflect the influence of other factors. Ideology can play an extremely important and positive role in an era of major change. But creeds such as fundamentalism and orthodoxy can also rally non-state actors, or even some states, to oppose and obstruct virtually all change, including the development of more co-operative relations with other groups or countries. The increasing influence of ideology today can be seen in the rising number of non-secular Islamic states and in the revival of nationalism in Central and Eastern Europe. Plainly, ideological motives have also fuelled international terrorism. The international political system is the ensemble of national actions and interrelations. As a system, it expresses the political characteristics of the era, articulates mutually acceptable forms and instruments for seeking advantage in the system, defines the contests, determines the choices available to states, and places limits on their aspirations. It can also be a source of major and sudden shocks in the global system. A vital task of international governance is to reveal accumulating tensions within the international political system and to prevent the outbreak of conflicts and violence by means of collective institutions and instruments.

The international economic system (or world economy) is the totality of global production, consumption, and exchange activities undertaken by micro-actors working within national economies and/or the world market. They are conditioned and interconnected both within nations and internationally by the diverse and increasingly globalised markets (in goods, capital, labour, and technology), and are influenced by the economic policies, international agreements, and other actions of various national macroeconomic and international organisations that manage co-operation regimes.

The state-centered character of the international political system is in increasing conflict with the transnational nature of the world economy. This conflict is aggravated by the dual-track character of the international economic system, with growing technological and income gaps and inequalities between the richer and poorer countries. The international economic system of the late 20th century is a highly complex formation. It is comprised of about 200 political units, national markets, in the framework of which an unspecified, but very large, number of micro-units create the global product. They are all parts of the "world market". The number of consumers is over 6 billion. Behind this magnitude exist immense inequalities and quality-of-life

---

[4] John Spanier, *Games Nations Play: Analyzing International Politics* (New York: Holt, Rinehart and Winston, 1984), p. 91.

differences. Ancient technologies, the dominant tools of production used by poorer regions of the world, today coexist with highly productive, modern technologies – sometimes within the same countries. Famine and poverty coexist with unprecedented levels of welfare.

The world market comprises different sets of relations, like monetary, trade, and technology relations, which are themselves special systems regulated by the market and by co-operation regimes. These sets of relations have become vitally important to the existence of states. Economic relations are the media for interdependence and competition. Spillovers of economic shocks and crises are communicated or transferred by them.

Among the different actors in the system, there are economic and technological superpowers setting the norms, and there are dwarfs, whose yearly output is smaller than the annual cash flow of a medium-sized supermarket in any developed industrial country. The contrasts are not less dramatic on the micro-level: there are both global giants (transnational corporations) and bare-footed entrepreneurs in the informal sectors of developing countries.

The world market, and its way of functioning, is a source of opportunity, income, and wealth; however, it is also a source of concern for many countries. Major changes take place in the global economic system as the result of radical technological innovations, the emergence or decline of major powers (competitors), and fundamental policy changes by the key countries of the system affecting income, output, trade, and investment. Changes are also interrelated with the global political system in terms of the role of economic power, the sources of instability, and the implications of political and economic conflicts and competition. The international economic system and the ecological system are closely interrelated by the processes of production, consumption, trade, capital movements and migration.

Past theories of international relations have overlooked the global ecosystem as an integral component of the global system. The natural environment has mistakenly been presumed to be the system of "global commons", an inexhaustible source of natural resources; at best, it has been dealt with as a "global commons" that either should, or should not be managed by co-operation regimes. Recently, however, deepening global ecological crises, as well as existing and potential international disputes over ecological problems, have changed the views of some scholars. The view of the ecosystem as an integral part of the global system, as a subsystem with special characteristics and postulates, is becoming widely shared, as seen in the development of international environmental policies, co-operation regimes, and law, and in attempts by grassroots organisations to safeguard the environment.

The global ecosystem (the atmosphere, hydrosphere, geo-sphere, and biosphere) is both the natural environment that sustains human society and the sum of interrelations between society and that environment. It has been characterised as a "self-organising" or "self-regulating" system, in which the biosphere has become an increasingly active element. The global ecosystem is a highly complex mosaic of regional, sub-regional, and national micro-systems where factors that have diverse environmental consequences interact. These micro-systems affect the global system differently, but they are interconnected and mutually influencing. The macro-system they form is a cumulative global network, which in turn influences how the micro-systems function.

A major conflict exists between the functional requirements of the global ecosystem and those of the global political-economic system. The basic requirements for sustaining the ecosystem are relative stability and ecological harmony, or balance. The ecosystem changes when major imbalances emerge as the result of human actions or natural catastrophes. As a complex system, the ecosystem is stabilised by "feedback loops" (the corrective reactions of natural or human forces). In general, the dynamics of nonlinear systems are chaotic. Stability under such circumstances implies that trajectories of disturbance remain within a relatively well-defined framework. Environmental catastrophes are disturbances that cannot be contained and thus radically affect ecological balance. As a result of extensive human economic activity, the feedback linkages with the biosphere are changed radically. The needs of the political-economic system are dynamism, expansion, growth, and greater profit margins. This is often achieved at the expense of the ecosystem. Harmonising the two sets of requirements is painfully difficult, requiring deliberate, well-co-ordinated international actions for achieving ecologically sound schemes for sustainable economic growth. It calls for responsible collective governance.

A widely recognised problem in social science analysis is defining terms and categories. This problem is even more difficult in the analysis of different systems. In social sciences, researchers often work with analytically imprecise categories that are understood and applied differently by various schools of thought. For example, the concept of the increasingly fashionable categories as globalisation, governance or sustainable development have yet to achieve a universally accepted definition.[5]

[5] A paper presented at the World Bank's 1991 conference on development economics emphasised that governance:

is not a word that has been used extensively in the past by political scientists and its recent appearance in popular usage has not been very rigorous. It has become in many ways both all-embracing and vague. According to the Oxford Dictionary, governance means "the act or manner of governing, of exercising control or authority over actions of subjects; a system of regulations." In essence, therefore, governance may be taken as denoting how people are ruled, and how the affairs of a state are administered or regulated. It refers to a nation's system of politics and how it functions in relation to public administration and law. Pierre Landell-Mills and Ismail Serageldin, *Governance and the External Factor.* (Staff Papers, The International Bank for Reconstruction and Development [The World Bank], 1992), p. 304.

An associated variable of some complexity in defining terms is the diversity and polyglotism of human cultures. Naturally, conceptual frames of reference and nuance vary by culture; a given intellectual construct in English may represent a different notion and be improperly interpreted and apprehended in French, Russian, or Swahili. For example, in certain languages "governance" simply means "the management of a household." Because of cultural differences, even seemingly opposite concepts as "chaos" and "order" are not necessarily understood dichotomously. In Chinese, the character for crisis simultaneously represents chaos and opportunity.

Similarly, concepts of "anarchy," "chaos," the "global system," and "world order" are neither easily transferable nor universally acceptable frameworks for students of international affairs. Indeed, even members of the same socio-linguistic group who accept the necessity of applying a systemic approach to the study of international relations are not always in agreement over the meanings of chaos and order.

Cultural differences go beyond mere linguistic differences. Human beings, who are in the final analysis the actors on the stage of international relations, are members of societies within which values, ideologies, customs, and history condition their ways of thinking. It is not the task of this study to discuss the extremely complex role of culture in international relations. However, how the many political cultures influence the decision-making process and how political transactions are affected by biases and predispositions remain fundamental questions. Culture, together with other key factors (geographic and historical conditions, for example) is one of the most enduring variables in conditioning changes and in influencing the forms and content of governance.

International relations in politics, economics, or other areas, have always developed as different forms of human interactions. A broader understanding (beyond the implications for the quality of life of the individuals) and clearer articulation of the human dimension of international change is a fundamentally important requirement in international life, and is especially important to the analysis of the development process. In spite of the significant material progress on global level, there is an increasing concern in most countries regarding the deterioration of the living conditions, due to economic decline, worsening income distribution, both in its direct and indirect forms. The patterns of development prevailing since the early 1980s have failed to lead to significant, favourable improvements in the complex linkages between economic growth, the well-being of the individuals, families, and communities. The globalisation of poverty, the dominating problems of the international system of the early 2000s suggest that global changes will be characterised by a "search for security" with "security" being understood multi-dimensionally and comprehensively. The need for dealing with security issues in a comprehensive, though unconventional, multidimensional way is the only general conclusion that can be drawn from any reflection upon the many changes taking place. A multidimensional framework would include the security of individuals, nations, regions, and the international community. It is one that would manage or address interconnected issues as well as singular, autonomous problems. The comprehensive character of the search for human security must also include such important areas as the sustainability of the ecosystem, issues of food security, the security of oil and raw material supplies, access to new technology, and the institutional reliability of international co-operation under different frameworks. These and other factors imply an increasing need for the efficient handling and management of changes at all levels, especially in those areas, which most directly influence the present and future conditions of people. The current phase of development in the world calls for a new, integrative, cross-disciplinary approach to global change. As a concept, global change can be understood as a process that modifies the characteristics and functioning of human society in the majority of the world's countries or in the biosphere. The process of change has gradual and sudden, reversible and irreversible, and quantitative and qualitative components that result in a process of profound, multiple transformations in a number of areas. The beginning of the 21st century brings a rare coincidence of transformations in almost all the crucial dimensions of human action. This applies to the global increase, age-structure, movement and settlement patterns of the population, to the role of various forms of organisation and interaction in societies, to the development and use of new knowledge, and to all areas related to these.

The growing interdependence and interaction between the different actors, functional areas and problems of the international system blended local, national and international trends in a historically unprecedented way. Although the intensity of the process has varied in time and space and in the different areas of economic and social change, it has influenced the character, intensity and patterns of global economic and social development.[6] The fun-

---

[6] The degree of integration in the world economy at the close of the 20th century coincides in many respects with the conditions before 1914. Some historians have seen the period 1870–1914 as a golden age of global integration. Imperial systems, the gold standard, low barriers to international trade, free international movement of vast sums of long- and short-term capital, and unparalleled intercontinental migration produced rapid world economic integration. Disintegration ensued between the wars, but integration resumed, albeit more slowly, after the Second World War. However, it took different forms from the ones it had taken before 1914, due to political impulses, an unprecedented surge of scientific and technical development, and rapid expansion of the market.

damental changes known as globalisation will probably be greater than those of any previous social transformation have been. Societies are changing in almost all the dimensions in which they function. The transformations include demographic processes, population growth, urbanisation, urban growth, major structural changes in society and the economy, and radical changes in the technological and production base, including the organisation of production and markets, entrepreneurship, employment and the international division of labour. The process and its consequences are realigning societies within the hierarchies of wealth and power. They are also bringing about qualitative changes in the political, military, cultural and institutional dimensions of human life.

In the eyes of the public, the most important areas of globalisation are money, capital, information flows and the media, while the essential players are the transnational corporations. International organised crime is also perceived as an unwelcome inhabitant of the "global village". The role of transnational corporations has often been cited as the main factor contributing to the globalisation process. Their role is certainly crucial in a number of areas, such as trade and investment, organisation of production and markets, and homogenisation of consumption patterns. Transnationals are important sources of new useful knowledge, embodied in new products and processes. This makes them the main force behind the transition to a new technological era, which is a special part of global transformation. Ultimately, however, the indispensable component of globalisation has been the liberalisation process, decided and implemented by governments. Governments are not neutral actors, of course. They are motivated by specific interests, and represent and express specific values. Liberalisation, too, reflects a consensus on specific interests and values, not necessarily shared by all.

Globalisation has been often presented by analysts, even in economic literature, either as a self-generating, irreversible and spontaneous process, unleashing uncontrollable forces, or as one managed by the great powers and the transnationals in a secretive and undemocratic way.

To conceptualise its human dimensions, I define globalisation as a higher stage of internationalisation. This roots globalisation in the long history of modern civilisation, where people and their communities have encountered other groups through trade, migration and conquest.

Internationalisation took two main directions. Pointing inwards, there was an increase (or penetration) of external sources of goods, capital, services, technology, ideas, information, etc. into the domestic consumption of a country. Pointing outwards, there was the predominance of world-market outlook among countries and global expansion of firms in trade, investments and other transactions (at corporate level). The main consequences of internationalisation were an increase in the interdependence of states and the spatial and institutional integration of markets.[7] The beginnings were connected with modern industrial development and the birth of the world market. The process of internationalisation can be seen as having various stages. Its nature at any particular stage was determined by the socio-political framework prevalent at the time. Internationalisation essentially promoted economic progress. It increased the exchange of material and intellectual values and encouraged contacts among peoples. But the process was always bound by specific economic and socio-political frameworks. The historical patterns of internationalisation proved that the nature of the process and the interests and the value system attached to it deprived certain groups of countries of its benefits.

Internationalisation developed at an unequal rate, with major setbacks occurring in technology, economics, finance, trade and culture. It was held back and even reversed for a time by the world conflicts of the 20th century. The period between the two world wars can be seen as one of retreat for internationalisation.

The process gained new strength in the post-Second World War era, particularly since the 1960s. Globalisation of economic growth in recent decades has been promoted above all by foreign direct investment. One important consequence and manifestation of the process has been the emergence of global problems. The unprecedented opportunities, the risks and the real and potential conflicts related to the various dimensions of the globalisation process cannot be addressed through the traditional orthodoxy of economics or by the bureaucratic approaches of governments constrained by short-term interests. Globalisation requires global thinking – seeing the world as a whole. This is indispensable to the management of global problems and maintenance of policy dialogue in vital fields of global security and co-operation. Without the requisite co-operation, global insecurity will grow and internal and external tensions and conflicts evolve from the globalisation process. These, along with the unequal benefits of globalisation, may undermine and reverse the process itself. National institutions are often not prepared for dealing with the tasks

---

[7] There is no exact, universally accepted definition of the process of internationalisation either. Efforts to provide a single measure of its achieved level are combinations of a number of indicators, whose weighing rest on subjective judgement, not on any scientific basis. Here as in many other cases in the social sciences, the process can be characterised only by reference to certain direct or proxy indicators. Internationalisation, on a level of the world economy and national economies, means an increase in the importance of exports and imports of goods and services and in information, knowledge and foreign investment flows into the system, and integration of state functions across jurisdictional boundaries. The main quantitative indicators used for the degree of internationalisation of a national economy are foreign-trade volume and its proportion of gross output and consumption, external capital investment flows, the import element in the new technologies applied, and labour-force migration. Global aggregates of these data are proxies for the degree of internationalisation of the world economy.

imposed by constant structural adjustment and other pressures related to the liberalisation process and deregulation, or the problems arising out the new forms of interconnection in increasingly competitive global markets. However, globalisation is not a linear or irreversible process. It may be reversed by major economic or political disruption, crisis or conflict, which in turn could lead to the disintegration of the world economy or the collapse of existing institutional structures. Universalisation is an important carrier and expression of the globalisation process. The concept is used in three important dimensions. One dimension is related to the modality of global development. Are there alternative models of modernisation or only the one characterising the main industrial countries? Will development follow universal patterns in a globalising world or as in the past it will be diverse? The other dimension of universalisation is related to the technological transformation and the spread of "global products" and production patterns, the standardisation of production and consumption. The third dimension is connected with the convergence of policies across national boundaries due to multilaterally agreed patterns, growing identity or similarity of national economic regulations and institutions or the spread of values and modes of doing things, encompassing the universal approach to human rights.

The process of internationalisation has developed a great number of interactions between the different societies and cultures and among various actors in various fields. Some of these are integrative, while others can lead to disintegration and fragmentation. These do not necessarily develop as contradictory processes that crowd each other out. The complex character of such relations is especially apparent in the human dimensions of the changes that relate more directly to globalisation. Some oft-emphasised issues here are the emergence of global problems, such as environmental degradation and population growth, whose management requires global co-operation. International organised crime is also a by-product of the globalisation process and the related interactions. Modern means of transport, advanced communications and relaxed frontier controls have created unprecedented opportunities for organised crime from Italy, Russia, South America and Asia to expand into new territories and markets and to launder their illicit earnings. Crime is also helped greatly by international migration.

Some social scientists consider globalisation, with its pervasive, multidimensional and multi-level consequences, as a new paradigm that will replace the traditional approach of analysing social processes in national framework. I do not intend to discuss in this book the paradigm theory, popular though it has become in some schools of social scientific thought. Scholars are generally inclined to use a central hypothesis in their research like the trunk of a tree, on which they can develop the branches and flowers of their arguments. The social sciences have never been able to build on a single central factor. Societies are complex systems influenced by several factors and the interactions between them. The world in the 21st century is marked also by fragmentation and disintegration, often related to conflicts caused by the globalisation process. Globalisation has to be analysed together with the other critical trends in society.[8]

Changes in the various dimensions of globalisation are also influenced by several factors. The technological dimension of globalisation, for example, produced a new, interactive information sphere in the life of individuals, business and institutions, and made these interactive capacities indispensable to co-operation and competition. It has stimulated the reorganisation of production and markets into networks and fostered a process of international mergers and acquisitions. The demand for new skills and the emergence of distance working and electronic commerce all relate to this new information sphere. Most recent trends in almost all spheres of human existence, from human reproduction to global cultural co-operation, are included under the "umbrella" of globalisation. It is seen as a long-term, structural and normative change, so broad and ill-defined that it can cover practically everything. The disintegration and fragmentation that influence the changes and relate to the consequences of globalisation are often disregarded. This is a grave methodological and conceptual error, particularly from the human-development perspective. Integration is connected more with the interests and values of the beneficiaries of globalisation, while fragmentation is often the result of the efforts of the losers, whose number is quite large. The simultaneous effects of both trends result in political and economic, social and psychological discontinuities as well as newly evolving factors and continuities. All these make the process of change complex and difficult to conceptualise.

This study looks at the new global interactions mainly in terms of the human dimensions of the changes. These include the causes and consequences of human actions. Human beings are multidimensional actors. They emerge from nature and transform nature. As producers and consumers in a specific socio-economic environment, they develop and form their economies and are the objects and subjects of any purposeful economic activity, including innovation or the process of creative destruction. They are agents of conflict, though agents also of conflict management and resolution. These and other elements of human behaviour influence the international aspects of the human dimensions of economic change. The human aspects of changes include both the consequences of human action and the influence of these on the quality of life, and in the final analysis, on the issues that influence human survival. The world orders comprise the global framework for human actions.

[8] See, for example, Rosenau, 1990.

26

PART I

THEORIES, CONCEPTS AND CHANGING TRENDS

1. CONCEPTS AND REALITIES OF WORLD ORDERS

The rationale of the "world order" concept

In the jargon of journalists and politicians, the "global system" and "world order" are often misapprehended as interchangeable categories. Given that the concept of "world order" is abstract and has been defined in many different ways, it is perhaps not surprising that this confusion exists.

According to its broader meaning, "world order" is the totality of globally valid norms, rules, and international codes of conduct generally observed by those states and transnational actors for whom they were designed in the international public policymaking process. According to its narrow understanding, "world order" is the entirety of legally binding rules and institutions that regulate interstate relations. While there are many other definitions for "world order", Hedley Bull's can be used as a point of departure. Bull defined international order as "...a pattern of activity that sustains the elementary or primary goals of the society of states or international society."[9]

International norms and rules are usually based on the specific interests and values of major powers, and, secondarily, on those of the whole international community. Effective sanctions to the violation of norms, rules, and codes, can be applied by a legitimately established international authority, by a coalition of states taking enforcement action, or by a single state willing and able to assume the role of international policeman.

While order is generally considered to be a static concept, no "world order" could ever be considered static. Indeed, the ability to adjust to and promote change is an important factor that accounts for the survival and durability of world orders. Order and disorder, as well as predictable and unpredictable events, are not completely exclusive notions in a complex global system. To a certain extent, individuals and groups have an immeasurable number of opportunities to react – rationally or irrationally – to

---

[9] Hedley Bull, *The Anarchical Society: A Study of Order in World Politics* (New York: Columbia University Press, 1977), p. 8.

domestic and international issues according to their intellectual capacities, cultures, and habits, being motivated by specific interests and goals. Behind their reactions, however, are the regulating forces, which represent constraints to their actions and influence the outcomes of their efforts.[10] Rules, norms, and regulating forces provide for some form of decentralised governance and order, and are thus valued by international actors.

In an interconnected and dynamic global system, there are unpredictable processes that can neither be prepared for, nor even anticipated. Therefore, regulating forces notwithstanding, any global order can only be relatively stable.[11]

The debate about order and chaos, and anarchy and governance, is far from being of only theoretical importance. If the international system is determined by disorder and anarchy, then everything – international violence, the threat and the use of force, terrorism, and international sanctions – would be legitimate instrument of statecraft, deterrable only by the punitive responses of other states. Order, however, implies institutionalised rules and a disciplined, accountable community of states. Order is a form of collective "self"-control, an ethic of sorts ascribed to an international consensus on norms and, partly, on a codified legal framework.[12]

In order to understand the new problems and postulates at the beginning of the 21st century it is necessary to raise some general, conceptual issues about the institutional "effectiveness" of the world order.

The criteria of "effectiveness"

There are two main issues related to the effectiveness of a world order. The first issue is the level of analysis: "effectiveness for whom?" The second issue is about the criteria used in defining effectiveness. Here, we are looking at the problems of effectiveness mainly but not exclusively from the perspectives of a complex and heterogeneous international community. There are no objective measures for evaluating effectiveness, nor can there be any, because the preferences of national populations (and of the political elite) may differ

---

[10] See James Rosenau, *Turbulence in World Politics* (Princeton: Princeton University Press, 1990).

[11] See R. J. Stoll, "System and State in International Politics: A Computer Simulation of Balancing in an Anarchic World", *International Studies Quarterly*, vol. 31, no. 4, 1987.

[12] A profound analysis of the views expressed by the different schools of thought on issues of order and anarchy is offered by Helen Milner, in her article "The Assumption of Anarchy in International Relations Theory: a Critique", *Review of International Studies*, vol. 17, no. 1, pp. 67–86.

greatly. For example, the ruling elite of totalitarian regimes usually have different preferences from those of democratic regimes.

From a democratic perspective, the effectiveness of the political system within a state is reflected, to a large extent, in the capabilities of government to accommodate, rather than suppress, differences in public opinion, and to maintain domestic political stability by way of a social consensus achieved at relatively low costs for high social benefits. This requires the prudent and rational use of power, a democratic sharing of responsibilities and power, and a high intellectual level of professionalism in governance. It also requires substantial flexibility in institutional structures, enabling the timely selection of the most necessary and important policies and adjustment measures at any given time.

These qualities can also be extended internationally, for a more effective international governance system. The indicators of political effectiveness here would also include a state's capacity to understand the nature of changes occurring in the international environment, and the capacity to influence them in order to avoid major crises. However, very few countries can decisively influence the international environment. Nevertheless, states can, either individually or collectively, prepare themselves to confront sources of instability and external risks and to mitigate the effects of crisis.

Is it sound to formulate an unambiguous and immutable set of "effectiveness criteria" that can be applied to any global order? Global orders are rooted in a given historical context. Their degree of effectiveness, therefore, must be measured against the operational performance required by those who are its architects and participants. Power has always been a critically important determinant in the establishment of global orders; therefore, aspects such as the source of power, its affirmative or cynical manipulation in instituting a global order, and the degree of acceptability of a particular power structure may offer some criteria for comparison and evaluation from a historical perspective.

The costs of sustaining the given order and the benefits it yields may be equally important and interesting criteria for historical, political, and socio-economic analysis. And yet, it seems impossible to establish concrete, "across the board" criteria for measuring the effectiveness of given orders or co-operation systems (or "regimes"), as there is perhaps more diversity between political-historical actors and their unique world orders, than commonality. Each set of criteria, therefore, must be specifically related to the major problems of a given historical era and to the particular interests of that era's main actors.

Having said this, what would be the criteria for a well-functioning world order in the current, post-Cold War period? In delineating these criteria (or postulates), it is necessary to do so not only from the viewpoint of individual nations, but also from the perspective of general human interests.

In political terms, the order must be effective in maintaining world peace, in preventing the abuse of power in international relations, and more particularly, in forestalling violent regional or global conflicts on the basis of mutual obligations, or of contractual and institutional guarantees for the security of each individual country. The order must be one that holds countries accountable for their obligations to provide these security guarantees. A successful global order must be authorised by mandate and have at its disposal effective mechanisms for the peaceful solution of international disputes, and for peacekeeping and peacemaking operations.

From an economic point of view, an effective order should promote relatively widespread development of the national economies comprising the system. This can be done by facilitating the international flow of labour, goods, services, technology, and capital. A good order would assist in staving off international economic crises, trade wars, and any other disruptions to economic transactions.

With respect to the human dimension, the order must help establish international institutional guarantees against the violation of human rights (broadly defined), and should be patterned along principles of human solidarity that would facilitate collective action in global disasters and emergencies. A 21st-century global order must also direct the collective responses of countries to the problems of the ecosystem for the protection of the interests of future generations.

These criteria imply that a new, more efficient world order in the 21st century cannot merely be a functional improvement upon the post-World War II order. Significant changes would be required in almost all important areas in order to satisfy them. However, the world is unable to organise itself completely anew, to start from a blank page of a book, when the very character of its institutions and leaders are products of 20th-century history. Even so, the world must realistically address itself to the changes that will transpire in this decade, changes that will probably be gradual and incremental, especially vis-à-vis the pressing demands that the evolving order must attempt to satisfy.

It follows from the above criteria that efficiency in a global order must be evaluated first of all against the extent to which the norms and institutions that shape the order are able to constrain or discipline the behaviour of states, thus making states predictable, reliable partners. In the absence of a strong, norms-enforcing authority and an established code of conduct – both likely to remain absent in a global arena of constant change – what will be an acutely important requirement in the future is an enhanced quality of collective efforts to confront sources of international instability and manage risks that may otherwise result in global crises. At the beginning of the 21st century it is also evident that the criteria of effectiveness must be evaluated from the perspective of human beings, how it promotes their welfare and security. This postulate is a difference from the past. One must understand of course that each world order was designed to function in a unique historical environment.[13] The United Nations System was the first to proceed beyond the traditional world order approach where the political-military aspects of the given era predominated.

This order proved to be very durable, in spite of the historically unprecedented global changes and challenges that have occurred over the past decades. A few of the changes the United Nations has weathered, and challenges it has engaged, include the Cold War, different hot wars of varying degrees, a devastating peace-time arms race (begun in the era of conventional weapons and carried through into the nuclear and space age), the political decolonisation and birth of 120 to 130 new states, the population explosion, the new scientific and technological revolution with its pervasive social and economic impacts, the most widespread expansion of the world economy and of global markets in history, profound changes in the patterns of output, consumption, and employment, the evolving ecological crisis, the rise and fall of dictatorial regimes, and many other severe global problems.

A major reason for the global order, along with its international co-operation structure, was able to survive intact through this turbulent period is that the power structure was firmly supportive of it. Simply put, it satisfied the power structure's interests and expectations.

---

[13] Interestingly, world order concepts may have their genesis in the ideas of certain religions. Virtually every great religion has claimed that world conditions would improve, were its precepts to become universally adopted. For example, one world order concept with a religious base is "unity". Indeed, world religions have so operated according to the dogma of unity that those not of the faith are pressured to convert. Islam issued a "da'wat" – an appeal to all humankind to become Muslim. The traditional position of Roman Catholicism has been "extra ecclesiam nulla salus" – no salvation exists outside the church. In fact, the Roman Catholic church became the first real hierarchical transnational organisation controlling and co-ordinating its relatively autonomous units from Rome by establishing general norms, symbolic leadership roles, and a binding decision-making process. The church has also created a global redistribution network for human and material resources between Rome and the semi-autonomous units.

On the basis of religious ideals, St. Augustine postulated the concepts of the City of God and the City of Devil. The former was a sphere where all faithful Christians would reside, and was free of violence and corruption. It was thought to be a sphere that could be reafied in the social formations of that time. Medieval Christian empires held to the firm belief that such a world was to be hierarchically organised, unified by a common faith under the joint moral code of the emperor and the Pope.

The world order based on the United Nations system, which has survived major global upheavals since its inception has arrived at a new turning point at the end of the 20th century. The new realities and dangers have a particular influence on the human dimension of change.

Ideologies and theories: the issue of relevance

Transformations can be seen as attempts by society to deal with challenges or as spontaneous responses to limited or non-existent adjustment capabilities in previous systems. Transformations are seldom premeditated, well designed or well organised. The different groups in a society react to the factors necessitating a transformation in different ways. Studying transformations involves studying structures and structural changes. These complex new problems present difficult and important tasks to the social sciences.

Are the social sciences any better prepared to address such issues than they were in the past?

Science amounts to more than the results of generalised empirical study or the product of previously devised theoretical models and hypotheses. Scientific progress and discovery form a process of constant confrontation of theories with realities and with earlier hypotheses and laws, resulting in a more profound understanding of nature and society. In this respect, the various scientific disciples resemble each other. Critical analysis is especially important for the social sciences, which are exposed to the dangers of pressure from various systems of values.

The progress and performance of a science must be judged in relation to its subject, its earlier capabilities and achievements, and its relationship to other disciplines.

Considerable progress has been made in the social sciences in the second half of the 20th century. This has been reflected in various ways in their analytical, interpretative, normative and problem-solving capabilities. However, the changes have widened the range of issues researched, improved their theoretical foundations and methodology, approximated these more closely to reality, radically improved the statistics available, facilitated comparative analysis, increased differentiation, and multiplied the number of researchers and research and teaching establishments. The last has helped to bring about a much wider range of approaches and schools of thoughts.

Research on modernisation and the complex issues of economic development, social transformation and cultural change has shown up the limitations of various one-dimensional, universalistic approaches. The differentiation among the social sciences implied theoretical diversification that has led to the development of new disciplines, such as international economics,

34

international sociology, environmental economics and so on, and brought the end of the traditional focus on Europe.

The social sciences have traditionally been critics of existing institutions and socio-political and economic regimes. While this critical stance remains important and even indispensable, there has been ever-stronger demand for the problem-solving abilities of the social sciences. This has resulted in a split within disciplines. Some work mainly as social critics, exploring the contradictions, origins and consequences of systems and the changes that are feasible and desirable. Others focus on solving current problems and seeking acceptable alternatives, within the prevailing framework of regulating forces and values.

There has been another shift in attitudes and value system in the social sciences, related to its problem-solving role: a shift from a traditional pessimism to a qualified optimism. Followers and advocates of mission-oriented theories have always been more optimistic in their normative work. Meanwhile there has been a recognition and theoretical acceptance of multi-dimensional interdependence with other species of the biological system, involving a better understanding of the finite life-sustaining capacities of the Earth. The result here has been not only conceptual changes, but also a number of new fields of studies, related to the interactions between the ecosystem and society, of which environmental economics is probably the most developed.

The new relations of the social sciences to nature were probably important factors in their interrelations with the disciplines that study nature, the physical world and the bio-system, for good reasons. The social sciences learned from the other disciplines, notably about the necessity of qualifications and the importance of empirical research, and in their efforts to introduce mathematics and modelling. Other fields where innovations in the social sciences came from other disciplines include recognition of the relative nature of social time, the introduction of system theories, and the concept of complex interactions between order and chaos. The changes in the natural sciences and the recognition of the constraints on their ability to comprehend and explain the world through a few fundamental laws have resulted in some convergence of approach to uncertainty.

Of course there will always be differences between the social and the natural sciences in methodology, in the way they evolve, in the forms their discoveries take, in the role and character of their experiments, and in the part played in their applications by vested interests and value systems. In the social sciences, experiments resulting in new discoveries are usually thrown up by history, rather than made in laboratories.

A role is also played by the information revolution, which facilitates research, simulations of complex systems, and collection, processing, analysis, storage and dissemination at an unprecedented scale. By connecting up the globe, including the main centres of research, it becomes another source of convergence.

The role and usefulness of ideas, values and knowledge in shaping the world orders and their evolution has often been questioned but particularly in the era of great social transformations. The relevance of different theories, related to the world orders and their transformation became also an important issue whenever reality contradicted the views of the mainstream. Some scholars had always doubts about them. Raymond Aron in one of his essays written in 1967 pointed out that few words were more ambiguous and more promiscuously overused than theories.[14] He noted that the first meaning of theory in Greek philosophy was contemplative knowledge. "Theory" as a concept of course in itself has different meanings in the various schools of thoughts. It is considered by some as a coherent group of general propositions used as verified or established explanations or principles for known facts or phenomena, it is also used as an abstraction, based on observed experiences and facts or as a hypothetical, speculative framework of thinking. In social sciences it is a value-loaded concept, influenced by interests, ideologies and norms. For many modern scholars in social sciences theory is a hypothetical, deductive system on the basis of which they could predict. At the time of important historical changes there are always problems with the relevance of theories related to social change. During the second half of the 20th century modernisation theories have been "popular" in explaining social transformations. They embraced a considerable range of interpretations. Some of them attributed great importance to socio-political factors, others examined the capacity of the given society to take advantage of the possibilities offered by the advancement of knowledge in political, economic and social terms. Most of the different approaches converged in looking at the importance of the institutions, including the differences between the institutional heritages of the Western and non-Western societies. A great number of "transformation studies" have drawn theoretical and conceptual inspiration from Karl Polanyi's "Great Transformation," even though he gave insufficient attention to events, social conflicts and the major actors in the process.[15]

The rise and fall of ideologies related to systemic changes have been one of the most complex and controversial components of human history. There had been different "model" causes and consequences of this process. Many of the ideologies, which wanted to create societies intended to meet all

---

[14] Raymond Aron: "What is a theory of international relations?" *Journal of International Affairs*. XXI (2) (1967) pp. 185–206.

[15] Karl Polanyi: *The Great Transformation* (Boston, Beacon Press, 1944).

human needs were in many cases utopias. Noble ideas of equality, solidarity and fraternity have been appropriated by lawless dictators and their implementation culminated in oppression and terror. Some of the doctrines and practices served the supremacy and superiority of a nation or a social group. The collapse of the etatist-socialist regimes in Eastern Europe has been one of the dramatic events in the process. The influence of the Marxist ideology on systemic changes was probably the most profound and far-reaching in modern history. It is quite natural that there are different interpretations of its historical destiny. Thurow in his popular book "The Future of Capitalism" considered the collapse of the communist regimes as the victory of individual values over social values. Besides, he wrote "The rich were smarter than Marx believed."[16] An other analyst raised basically similar questions. Marxism proceeded with phenomenal speed he wrote, and added "Both the tempo of Marxism's earlier triumphs throughout the world and of its present day disestablishment are bewildering. Was Marxism a short-lived delusion, an aberration in modern history? Did it leave behind anything worth preserving? Was its failure the consequence of its unfortunate application in vast land masses like Russia and China with deeply ingrained authoritarian traditions and political economies that foredoomed the effort from the outset?"[17] His answer is rather open ended: "Since there are many chambers in the house that Marx built" some of his ideas may yet find a place in secular and religious humanism. An African Islamic scholar Ali A Mazrui raises similar questions, but his answers to the question "Is Marxism Dead?" are more concrete. He underlines that "the concern about economic disparities has not been invalidated." "Marxism as a methodology of analysis" is still valid, but Marxism as an ideology of development has been discredited." "The Marxist baby is being thrown out with the Leninist bath water."[18] He suggests that Marxism may survive in Asia and remain marginal in Europe.

The various ideologies of liberalism-neocapitalism, may not be effective in addressing the concerns of the developing world, like poverty, polarisation, deprivation, and mass unemployment. Nationalism, fascism, and anarchism, as other ideological movements, preach fanaticism in different forms, like racism, ethnic hatred, or religious bigotry. Lamentably, these ideological movements are gaining ground in some countries as the result of growing socio-economic problems, and political gridlocks. These ideologies also can-

[16] Lester C. Thurow: *The Future of Capitalism.* N.Y. Penguin Books, 1996, pp. 4–5.

[17] Frank E. Manuel: "A Requiem for Karl Marx," *Daedalus,* vol. 121, no. 2, 1992, pp. 7–8.

[18] Ali A. Mazrui: "Islam and the End of History," *The American Journal of Islamic Social Sciences,* vol. 10, no. 4 (Winter 1993), pp. 11–12.

not be expected to encourage solving the problems of poverty, environmental degradation, and crime.

Pope John Paul II has squarely identified the problem: "The Marxist solution has failed, but the realities of marginalisation and exploitation remain in the world, especially in the Third World, as does the reality of human alienation, especially in the more advanced countries. Indeed, there is a risk that a radical capitalistic ideology could spread which refuses even to consider these problems, in the a priori belief, that any attempt to solve them is doomed to failure, and which blindly entrusts their solution to the free development of market forces."[19] And, of course, more than a few ideologies have a priori biases that make them as non-responsive to basic problems as capitalism.

In the early 2000s, there are many large and small groups with different variations of ideologies like environmentalism, globalism, regionalism and feminism. The globally organised churches, which are very active internationally, may offer cohesive ideological response to many issues of the present and future. It is an open question to what extent their approaches will be interwoven with their traditional beliefs and will be sufficiently encompassing to solve modern problems. Churches might also be limited in action by the interests of their various constituencies, including their fundamentalists.

The future influence of theories and ideologies on the issues of development and modernisation are particularly important questions. Will these processes be influenced much more by the pragmatic experiences than by ideologies? Will they develop under the influence of the conflicts and social changes attributed to the globalisation process? (The influence of the conflicts in a way was already visible in the "universalist" and the "particularist" approaches. The universalists put the emphasis on the role of the market which implied the replication of the path of advanced industrial countries. The particularists recognised the diversity in the political, economic and institutional experiences, goals, instruments and outcomes.)

The debates of the strategic conferences organised by the UN in the 1990s were influenced by both above trends but looked at the issues of development and modernisation as an interactive global process of human actions. They indirectly suggested an integrated and integrative approach. The main common element in those debates was the emphasis on the human dimension of the development and modernisation process. This implied not only more human centred approach but also the necessity of understanding better

---

[19] John Paul II, On the Hundredth Anniversary of Rerum Novarum. "Centesimus Annus", *Encyclical Letter,* May 1, 1991. Publication 436–438, Office for Publishing and Promotion Services, United States Catholic Conference, Washington D. C., p. 82.

the role of culture in the similarities and the differences of human interactions in the process of transformation and change in the different societies. As for the relevance of the different schools of thoughts and theories explaining the changes, I consider the views of Douglas North, a recipient of the Nobel Prize which he expressed in a paper presented to a conference on Public Choice Theories and Third World Experiences at the London School of Economics as a critique of the existing theories. He wrote: "There is no greater challenge facing today's social sciences than the development of a dynamic theory of social change ... and give us an understanding of adaptive efficiency".[20] There is even less agreement about the relevance of theories concerning the nature and management of future systemic changes and social conflicts. It is evident that a new agenda of research is needed for the better understanding of their dynamics in the era of globalisation and intense competition between countries and firms.

The chronology of change was also an important issue in all social sciences. The search for objective criteria became in itself an interesting theoretical issue. One of the pioneers of international macroeconomic research, Simon Kuznets, defined an economic epoch as a relatively long period, possessing distinctive characteristics that give it unity and differentiate it from epochs that precede or follow it. Economic epochs, Kuznets added, can be distinguished at various levels of social life and associated with the interplay between technological and social change. They affect a variety of social units and states, and the different communities within them.[21] Other schools of thought relate phases of development to the introduction or spread of fundamental technical or institutional innovations,[22] or to scientific discoveries of epoch-making significance. Another approach is to examine the primary techno-economic sectors that typify an era, whether they are agricultural, industrial, postindustrial (service economy), or hyper-industrial (where services are transformed into mass-produced consumer goods).[23]

[20] Douglas C. North: The New Institutional Economics and Development. Cited by Forum. *Newsletter of the Economic Research Forum of the Arab Countries.* vol. I, No. 2, p. 5. (May 1994).

[21] See Simon Kuznets: *Modern Economic Growth: Rate, Structure, and Spread* (New Haven: Yale University Press, 1966), pp. 1–8.

[22] See N. D. Kondratieff: *Die langen Wellen der Konjunktur* 56 (Tubingen: Archiv für Sozialwissenschaft und Sozialpolitik, 1929); D. Landes: *The Unbound Prometheus: Technological Change and Industrial Development in Western Europe from 1750 to the Present* (London: Cambridge University Press, 1969); W. W. Rostow: *Theorists of Economic Growth from David Hume to the Present, with a Perspective on the Next Century* (Oxford: Oxford University Press, 1990), pp. 486–508; and Joseph A. Schumpeter: *Business Cycles: A Theoretical, Historical, and Statistical Analysis of the Capitalist Process* (New York: McGraw-Hill, 1939).

[23] See J. Attali: *Millennium* (London: Times Books/Random House, 1991), p. 10.

Many scholars consider the great shocks of history (wars, economic catastrophes, or major crises) as signals of new phases. Angus Maddison distinguishes four phases of development in the 20th century: the phase of the so-called liberal order, from the 1870s to 1913; a period of conflicts and autarchy, from 1913 to 1950; the "golden age", from 1950 to 1973; and a period of inflation and slow world economic development, which began with the oil crisis of 1973 and the disintegration of the international financial system. During the golden age, the liberal relations characteristic of the beginning of this century were restored, and, moreover, restored under more favourable conditions than before. Governments undertook programs that encouraged economic growth and sought to sustain full employment at the same time as the financial system was functioning relatively well, the colonial system was dissolving, and the world was becoming, generally speaking, more democratic.[24]

The theory of long waves or cycles,[25] which has disappeared and reappeared in social science analysis for decades, is another framework for studying the historical interrelationship of political and techno-economic changes.

---

[24] See Angus Maddison: *The World Economy in the 20th Century*. OECD Developmet Center, 1989.

[25] The elaboration of the long cycles theory is credited to the Russian scholar Nicolai Kondratieff, who concluded that the development of the capitalist system is not linear, but cyclical. Short waves of development of one-and-a-half to three years are matched by economic cycles of seven to eleven years and social and economic cycles of about fifty years. Kondratieff believed that recoveries occur more often in the upward trend of long cycles than in the downward trend, which corresponds to much suffering, particularly in the agricultural sector. The phase of decline is noted for its many innovations, technical and other, that are employed on a mass scale at the beginning of the subsequent phase. The upward trends represent phases of growth that strain economic resources. In these phases wars and revolutions break out, which in turn influence development.

Long cycles have been examined by several other experts, including J. A. Schumpeter, P. G. Mensch, and W. W. Rostow. Christopher Freeman and Carlota Perez have also sought to explain the causes of long cycles; their technological, economic, and social peculiarities; their political-economic consequences; the corporate organisational forms within them; power relations; and international organisational structures and institutions. According to these authors, the first cycle began in the 1770s–1780s (the beginning of the manufacturing industry) and lasted until the 1840s, with rudimentary mechanisation as its technological basis. The second cycle lasted until the 1880s–1890s, and had as its base the development of steam engines and railways. The third cycle lasted until the 1930s–1940s, its base being the electrical and heavy machine industries. The fourth cycle came to a close in the 1980s, and had the characteristics of mass production, the development and distribution of road and air transportation networks, and the synthetic chemical and nuclear industries. The fifth cycle began in the 1980s, and is being fed by information and communications engineering, the microelectronics industry, the biological revolution, and space technology. See Christopher Freeman, ed., *Long Waves in the World Economy* (London: Frances Pinter, 1984).

Long cycles are usually discussed around the time of major global changes; discussion ceases once continuity sets in to distinguish a certain era. Debates about long cycles and the beginnings of new phases have become more animated since the early 1970s, particularly under the effects of the international oil crises of the early 1970s and 1980s. Those crises, as well as other developments of the 1970s and 1980s – the sudden break of the golden age of world relations, the slowing of development accompanied by rapid inflation (stagflation), the increase in unemployment – drew the attention of analysts, who set out to seek causal explanations of these phenomena.

Although the theory of long cycles may be attractive to students of historical determinism, because of differences in the causes of phase-particular developments, one cannot identify any precisely recurring cause-and-effect relationships. In fact, the causes and effects referred to in the theory are often confused. For example, innovations appear in different national and global settings under different conditions, but their frequency of occurrence in the various cycles is the consequence of different variables. The characteristics outlined by Christopher Freeman and Carlota Perez are so diverse that little cyclicity can be identified.[26] Nevertheless, Freeman's and Perez's criteria are suitable for characterising various phases in economic and technological history. These issues are also relevant in the context of the dynamics of change and the ongoing transformations. Does the new era, characterised by different catchwords: as the stage of globalisation, the "post-Cold War" era, the epoch of the new technological revolution, the information age or the age of knowledge represent a special new stage in human development?

[26] See *ibid.*

2. INTERNATIONALISATION, INTERDEPENDENCE AND THE GLOBALISATION PROCESS

The theory of systems analysis conceives a system to be a total sum of interdependent variables (elements and blocks), with a structure consisting of the cumulative totality of the functional interdependent variables. The concept of "internationalisation" or "globalisation" of interdependence emerged in economic and political science since the 1960s, as a term characterising the new alignments between countries, the increasing impact of one state on another through various actors and channels. Interdependence featured as an issue mainly in the writings of the school known as international political economy, and mainly in terms of the outcome of distributive relations among states.

The concept of interdependence has been welcomed as a new discovery by some social scientists. It was extremely popular in the golden age of the 1960s and appeared in the new framework of the 1970s amidst the problems and crises of the world economy. However, interdependence is not a new notion. The causes behind the internationalisation of economic development under the then prevailing conditions of capitalism were understood and illuminated a century and a half ago in Marxist political economy. In the Communist Manifesto, first published in February 1848, Marx and Engels write, "The bourgeoisie has through its exploitation of the world market given a cosmopolitan character to production and consumption in every country ... New industries ... no longer work up indigenous raw material, but raw material drawn from the remotest zones; industries whose products are consumed not only at home, but in every corner of the globe ... In place of the old local and national seclusion and self-sufficiency, we have intercourse in every direction, universal inter-dependence of nations." They added that the same process was taking place "in intellectual production. The intellectual creations of individual nations become common property" (Marx and Engels, 1971, p. 36). Since the formulation of these ideas in the last century, the process has advanced further, albeit with many distortions and disruptions.[27]

[27] See Simai (1981) and (1994).

Since the 1960s, a voluminous literature has appeared in economics, political science and related disciplines in the industrialised Western countries on the notion of international interdependence. The expression has also gained currency among politicians and in the media. The literature has contributed to a better understanding of the world system, but it has also created confusion and in many cases reduced the concept to the plane of pseudo-scientific platitudes. Nonetheless, several authors have made meaningful attempts to comprehend the implications of international interdependence and arrive at a definition of its concept. One of the most comprehensive appeared in a report to the US legislature some years ago (USGPO, 1976). Interdependence has a great many meanings. It is described as a dynamic condition system, on which the forces of growth and change compel the states and peoples of the world to depend more on one another for their security and welfare, while they also (and decisively) rely on themselves. Thus interdependence also implies both self-reliance and bi- and multilateral co-operation.

This definition is correct in the sense that interdependence is a multidimensional notion, but for a concrete analysis, it must be defined more precisely. The interpretation is also one-sided, because it fails to take into account the stages in the process, with its divergent intensities, degrees of importance and consequences of relations. It does not explain, for example, historical changes in interstate relations, and it is problematic because it equates actual mutual dependence with one-sided dependence. An alternative definition was provided by Yoshikazu Sakamoto (1974). First: interdependence may have a negative and positive face. The former refers to those interactions that arise from mutual withdrawals and mutual denials, while the latter to those from expectations connected with mutual benefits. Secondly: interdependence may be symmetrical and asymmetrical. The former indicates that interdependence takes place on equal terms while the latter means the interdependence is unequal.

The combination of these two criteria leads to the following possible subnotions:

- Negative symmetrical interdependence, exemplified by nuclear deterrence existed between the United States and the Soviet Union.
- Negative asymmetrical interdependence, represented by the colonial system.
- Positive symmetrical interdependence based on equitable partnership relations, e.g. horizontal division of labour among the developed countries.
- Positive asymmetrical interdependence found in the framework of the European Union, between the small and large member-countries.

Sakamoto's definition describes all forms of international relations or interstate effects as interdependence, irrespective of their character and intensity. It is important to note here that, while cases of negative symmetrical, negative asymmetrical, and positive symmetrical interdependence are rather common in history, few successful examples of positive asymmetrical interdependence relationships can be recognised between the North and the South without asymmetrical dependence assuming a dominant role. The question is this: is a positive asymmetrical kind of co-operation possible, and is it a politically and economically realistic objective?

The pioneers of the notion of interdependence in American political science were Keohane and Nye (1977). They state that interdependence, defined in the simplest way, means mutual dependence. "Interdependence in world politics refers to a situation characterised by interactions among states of agents … of world politics … in the different countries. We do not confine interdependence to mutuality. Such a definition would presuppose that a policy concept is useful only where threat by military power is rare and the level of conflicts is low." However, the concept expressed by Henry Kissinger was not far from the views of Keohane and Nye: "The traditional themes of foreign affairs – power relations among the leading countries, the security of states – no longer define out dangers and possibilities. We are entering a new era. The traditional international structure is decaying. The world has become interdependent in the fields of economy, telecommunications and human endeavours" (US Department of State, 1975, p. 1). Kissinger (1995) also emphasises the growing internationalisation of national politics. Interdependence has undermined even more the effective sovereignty of states in their economic transactions, he notes.

There is an extremely complex range of problems relating to the management of "mutual dependence" or interdependence. For interdependence brings mutual vulnerability, as a new dimension of the political, economic and environmental security of the interdependent countries. Since the activities and existence of one state interweave in a complex fashion with those of other states (and social classes and groups within them), that state's objectives in several areas can be attained only if the impact of other countries is taken into account. Such an impact may occur in the political and economic fields and in environmental management, and not necessarily in a symmetrical way. Interdependent relations may increase the coincidence of interests, but it may also give rise to tensions and conflicts. The ways countries interact may engender chaotic relations in international life and mean that they lose control over many areas of national life. Interdependence may provide an incentive to some countries to be less dependent, but it may also stimulate collective policymaking and action. The international consequences of interdependence are notably important in relation to global problems, which create interactions between states and make co-operation between them essential. The degree to which global development is environmentally and socially sustainable depends largely on the capabilities of nations for managing their interdependent relations.

Managing interdependence calls for suitable national institutions and international, multilateral organisations, to provide a framework for developing mutually accepted rules, norms and co-operation forms. These must perform international harmonisation of the cost and benefits, so that conflicts emerging in political or economic relations can be resolved equitably. Success with this presupposes greater co-ordination of economic policies. The concept and practice of global governance that is emerging is in fact a requirement for the management of interdependence.

All these and other changes are interrelated with the ongoing transitions and transformations in the human dimension of globalisation at the early years of the 21st century, which are the main issues of this book. They include the interactions between environmental, technological, economic and social changes, and the population trends, with the transition to a new, global population cycle. Other aspects covered relate to urbanisation and the evolving patterns of settlement, complex issues concerned with employment and internationalisation of labour markets, and the problems of governance and the civil society.

3. THE NEW TRAJECTORIES
OF SOCIAL TRANSFORMATION

*The sources and consequences of social changes and
mounting inequalities*

Recorded history begins in a world divided into small and large communities across different continents. During the next couple of milleniums each succeeding epoch has added opportunities for some communities to progress and expand or destroyed the conditions for them to do so. The communities have also changed. Families remained for a very long time the most lasting formations but their role and structure had been also transformed by the different turns of human history. City states became regional empires. New empires emerged and disintegrated, global empires flourished and perished. Nation states developed on their ruins. Over the last half-millennium, there has been a protracted decline of great empires, beginning with the collapse of the Spanish Empire, and ending with the disintegration of the Soviet Union.

Economic development had been the most important factor in changing societies. It has involved different social, structural, institutional, technological transformations. The main trajectory in economic development is economic growth.

Economic growth was slow almost throughout human history up to the Industrial Revolution. It was so slow, in fact, as to be imperceptible within the life span of an individual, so that contemporaries did not notice it at all. This gradually changed after the mid-1700s, but the progress was neither constant nor general. The ups and downs of cycles, recession, stagnation, man-made and natural disasters, "golden ages" and "muddling through" made human life insecure, in an ever less predictable and manageable environment. Institutions were established and responded with varying efficiency to the challenges of the epoch, changing under new pressures, as their communities were transformed.

The meeting of basic needs as a global right was stated in the Universal Declaration of Human Rights of 1948, which explicitly expressed the social dimension of human rights. This dimension was reaffirmed more emphatically in the international covenants of 1966, especially the International Covenant on Economic, Social and Cultural Rights. Several years later, the fundamental concept of the right to development began to emerge in that context.

In the world after the Second World War, the Universal Declaration of Human Rights reflected an important recognition by countries about the role of welfare, democracy and human security in the sustainability of global peace. A fundamental place in the standard-setting activities of the United Nations was taken by the idea of social development. As early as 1954, the United Nations prepared an interesting report on the measurement of social progress, or as the title put it, "International Definition and Measurement of Standards and Levels of Living" (UN, 1954). This listed the perceived components of the level of living, resulting from the peculiarities of environmental conditions, cultures, values, economic, political and social conditions. It included (1) health, including demographic conditions, (2) food and nutrition, (3) education, including literacy, (4) conditions of work, (5) employment situation, (6) aggregate consumption and savings, (7) transportation, (8) housing and household facilities, (9) clothing, (10) recreation and entertainment, (11) social security, and (12) human freedoms. The report was a largely statistical exercise that advanced collective thinking in international organisations and countries and the development of the statistical indicators. Later, a number of social goals were included in the targets of Development Decades. Some UN agencies, such as Unicef, the WHO, the FAO and the ILO, tried to develop or recommend policies along the lines of the standards established in 1954, to redefine the goals of development. Thus the UN system was working for social progress in a number of areas, with the UNDP, the Unicef, the ILO and the Unesco leading the way.

Social issues gained particular importance at the strategic UN conferences held in the last decade of the 20th century. Global conferences have been organised by the UN also before the 1990s. Even some of the old themes of the end-century world conferences reflected however the postulates of the new era. Some of these conferences were global summits with the participation of heads of states and prime ministers from the majority of the states. The great difference was however the increasing participation of the non-governmental organisations, representing the civil society of the countries. The first World Conference on Children in 1990 introduced new commitments for national governments to monitor of, and report regularly on the situation of the children. At the Conference on Environment and Development in Rio de Janeiro in 1992, the relationship between the human being and the environment was raised in such a way that the relations between social and environmental issues gained central importance. The human and ecological dimensions of sustainable development have been organically linked. A new International Commission on Sustainable Development was established. The Human Rights Conference in Vienna in 1993 reiterated the organic relations between human development, participation, security, sustainability and the guaranteed human rights. The emphasis on the universality, inalienability and indivisibility of human rights and the essential need for a comprehensive approach to the related issues have been particularly important messages to governments and the civil society actors in the new era. The demographic aspects of global development were raised at the Cairo Population Conference in 1994 again in the context of social policies. The conference reflected also those political and social problems which divided the population of the world in the important issues of birth control and family planning. The 1995 Social Summit in Copenhagen was the first occasion at which global social-development issues were raised, discussed and treated in a comprehensive, coherent framework. Three important governing ideas and three priorities were defined. (1) Only within a social order based on justice can individual human beings reach their full potential. (2) Economic progress is impossible without progress in the social sphere. (3) Social development should be the political response of the international community to the socio-economic challenges of globalisation. Accordingly, the three priorities set were to provide social protection for the individuals, to assist social integration and to maintain social peace. The documents and the debates revealed the fact that social protection, employment and globalisation are closely linked. Competitiveness is a crucially important factor in the world of the 21st century. Firms which strive to remain competitive often consider social protection contributions as costly impediments. It has been emphasised that the costs of social protection should be weighed against the costs of not providing it. Social protection is not just an issue related to well being. It is a source of higher labour productivity, greater social cohesion and of other positive outcomes directly or indirectly promoting competitiveness. These priorities have raised the question of interaction between political and social issues. On the one hand, harmonious social development requires a stable political environment, while on the other, political stability calls for a healthy social environment. A state in which inequality and privilege predominate runs the risk of social upheavals and instability. A state that does not allow satisfactory social integration and fosters massive exclusion leaves itself open to unexpected social outbursts. Nations such as these accounted for most of the armed conflicts in the 1990s. The Beijing conference on the status of women in 1995 addressed 12 areas of critical concern to women: the survival and development of the girl child, poverty, education, health, violence, armed conflicts, employment opportunities and discrimination, economic and sexual exploitation, women and the media, participation in political decision-making, specific strategies in different situations and the legal framework. Habitat II in 1996 in Istambul was focussing on the key socio-economic problems of urban transition and on the critical issues of urban poverty. The new problems and dimensions of global food security have been the main topic of the World Food Congress in Rome in 1996.

Despite all the problems with the implementation and compliance, the recommendations of the strategic conferences stimulated national policies and actions and have yielded improvements in some areas. For instance, the 1990s have brought increases in life expectancy at birth to about 30 countries, including 17 in the developing world. The proportion of the world population with access to safe water nearly doubled in 1990–99. Adult literacy reached 76 per cent. Per capita food production increased by about 25 per cent between 1988–2000. The unprecedented global spread of democracy, however, did not strengthen adequately the self-correcting mechanisms of the societies that replaced the authoritarian regimes (UNDP, 1999). Society at the beginning of the 21st century still faces important questions. Are the existing and evolving institutions of the community conducive for human welfare? What are the sources of success and failure in the evolving system? There is a widespread perception that society in such countries is threatened from numerous directions.

Frank Knight, a celebrated American economist in the 1920s and 1930s, used to say that progress is not a question of happiness, but of what people are unhappy about. There are many sources of discontent in the world of the early 21st century. Most of them relate to the specific problems of countries and regions, but some are global. Inequalities and their consequences, for instance, cut across the bounds of communities great and small. Here are some examples:
- Many countries are suffering economic decline or stagnation, with falling per capita income, investment and consumption. Of 95 developing countries monitored by the UN in the second half of the 1990s (UN, 2000a), one-third were experiencing a decline in per capita GDP. These countries, most of them in Africa and the Middle East, contained about 22 per cent of the population of the developing world.
- There is persistent and often growing poverty in many parts of the world. According to more recent UN data, 1.3–1.4 billion people live on less than US $1 a day and about 840–900 million are malnourished, of which about 160 million are children.
- There is large-scale unemployment and under-utilisation of human potential, coupled with diminishing job insecurity. There is also an increase in sexual and commercial exploitation of women and children, with more than 250 million child labourers.
- Various forms of discrimination are prevalent, particularly on a gender basis, leading to marginalisation and social exclusion. The most dra-

matic change in the second half of the 20th century took place in the family. Families now face many pressures, including shrinking family size and the disappearance of the extended family. This process is more advanced in the developed world and the urban centres of the developing countries. The divorce rate is rising and so is the proportion of single-parent families. The traditional structures of solidarity and consensus building are weakening. At the same time, there is a growing sense that human beings need to belong to their communities and participate in them.

– There have been cuts in real expenditure per head on education and health in many countries, and a general neglect of social-development issues. In the second half of the 1990s, close to 900 million people lacked access to basic health services and 2.6 billion to basic sanitation (UNDPI, 2000). Between 1990 and 1997, the number of people infected with HIV more than doubled. Around 1.5 billion people alive today are not expected to survive to the age of 60. About 260 million women are not expected to survive to the age of 40.

Behind all these problems lies a general international socio-economic problem of the early 21st century: the increasing income and wealth inequalities between and within countries. A recent UN report (Unicef, 2000) described the situation as an undeclared war on women, adolescents and children, whose rights are threatened and development prevented by poverty, chronic social instability and preventable diseases. The policies and strategies must address both the causes and effects of it to build an appropriate framework for concrete actions.

The secretary-general of the UN, in his report to the Millennium Assembly (UN, 2000b) stated that the 20th century had ended without liberating humanity from dramatic inequality. However, his report failed to give a convincing explanation why this had happened. The world as a whole has become wealthier than it was a hundred years ago. Global GDP in 1999 was about US $35 trillion, which was almost 20 times higher than in 1900. Per capita world income was about $5600 in 1999, as opposed to $1410 in 1900, at comparable prices, so there is about four times as much GDP per "average person".[28] The secretary-general's report sheds interesting light on how the average person fares at the beginning of the 21st century:

[28] The concept of an "average person", by the way, was introduced by a Belgian statistician, Adolphe Quetelet, in 1831. An astronomer by training, he became interested in scientific analysis of social questions. His fictional average person, representative of a group, is still a useful concept, for global social analysis as well. For information on Quetelet and his concept, see Stigler (2000).

"For the United Nations, success in meeting the challenges of globalisation ultimately comes down to meeting the needs of peoples. It is in their name that the Charter was written; realising their aspirations remains our vision for the 21st century. But who are we, the peoples? And what are our common concerns?"

"Let us imagine, for a moment, that the world really is a 'global village' – taking seriously the metaphor that is often invoked to depict global interdependence. Say this village has 1000 individuals, with all the characteristics of today's human race distributed in exactly the same proportions. What would it look like? What would we see as its main challenges?"

"Some 150 of the inhabitants live in an affluent area of the village, about 780 in poorer districts. Another 70 or so live in a neighbourhood that is in transition. The average income per person is $6000 a year, and there are more middle-income families than in the past. But just 200 people dispose of 86 per cent of all the wealth, while nearly half of the villagers are eking out an existence on less than $2 per day."

"Men outnumber women by a small margin, but women make up a majority of those who live in poverty. Adult literacy has been increasing. Still, some 220 villagers, two thirds of them women, are illiterate. Of the 390 inhabitants under 20 years of age, three-fourths live in the poorer districts, and many are looking desperately for jobs that do not exist. Fewer than 60 people own a computer and only 24 have access to the Internet. More than half have never made or received a telephone call. Life expectancy in the affluent district is nearly 78 years, in the poorer areas 64 years and in the very poorest neighbourhoods a mere 52 years. Each marks an improvement over previous generations, but why do the poorest lag so far behind?"

"Because in their neighbourhoods there is a far higher incidence of infectious diseases and malnutrition, combined with an acute lack of access to safe water, sanitation, health care, adequate housing, education and work."

"There is no predictable way to keep the peace in this village. Some districts are relatively safe while others are wracked by organised violence. The village has suffered a growing number of weather-related natural disasters in recent years, including unexpected and severe storms, as well as sudden swings from floods to droughts, while the average temperature is perceptibly warmer. More and more evidence suggests that there is a connection between these two trends, and that warming is related to the kind of fuel, and the quantities of it, that the people and businesses are using. Carbon emissions, the major cause of warming, have quadrupled in the last 50 years. The village's water table is falling precipitously, and the livelihood of one sixth of the inhabitants is threatened by soil degradation in the surrounding countryside."

"Who among us would not wonder how long a village in this state can survive without taking steps to ensure that all its inhabitants can live free from hunger and safe from violence, drinking clean water, breathing clean air, and knowing that their children will have real chances in life?"

"That is the question we have to face in our real world of 6 billion inhabitants" (UN, 2000b).

Nonetheless, averages become insufficient to explain reality in an era of increasing inequalities. They also offer little help with setting social targets.

The advantages of the developed countries increased further and faster during the 20th century, with the exception of short periods. There has been some convergence in per capita incomes within the group of developed countries, but the income gap between developed and less developed countries has widened dramatically. According to economic historians, the income ration of the poorest to the richest country was 1:3 in 1820, but 1:78 at the end of the 20th century. UNDP studies suggest that the richest 20 per cent of the world were consuming about two-thirds of the goods and services, while 60 per cent of the world's population received less than 20 per cent in the last decade of the 20th century (UNDP, 1996, 1997, 1998, 1999 and 2000).

One of the consequences of the growing inequalities is the persistence and increase of poverty. Poverty increased fastest in the 1990s in some of the former socialist countries. This was reflected in a decline of family incomes, increasing mortality rates, deteriorating health conditions, and in many countries, declining education standards.[29]

There are various definitions, sources and faces of poverty on the globe. Most international organisations define poverty as the inability to attain a minimum standard of living. A more comprehensive approach was developed in the research programme on hunger and poverty conducted by the World Institute for Development Economics Research of the United Nations University.[30] It included in its analysis of poverty such factors as access to health care and economic resources, various forms of livelihood, income, wealth, access to education and skills, level of functional literacy, social mobility, exclusion, discrimination, social integration, housing, security of life and property, human rights and political participation. It was found that the most important factors causing poverty were economic decline, stagnation or slow economic growth, unemployment, discrimination on grounds of

---

[29] For details, see Unicef (1999a).

[30] This was the widest-ranging research programme on poverty to be conducted within the UN system. The large international, interdisciplinary research group was headed by the Indian economist, Amartya Sen. See Wider (1994), p. 15.

gender, religion or ethnicity, social exclusion, and various systemic factors resulting in great inequalities in the distribution of incomes and welfare.

International experience shows that the market system can only reduce poverty under certain conditions, unless there are deliberate policy drives to do so. Poverty is usually moderated if economic growth is fast and widespread. Research work on the interrelations between growth and poverty in specific developing countries revealed that a growth rate of 10 per cent reduced the poverty headcount (the percentage of the population living on less than $1 a day) by 9 per cent in countries where income was fairly equally distributed. However, in countries with highly unequal distributions of income, a growth rate of 10 per cent reduced the poverty headcount by only 3 per cent.[31] In the early stages of the 21st century, amelioration of poverty will require extended, sustainable GDP growth of 2–3 per cent a year in the industrial world, 4–5 per cent in the developing countries and 3–4 per cent in the transition countries. Such growth should also result in a rapidly increasing demand for labour. The other condition for moderating poverty in a market system concerns rural communities and relates to the availability of vacant land for the rural poor. The third condition is a supply of capital accessible even to poorer entrepreneurs. A general condition is empowerment, for which the main instrument is a widespread, free system of education able to provide functional literacy. However, poverty is not just a problem of low incomes. It is also inherent in a lack of social services and health care, and for many millions of people, it takes the form of social exclusion and marginalisation, with deprivation of fundamental rights. "Pro-poor growth", a concept introduced in the 1990 World Development Report (World Bank, 1990), cannot be confined to growth rates.

The spread and growth of poverty has often been blamed on the process of globalisation. In the global market system, all economic interaction, trade, capital flows, and even migration between countries have their winners and losers.

The research work undertaken so far on the social aspects of globalisation is still not sufficiently widespread and complex for a convincing, unambiguous verdict on this issue. The influence of globalising economic forces on societies depends on many internal and external factors. Liberalisation, for example, which is one of the important pre-requisites of globalisation, has brought greater inequalities in primary incomes in countries with a weak competitiveness.[32] One empirical study on several countries found that wages fell as the participation rate in the labour force increased. Some of its

---

[31] See Hammer et al. (1999), pp. 547–63.
[32] See Berg and Taylor (2000).

findings confirmed earlier hypotheses, for instance, that the process had a particularly adverse impact on unskilled labour. Wage differentials between skilled and unskilled workers tended to increase. The consequence of liberalisation in advanced countries is different. There it promoted some convergence of incomes among the industrial countries, according to the study (Ben David, 2000).

It would be necessary to pay more attention to the role of internal factors, which are hampering the potentially positive influence of globalisation on modernisation and development particularly in the former socialist states and in many developing countries. Modernisation is of course not only technological or institutional change. It is as much related to changing human attitudes. In this context, the modernity syndrom of individuals in its Western understanding was characterised by one author as

- openness to new experience, both with people and with new ways of doing things, such as attempting to control birth;
- the assertion of increasing independence from the authority of traditional figures like parents and priests and a shift of allegiance to leaders of government, public affairs, trade unions, co-operatives, and the like;
- belief in the efficiency of science and medicine, and a general abandonment of passivity and fatalism in the face of life's difficulties;
- ambition for oneself and one's children to achieve high occupational and educational goals;
- liking people to be on time and showing interests in carefully planning affairs in advance;
- showing strong interests and taking active part in civic and community affairs and local politics;
- striving energetically to keep up with the news and within this effort preferring news of national and international importance over items dealing with purely local affairs.[33]

It is of course an open question to what extent those characteristics are compatible with different traditions and are they shared by the different generations? In the case of Japan for example it was underlined that certain components of traditional attitudes were instrumental also in the modernisation process, like for example the openness to education and the subordination of individual interests to the community. It is also an interesting question: do personal characteristics in the modernisation process change or induce individualism or collectivism and solidarity, do they facilitate the harmonisation between individual and social goals, attitudes toward poverty, exclusion, etc.

---

[33] M. Havelsrood: *Controversies concerning the relationship between education and development.* (Paper presented to the 11th General Conference of IPRA. 1986), p. 5.

There is for example and increasing opinion which attributes poverty to structural causes rather than to the properties of the individuals concerned. In the conflict between traditional cultural values and modernity the impact of these types of changes must also be better understood.

In the context of the cultural factors, in an interesting book "Culture Matters", edited by L. E. Harrison and S. Huntington, the author of the chapter on Africa, Etounga-Manguelle, a distinguished expert from Cameroon for example, puts the emphasis on the following modernisation-resistant components of the African culture: the high degree of fatalism and irrationalism, focus on the past and present and not on the future, excessive concentration of authority and power, a communitarianism that suffocates individual initiative, disregard for the economic realities of life. The African nightmare, as he puts the combined effect of those factors on the nations south of the Sahara is however not confined to the region. Such problems as the focus on the past or the disregard of economic realities are characterising many other cultures also in other parts of the world.

Globalisation and changing social stratification

Taking a broader perspective, it becomes increasingly apparent that the social influence of the globalisation process cuts across the traditional social classes. In a simplified way, three main groups of the world population can be defined as emerging because of globalisation.

The first, which can be considered as globalised segment of society. This is a diverse group, topped by the "super-rich" of the world. The richest 225 people in the world have a combined wealth equal to the annual income of 47 per cent of the world's people. Two-thirds of these super-rich are the citizens of the industrial countries, while the remainder come from the Third World and the former socialist countries (UNDP, 1998). The most important and influential section of the group is the one that commands the hierarchies of the major institutions that have a fundamental influence on the political, economic and military processes of globalisation, through their role in decision-making. These people are also powerful enough to implement their decisions, due to their wealth, executive position or both. They are not solitary actors, but surrounded by specialists, advisers, consultants, scholars and institutions, and by the influential personalities in the media. Their power derives from a number of factors: personal wealth, the size of the human, financial, and material resources over which they dispose, and the political and military influence of these decisions on various countries. Gustave Speth, the former administrator of the UNDP, wrote, "An emerging global elite, mostly urban based and interconnected in a variety of ways, is amassing great wealth and power, while over half of humanity is left out."[34] The global profiteers and speculators often mentioned by the critics of globalisation comprise only a small part of the "global power elite" in the various societies. [35] Beyond the owners and managers of the 60,000–65,000 transnational corporations, there are 100–120 large international banks, auditing and consultancy firms, whose core executives also belong to the globalised group of society. According to UN statistics, the transnationals employ globally about 90 million people. Many of these work in sweatshops and cannot be considered as parts of the globalised society, but the small and medium-sized entrepreneurs who are their subcontractors belong to this group.

The global political elite is diverse and hierarchical. The role of the executive and legislative elites of the US, Japan, the main European countries, Russia and China are particularly important. Indicators such as presence in the General Assembly Hall during the speeches by heads of state at the UN Millennium Summit of the UN reflected well how the world "evaluated" the leading politicians of different countries, in terms of global hierarchies. Apart from the top elected and appointed part of the political elite, the globalised group can also be considered to contain the majority of leading members of the civil service, the top military elite and the academic community, as well as media figures and leading personalities in "global" religious denominations. Naturally, the benefits are also shared by family members of these people. The "globalised" segment can be estimated to include 15–20 per cent of the population in the industrial countries and much less in the developing world. Of course, there are great differences in income, power and influence among them. The Secretary General of the UN had an annual income of US$258,552 in 2000. The President of the Ford Foundation received US$487,500. The chief executive of Coca Cola had an annual income of US$4,440,000 and a personal accumulated wealth of more than 130 million dollars.[36] Some of them who share common interests in the globalisation process in the less developed part of the world are also billionaires. They also share a number of common values and convictions, and even use a common language. They form the most mobile part of their society. They project an image and concept of success measured in power and financial gains. There is also a poorer part of the group, whose livelihoods nonetheless depend on the success of the globalised sectors, so that they share certain interests in this context.

[34] *New York Times,* July 15, 1996. p. 55.

[35] Mills (1956) provides an authoritative account of the American ruling elite. It could still offer an interesting starting point for analysing the global power elite, which is an important task awaiting sociologists.

[36] *The New York Times,* April 1, 2001. pp. 10–12.

At the opposite social extreme stand a much greater number of people. They are mainly losers. These people are not simply excluded from the globalisation process and marginalised by it, but often (and increasingly) exposed to the global mass consumption and mass culture ideology, to a greater extent than the globalised group. They include the vast majority of the agricultural population, although the agricultural sector and agricultural population are also divided. Only a small minority is engaged in industrial-scale agriculture. The vast majority, including the masses of the rural poor, belongs to the informal economy. However, there are some interactions between the two types of agriculture. The tens of millions who have been squeezed out of agriculture by the technological and economic changes in agriculture can only find an alternative livelihood by migrating to urban areas.

The large, diverse non-globalised group in society consists of the unskilled, most small entrepreneurs (especially the "barefoot capitalists" of the informal sector), the urban poor, the unemployed, various ethnic minorities and the victims of social exclusion. Many people in this group are functionally illiterate, even in the industrial countries. According to an OECD classification, the proportion of the functionally illiterate comprises 20–40 per cent of the population in its member-states.[37] The proportion of this group is much higher in the developing countries. Those excluded include the "proletarians" of the professional world, such primary schoolteachers. Statistical estimates suggest that the group excluded from the globalisation process may comprise about 50 per cent of the world population.

The third group consists of those between the two previous groups or on the frontiers of them. This group is exposed to the opportunities and losses connected with the globalisation process, and tends to split. The well-educated and wealthier part will probably join the first group, as the knowledge-based economies open up new opportunities for them. The remainder will progressively experience the full disadvantages of the globalisation process.[38]

One of the big dilemmas for social scientists examining the social consequences of globalisation is to decide whether it will push humanity into stormy, turbulent waters? Can the process be managed in such a way as to reduce its detrimental effects and extend its opportunities to much larger numbers of people? These are not theoretical issues. They are closely related to such practical problems as the global organisation of production and the social responsibility and accountability of the business sector. Also an important practical issue is the functioning of government, particularly in such

---

[37] See Panos Institute (1999).
[38] See Drucker (1994).

areas as controlling market forces and the adverse consequences of global competition.

There are problems of different nature relating to the functioning of the political system. In the longer term, for example, this covers the question of whether global citizenship is a realistic concept. Some social scientists point to the way national citizenship emerged in past centuries via the modernisation process, based on three pillars built by different social struggles and reforms: individual and human rights, political participation and socio-economic welfare.[39] They note that all the issues central to the debates on national citizenship in past centuries are increasingly affected by global forces, which suggests it is time to focus attention explicitly and deliberately on global citizenship. However, such suggestions are not borne out by the realities or the social consequences of the globalisation process. Even in Europe, in the framework of the relatively homogeneous European Union, progress toward European citizenship has been slow, difficult and controversial.

Population trends and demographic factors will have a major influence on all other aspects of global change. They comprise also a vitally important part of global transformation.

[39] See UNRISD (1995), pp. 168–169.

4. THE POLITICS AND ECONOMICS OF THE CHANGING POPULATION TRENDS

Population dynamics influence all other aspects of global changes. They are also influenced by other, political, economic, technological and institutional changes and also by interests, values and ideologies. The size, structure and rate of increase of the world population have always been fundamental to an analysis of the human dimension of global change. The world's population problems received notable attention in the second half of the 20th century, generated debate far beyond the academic community of professional demographers. Doomsday pessimists, objective scholars, religious fundamentalists and racist extremists add strands to the global debate. Paul Erlich's famous book *The Population Bomb* (1968) offered a dramatic picture of the future, reflected in its title. *The Limits to Growth*, the first report of the Club of Rome, issued in 1972, states, "If the present growth trends in world population, industrialisation, pollution, food production and resource depletion continue unchanged, the limits to growth on this planet will be reached sometime within the next one hundred years. The most probable result will be a rather sudden and uncontrollable decline of world population and industrial capacity" (Club of Rome, 1972, p. 23).

An interesting side of the population debate in the 1960s concerned the limits of the Earth's capacity to sustain human life. Various studies took a great number of approaches. The central issues in the early years were energy and food, which prompted an overly optimistic, Utopian response from the Russian academic K. M. Malin in *The Life-Sustaining Resources of Mankind*, published in 1961. He estimated that the Earth could ultimately supply 58 billion people, if all its resources were subordinated to human needs.[40]

In a more recent book, *How Many People Can the Earth Support?* (Cohen, 1995), the American demographer Joel Cohen raises several related questions to do with alternative strategies. What level and distribution of material well-being are presupposed? What technology, domestic and international

---

[40] Malin (1961). The Hungarian edition of 1963 was consulted.

institutions, and political and economic arrangements will pertain? What will the physical environment be? What risks will be run and for how long? What values and quality of life are required? Cohen also asked pertinently how free society would be to answer to these questions. The work of Cohen and others shows there can be no easy, clear answer to the question Cohen puts.

Before embarking on more detailed discussion of what the size, growth and structure of the world population imply for the future, some qualifications to do with methodology and policies must be mentioned.

(1) Population projections have proved to be more reliable in anticipating or predicting changes on a global scale than political and economic projections, but even so, a number of the prognoses have turned out to be wrong. These have usually been overestimates, globally and regionally. (2) Population changes are important factors in shaping the prospects for the global economy, but demography remains only one of several factors. In a global economic context, demography has to be related to other processes, such as the availability of natural resources, the influence of technology change, the role of economic growth patterns, or the impact of social policies. (3) The pressure of demographic forces on the functioning of a society or an economy is more often indirect, manifesting itself through different problem areas, so that it is understood in a particular environment only after some delay. (4) Relations between demographic and economic changes are even more complex on the level of the global economy, because of the increasing global demographic diversity. (5) While population problems are potentially imminent and could become a source of dangerous conflicts, they may not influence national public attitudes and government decisions to the required extent, if attitudes and decisions are prompted, as usual, by shorter-term interests. (6) The attitudes toward population issues, especially family planning, have been influenced much by a variety of ideologies and sets of values. (7) All these problems are obstacles to managing population problems on a national and international level. Many states have national demographic policies, but no well-conceived, internationally co-ordinated activity has emerged.

By the end of the 20th century, the population of the world had surpassed the 6 billion mark. Historians put the world population at the beginning of the first millennium at about 300 million, and by the end of the first millennium, only a little higher. It then took about 800 years to reach 1 billion in the early 19th century. According to the same estimates, it therefore took 17 centuries to double the population of the world. During the past 200 years, on the other hand, there has been a six-fold increase in the population of the world.[41] With present fertility rates, it would double in 40 years. The 25 years from 1975 to 2000 brought the largest increment in world population experienced in any previous quarter-century of human history: more than 2.2 billion people. The increasing size of the world population poses a critical and historically unprecedented social, economic and ecological challenge, through increased pollution and requirements of food, water, energy, raw materials and space.

The world is approaching the end of a demographic epoch marked by an accelerating increase in the world population. The first scientifically important effort to understand the nature and dangers of this came from Malthus in 1797, in his famous *Essay on the Principle of Population* (Malthus, 1798). Malthus predicted an increase in famine and malnutrition due to an inequality between the population increase and the goods available. He believed that the population of the world would increase to saturation point unless natural forces checked its growth. The "positive check" of war, famine, plague, pestilence and disease should be allowed to counteract the increase "without let or hindrance", he argued. Malthus and his followers failed to predict two important things. One was that a growing population, under certain conditions, could have favourable consequences. The other was that population trends might also change over the years, as societies became more prosperous. In demographic terms, improved health and social services bring a decline in mortality that causes rapid population growth, but after a varying length of time, a number of general and specific factors cause a decline in birth rates that may even result in stagnation and a declining population.

There is historical evidence for the first assumption in late 18th-century England, where the population growth and subsequent stimulation of demand for food encouraged investment in agriculture. Thereafter, industrialisation increased employment and demand. The post-war baby boom in the United States likewise boosted investment, demand and employment. However, these events occurred in single countries. In the economy of the late 20th century, such favourable interactions were not present in the developing countries.

As for the second trend, the latest United Nations estimates and projections of world population show a continuing slowing of growth. It is projected to grow to about 8 billion in 2025 and 9.3 billion in 2050. The world population growth rate has declined from a peak of 2 per cent in 1965 to 1.7 per cent in 1980 and to 1.3 per cent in 2000. It is projected to decline to 1 per cent around 2020 and 0.5 per cent in 2050, with all of the population growth

---

[41] Quoted in *The Economist*, December 31, 1999, p. 13.

after 2025 occurring in the developing countries.[42] The process of demographic transformation is unequal. It may be the source of various social conflicts, if its implications are not understood and managed properly. The transition to the new era has started in the more developed countries and in many former socialist and some developing countries. The demographic transformation is related to improvements in health and changes in socioeconomic conditions. Also involved are such factors as the growing emancipation and social participation of women, urbanisation, the changing social division of labour, the spread of family planning, and many other specific changes.

[42] The Population Division of the United Nations prepared new long-range projections for the world population and eight major world areas for the period 1995–2150. The revised findings, published in UN (1999a, 1999b and 2000c), cover in detail Africa, Asia excluding China and India, Europe, Latin America and the Caribbean, North America, Oceania, and China and India (the only two countries considered separately). The projections include several scenarios for possible future growth of the world population. (a) The medium scenario assumes that fertility in all main areas will stabilise at replacement level (slightly over 2 children per woman) by 2050 or after. (b) The low scenario assumes that fertility in all main areas will fall short of the rate in the medium scenario by about half a child. (c) The high scenario assumes that fertility will exceed the rate in the medium scenario by about half a child. Also considered for illustrative purposes are (d) a constant scenario, where fertility is constant over 1995–2150 at the level it had in each main area in 1990–95, and (e) an instant-replacement scenario, in which fertility in each main area is assumed to drop instantly to replacement level in 1995 and remain there until 2150. All these scenarios assume that mortality declines steadily over the projection period, but for some, a variation that incorporates constant mortality over the period 2050–2150 at the level attained in 2050 is also considered for purposes of comparison. Normally, long-range projections are produced every five years. However, the changes introduced in UN (1999a, 1999b and 2000c) made early revision of these projections necessary. In recent years, a major reassessment of the prospects for fertility decline has taken place. By 1995, only 17 countries in the developing world, with less than 4 per cent of the world population, showed no signs of a fertility reduction. In many countries where fertility reduction had begun, the fall was rapid. Moreover, in countries already far advanced in the transition from high to low fertility, fertility did not necessarily stabilise at replacement level. The number of countries with below-replacement fertility is large and increasing. By 1995, 44 per cent of the world population lived in countries where fertility was at or below replacement level (2.1 children per woman). Forty-nine countries, including China, were in that group, and many had been experiencing below-replacement fertility for a decade or two. In 10 countries, fertility fell below 1.5 children per woman. Recent data confirms that low fertility has persisted. These developments justified the assumption that fertility would remain below replacement level over most of the 1995–2150 period in countries with below-replacement fertility today, incorporated into the medium projection of UN (1999a, 1999b and 2000c). The 1996 Revision in the same series had assumed a return to replacement-level fertility in all countries. Such differing assumptions have important implications for the long-term future. Whereas the medium scenario of the preceding long-range projections, consistent with the 1996 Revision, yielded a world population of 10.8 billion in 2150, the medium scenario of the present projection, consistent with UN (1999a, 1999b and 2000c), produced a population total of 9.7 billion, or 1.1 billion lower.

The new political economy of age composition

There are two important dimensions of the changes in the age composition: the large number of younger people which is a pressing problem in most of the developing countries, and the ageing, the growth of the elderly segment of the population, influencing mainly the developed part of the world.

This latter will be a global long-term consequence of the demographic transition. Some of the developing countries are already facing the problems of ageing. In fact they are in the pincers of the changing population dynamics. The median age of the world population was 23.5 years in 1950 (21.3 in the developing and 28.6 in the developed countries). In 1999 it was 26.4 years (24.4 in the developing and 37.2 in the developed countries)[43]

Relatively high fertility rates and declining mortality rates in the developing countries mean the majority of them have a relatively young population, but the proportion of young people is declining also in these countries. The proportion of children and adolescents below the age of 18 reached almost 40 per cent of the population at the end of the 1960s and then began a slow decline. The age group still made up more than one-third of the global population at the end of the century, which reflects the trends in the developing countries. Meanwhile the proportion of the population below the age of 18 in the developed countries has fallen below 20 per cent. The average European woman bears 1.7 children during her years of fertility, as opposed to the 2.1 children that would be needed for full population replacement.

In spite of the overall decline in the proportion of children under 18, the current number of young people is over 2.1 billion which is the largest in the history of the world. Over 85 per cent of them are living in the developing countries where the child population is exposed to a great number of specific risk factors. In the developing parts of the world one-third of the births are not registered. The chance of a child to survive is affected by poverty, malnutrition, disease and conflicts. There are about 130 million children of school age who do not have access to basic education (about 60 per cent of them are girls). About 250 million children work and many of them are below the age of 10 and in workshops with hazardous conditions. Participation in armed conflicts influences also millions of children and youth. The mass migration from the rural to the urban areas is an other important source of difficulties. Child poverty, the commercial and sexual exploitation of children are not confined to the developing countries. Some 10 per cent of the children are liv-

---

[43] The World of Six Billion. UN Population Division, 1999. p. 31.

ing in families whose income is below the official poverty line in the industrial world.[44] Such challenges as limited resources available for education, inequalities in living conditions and opportunities, gender discrimination, juvenile delinquency, growing incidence of drug abuse, HIV/AIDS, limited employment opportunities, youth unemployment are global problems for the young people with adverse influence on the development of future generations. The problems of young people in the early 21st century have a number of characteristics specific to different regions. An important group among them consists of those between the ages of 10 and 19, who comprise about 20 per cent of the human race – 1.2 billion people. They represent a vital global resource but remain extremely vulnerable. The latest statistics show, for example, that 70 per cent of all premature deaths among adults result from behaviour that began in adolescence, such as the contraction of HIV or the use of tobacco. Every day, more than 7000 young people become infected with HIV, which now accounts for 50 per cent of all new infections with sexually transmitted diseases. The HIV infection rate among adolescent girls is up to five times as high as for boys. Altogether, some 10 million adolescents carry HIV and the number continues to climb. Meanwhile, over 100 million adolescents are exposed to the effects of armed conflict, as child soldiers, porters, sexual slaves or refugees. One in every 10 births is to an adolescent mother, and at least 60,000 adolescent girls a year die from complications in pregnancy or birth. Up to 4.4 million girls, between the ages of 15 and 19, undergo unsafe abortions every year. Some 300 million adolescents use tobacco, of whom half will die of tobacco-related diseases later in life. Traffic accidents are the leading cause of death among young men world-wide. The fatalities are often related to the use of alcohol and other drugs. There are at least 70 million child labourers between the age of 10 and 14.[45]

The implementation of the provisions in the Convention on the Rights of the Child (the most widely ratified global legal instrument), will have to be better supported by national children- and youth-friendly policies and actions.

Another important indicator of change and divergence in population trends is the number and proportion of people of working age (between the ages of 15 and 64). The proportion of this age group increased on a global level from 57 per cent in 1970 to 62 per cent in 1990, and reached 64 per cent in 2000. In the developed countries, it has remained relatively high (close to two-thirds of the population), but in the developing countries, it increased from 54.4 per cent in 1970 to over 60 per cent in the year 2000. Between 1970

---

[44] The State of the World's Children. (New York: UNICEF, 2000).
[45] The State of the World's Children. (New York: UNICEF, 2000).

and 1990, the working age group increased by about 1140 million persons, to more than a billion in the developing countries. According to the UN population projections, the number of people of working age will have increased by 1360 million between 1990 and 2010 (more specifically, by about 620 million in the 1990s and 740 million in the first decade of the next century). Only 4.7 per cent of the increment will be in the developed world and more than 95 per cent in the developing countries, where the increment will be about 1300 million. The developing regions where the population of working age increases most rapidly will be the Middle East, South and Central America and certain African countries. The biggest absolute increments will be in South Asia and China.[46]

Ageing is also a complex issue. Its political and economic consequences are often treated in a simplified way confined to the demographic aspects and to the potential difficulties. Orio Giarini, one of the important experts of the problems related to ageing, drew the attention to some important shortcomings. "This phenomenon is frequently described in traditional terms. It is, for example said that society is ageing. If what is meant is merely that most people today achieve an older age than they expected to 50 years ago, then the statement is acceptable. But in itself, the expression 'ageing society' is somewhat inappropriate. We must first recognise that there has been an increase in the length of the life cycle which probably counts as one of the greatest achievements of the 20th century. Second, it must be observed that what is really becoming older is the notion of age itself. We only need to read the European literature of the last century to learn how people felt at 40 years of age. It is also clear that the onset of physical and mental decline has been pushed back far later than was hitherto the case. In other words, at 50, 60, or 70 years of age, we are much younger today than we would have been at those ages in the not so distant past. Therefore our societies are in a sense getting younger because we live longer and better … Failure to understand the situation in these terms can lead to serious mistakes: on one hand, we tend to marginalise far too early a growing part of the population (those over 60) while on the other, we quickly run aground in the political debate about how far the younger generation should pay for the older. On both accounts, we find we have entered a dead end street."[47] As for the developed industrial countries, one may share the views of Mr. Giarini. In global perspective, the problems are more difficult and complex.

---

[46] The sources for these data include Human Development Report UNDP (1991–1999 volumes).

[47] Orio Giarini: Promoting gradual retirement in a counter-ageing society. Paper presented at the Policy Summit of the Global Ageing Intitiative. Zürich 22–24 Jan. 2001. p. 2.

There has been an expansion at the top of the population chart. The proportion of the world population over 60 years of age was 8.3 per cent in 1960, but 9.2 per cent by 1990 and about 10 per cent by the end of the century. In the 1990s, there were close to 620 million people in this age group, which was about 140 million more than in 1990. The over-60 age group makes up almost 20 per cent of the population in the developed countries, but only about 8 per cent in the developing world. By 2050 it will be more than double of the present proportions.

Another factor behind the ageing of the population is the improvement of health and social services, which reflects general human progress. Two-thirds of those who have ever survived to the age of 65 or over are alive today. Some developing countries, such as China, will have to face a double population pressure, as the young and the old age groups increase simultaneously.

The "political economy" of the changes in the age structure calls for deeper study of the process. One important issue is the shift in the borders between generations. The faster rate of technological innovation and the shortening of technological cycles mean that younger people will play a much greater role at the workplace due to their more up-to-date skills. The economics of population ageing has other dimensions as well. There have been four factors in the past, which helped the societies to handle the problems of the elderlies: the efforts of the individuals and the families, the capital, which has been accumulated over the working years, the social infrastructure and flexible labour market policies facilitating the extension of active participation.

Ageing increases the dependency ratios and places a greater burden on the groups of working age. The influence of the increasing segment of the older population increases the need for restructuring social expenditures to concentrate on special health and other services needed by the higher age groups. More than half of the social and health expenditure is already being spent on such services in some countries.

The challenges and problems caused by the decline or ageing of the population differ, of course, from those caused by the continuation of population growth. The latter brings an increase in the proportion of people of working age and a demand for new employment opportunities.

One of the challenges related to ageing is the management of intergenerational conflict. The increase in the number of dependants and the growth of health expenditure and pension outlays place additional burdens on the working population. This has to be done in a way that does not damage the chances for the younger generations to improve their living conditions. The social, economic and ethical issues of intergenerational responsibilities are far from abstract or theoretical in nature. The redistribution of incomes and reassessment of established policies, such as the appropriate ages, types or

66

nature of retirement and labour-force participation by the elderly, are important and difficult policy issues.

From among the four factors, the higher average age and the extension of
human capacities to work present new kinds of employment issues not only
for the older groups of the population. The age group which is taking shape
in the labour force is the new middle aged, between the ages of 55 and 75,
who are becoming much more active and looking for a productive role in
society rather than retirement influences the employment opportunities for
the younger people. The new middle aged will remain characteristic for a
time in a number of developed countries.

There are different possibilities for adjustment in the different specific situations. In countries where shrinkage of the groups of working age represents a more serious problem, there is a push to increase productivity by
innovation and by an accelerated mastery of new technology. This may impel
some countries to phase out and redeploy labour-intensive activities to other
countries and concentrate on high value-added production and services. In
the developing countries, the increasing number and proportion of people of
working age reduces the demographic dependency ratios. This could be
favourable to economic and social development, but only if a sufficiently
large number of new jobs can be created.

There are other approaches which are possible or already implemented in
some countries facing the problems of ageing. The first is artificial interfer-
ence in the population cycle: limiting the possibilities for family planing and
stimulating population growth. The second is to increase the productivity of
the working population by improving education and investing in technology. The third is liberalisation and selective stimulation of immigration. Each
of these courses implies social costs and may give rise to problems. Various
studies published by international organisations place emphasis on the
potential role that international migration could play in offsetting population
decline and ageing. As the age structure of immigrants is usually younger
than that of the host country, a more liberal immigration policy is the fastest
way to increase the number of the younger population. Most of these studies, however, pay little attention to analysing the economic costs and political and social implications of this alternative.

In the global discussion on the problems of ageing a new global plan of
action has been suggested by a number of countries which could change the
one-sided view mentioned by Giarini and put the emphasis on the active role
of the elderly people. This would differ from the programme adopted in 1982
and developed further in 1992. In this new plan of action, the societies would
facilitate that older people take on numerous responsibilities in which they
could utilise the accumulated knowledge, experience, capabilities and skills
at their command. These may vary from region to region and from culture to

culture in their specific character and content. The plan of action should of course pay due attention to the different age groups and health situations.

There is already a World Programme of Action for Youth to the Year 2000 and Beyond adopted in 1995 focussing on the welfare and living conditions of young people. It contains a number of recommendations for measures to strengthen national capabilities regarding youth and to increase the opportunities available to young people in the society. It identifies priority areas for actions, like facilitating education, creating employment, reduction of hunger and poverty, improving health services, organising and promoting leisure time activities, struggling against drug abuse and juvenile delinquency, providing special opportunities for girls and young women and promoting the full and effective participation of young people in the society.

Toward a globalised urban world

Before reaching the anticipated level of stagnation and decline, the world will still have to face the problems caused by its increasing population. This will entail a greater demand for resources and a heightened stress placed on certain areas of the global resource economy and ecosystem. Resources connected with the food economy, especially soil, water and energy, are the most directly involved, in a complex, interrelated framework and in specific problem areas. Several international projections have drawn attention to the global consequences of deforestation (in Latin America and Africa), desertification (in Africa), and soil degradation (in almost all regions of the world), and of the large increases of water withdrawals for irrigation, industrial, and domestic use. Water scarcities may be an especially dangerous problem in the Middle East, North Africa, and Central and Southern Asia, and may develop into a source of international tensions and violence.

The other consequence of the changes will be an increasing polarisation of the population. Ninety-five per cent of the population growth in 2000–2050 will take place in the developing world and more than half of it in five countries: India, China, Pakistan, Indonesia and Nigeria.

The implications of the demographic changes are numerous. Above all, they are potential sources of conflicts, within countries and on a global level. There will be population pressures building up due to such factors as population growth, poverty, high population density, income disparities, lack of job openings, limited opportunities, unequal distribution of land and uneven agricultural development. These are already stimulating large-scale migrations within several countries and internationally. The internal migration consists mainly of movements to urban areas.

The 20th century saw a gradual increase in the urban population. In 1900, Britain was the only country in the world where a majority of the population lived in urban areas. By 2000, a large number of countries were in this situation, including all the developed countries, 17 of the 19 upper middle-income countries, 22 of the 40 lower middle-income countries, and 2 of the low-income countries (according to World Bank definitions). The urban transition process in the developing world has been also characterised as "de-ruralisation," since it covers not only urbanisation, but the disintegration of traditional rural life. As the result of the massive urban migration, the era of global transition to an urban society will be largely concluded within 25 years. In 1900, more than 80 per cent of the world population lived in rural areas. By the end of the 20th century, the proportion of the urban population had reached about 50 per cent. More than two third of the world's population will be living in urban areas by about 2025, as can be seen in *Table 1*. The global urban system will include 20–30 mega-cities, each with a population over 10 million, a great number of big cities with over a million inhabitants, and countless larger and smaller towns. The challenge of de-ruralisation has cultural, social, economic and political aspects. Most urban settlements in the developing world will draw in large numbers of the poor looking for a better life, and above all employment. The rapid growth of cities around the world is increasing the world incidence of poverty and poor living conditions. While cities cover 2 per cent of the world's landmass, they contain 50 per cent of the global population, consume 75 per cent of the world's resources and produce 75 per cent of its waste. Between 25 and 30 per cent of the world's urban population live in makeshift shanty towns and settlements that lack basic facilities such as sanitation, waste disposal and running water. More than half the urban population of Asia, Africa and Latin America lives in poverty.

It is becoming increasingly evident to social scientists that studying the socio-economic and political processes related to the cities of today is of fundamental importance to a better understanding of contemporary society functions and changes.

The two main sources of urban population growth are natural increase and urban migration. There is strong pressure behind internal migration from rural to urban areas in a number of countries. At the beginning of the 21st century, there are five main discernible factors behind the de-ruralisation process in the developing world. (1) The most frequently emphasised cause is rural unemployment, resulting from the mechanisation of agriculture and rapid population growth. (2) There is a shortage of arable land, aggravated by environmental degradation. (3) Rural areas are short of social services, particularly education. (4) Migration to the cities is often prompted by natural disasters, particularly recurrent droughts. (5) There is the significant fac-

Table 1
Regional trends in demography and urbanisation

Regions	1950		2000		2025	
	Popula-tion (mn)	Urban %	Popula-tion (mn)	Urban (%)	Popula-tion (mn)	Urban (%)
Africa	218.8	13.2	813.1	37.7	495.8	54.0
Asia	1367.7	16.0	3636.3	38.1	4960.0	54.3
Latin America	163.9	40.9	463.7	74.8	709.8	84.2
Europe	319.9	54.8	539.8	78.7	718.2	82.9
Former USSR	180.0	39.4	315.0	76.3	308.1	73.5
North America	166.0	64.6	296.1	86.4	369.6	85.6
Oceania	12.8	64.5	32.7	78.2	41.0	81.1
World	2501.2	28.6	6253.1	49.6	8294.3	64.1

Sources: WHO (1988) and UNFPA (1999).

tor of civil unrest. Most rural people displaced by internal conflicts move subsequently to urban areas.

Also important factors behind urban migration are the pull effects of urban life. Even in poorer countries, cities offer opportunities for better education and health, more effective family planning, and jobs. They have promoted faster emancipation of women. It is an important challenge for the political process to transform the potentials of urban settlements into realities and to make de-ruralisation manageable. Increasing and improving of employment opportunities is probably the main way to avoid the dangers inherent in urban transformation.

The process of urbanisation in a globalising world raises a number of new problems, unprecedented in many ways, which call for research and of course for action.

The challenges of urban transition

The scale and consequences of the ongoing mass-urbanisation process mean that it formed a hiatus in the history of human development. Urban living appeared profoundly unnatural to many past biologists and anthropologists, who emphasised that humans had evolved as dispersed groups ranging over wide territories. The population density found in the cities was seen as presenting dangers to human health in the form of epidemics and psychological stress. If the city were indeed an alien environment, the future of the human species would be in jeopardy. Historical experiences have shown that cities may not be biologically healthy for human beings, but they are a natural habitat for economic development and human culture. A disproportionately large number of human activities and achievements in economics, science, literature, music and so on have been accomplished in urban environments.

Cities around the world are entering a new stage of development in this new era. Most of the towns and cities that developed in the first half of the 20th century or earlier have been unable to absorb the successive waves of immigrants within their traditional frontiers. Instead, new satellite settlements have appeared on the peripheries, with already limited capacities to provide employment, food security, housing, sanitation and health care. The growth has been so fast that the authorities have been unable to extend and develop basic services to these peripheral communities, so that 20–60 per cent of each country's urban population live in substandard housing. The marginal segments of society are in an especially difficult situation. Squatters and slum-dwellers are the most dangerously exposed to the deteriorating environmental, hygienic and other living conditions of cities.

Apart from population growth and associated problems, many cities are beginning to experience greater social and economic diversity than ever before, especially in multi-ethnic countries. Many of them will remain industrial centres, but as in the past, there will also be "service cities," based on traditional and modern technical, commercial, administrative and other activities. This diversity will continue to be apparent for many decades to come in a juxtaposition of ultra-modern districts with shanty towns and slums, housing their "two nations" of poverty and wealth.

The acceleration and global spread of the process that has made the cities the centre of a number of human activities will be both the cause and the effect of highly complex socio-economic changes in the way societies function. In many parts of the world, the entrepreneurial city is emerging as a national or even international interest group. The political city is already a crucial force in the struggle to share and distribute national political power. The urban communities are also centres of organised crime and targets of terrorists. Cities have become engaged in international and national competition, for investment, central budgetary resources, foreign capital, and specific roles in the global market as centres of finance and trading. In some countries, they are also becoming competitive with central government in the field of economic distribution. These developments mean that the traditional management of cities is becoming a highly specialised, multifarious task of governance.

Urbanisation and socio-economic changes

An essential task facing institutions is to promote various rural-development initiatives, to slow migration to the cities. This cannot be achieved within agriculture. Meanwhile the problems of urbanisation call for an increase and an improvement in the opportunities offered by cities and anticipation and management of the new conflicts emerging out of urbanisation and the adverse consequences of urban development. This means providing the basic infrastructure, educational facilities, health care, nutrition and family planning, and creating jobs on a massive scale. There should also be decentralisation of administrative services and improved management of slum areas. The management of mega-cities is a specific issue in this context. Anticipating and managing conflict is a complex task in cities, which have historically been the centres of social struggles. Such struggles in the past tended to relate to employment or communal relations, such as ethnic and religious divisions and segregation. The new era will bring to the fore conflicts over "residential" issues, the huge income inequalities, and the highly unequal access to urban services, such as clean water, sanitation, health and education. These are often related to the communal problems and instances of social exclusion.

Significant progress has been made in various countries and cities to devise mechanisms to implement good urban governance. This progress can be categorised in three broad strategies, namely, to promote decentralisation and strengthen local authorities; to encourage participation and civic engagement; and to ensure transparent, accountable and efficient governance of cities. Most of the socio-economic problems connected with urbanisation have also been extensively researched. They include migration, employment and labour-absorption capabilities, the features of the urban informal sector, the infrastructure and urban services, and stratification of the urban population. Other topics include polarisation between rural and urban areas, housing problems, especially with urban slums, the specific problems of mega-cities, the management of urban communities and the environmental problems in cities. All these have received increasing attention in academic studies and practical work.[48]

Much less is known about what kind of interactions will develop in a predominantly urbanised world, between urban and rural communities and what role provincial towns, the small cities of the future will play. How will economic growth and the migration process influence their situation? The role of cities in the globalisation process is another important question whose implications need to be better understood.

---

[48] An excellent presentation of these issues is given in Kirdar (ed.) (1997).

One important economic issue is how urbanisation relates to growth and development. It has been generally recognised that the urbanisation process, in most cases, is instrumental in promoting economic growth in the new era, but there remains the basic question of whether urbanisation will also change the character of economic growth in the developing world.

Primarily, a better understanding is needed of how the urbanisation process will influence the supply of the growth factors – labour, capital, and technology – particularly in the developing countries. Will it radically change the deployment of economic activities by concentrating it in urban settlements? Will it promote and accelerate modernisation and structural changes in the economy? Historical experience shows that the unskilled labour force migrating in from the rural areas is increasing faster than the cities' capacity to absorb it. Here urbanisation is becoming a source of growth in the informal sector, where fewer skills are required. Urbanisation, of course, opens up greater opportunities to increase skills rapidly than the rural environment does, but this advantage takes time to develop. Patterns of savings and investment are also changing. Savings become more institutionalised through the development of banks. However, the cities call for greater savings and investment because of the growth of the infrastructure. In principle, the cities represent a better environment for the development of modern entrepreneurship.

Historical experience also shows that consumption patterns are influenced by urbanisation, which turns the subsistent economy into a market economy more rapidly than the rural economy does. A new urban consumer market emerges, marked by greater stratification and standardised consumption patterns. Satisfying the needs of the urban population calls for new distribution patterns, observed, for instance, in the supermarkets that are emerging also in poor countries.

Urbanisation also brings changes to the welfare effects of the growth process. Analysis of the welfare effects often focuses more on the issue of growing rural poverty, but it is important to add that a new urban middle class is also emerging. In some countries, such as India and Brazil, this urban middle class has become a big factor in the domestic market. Its special needs in consumption, education, transport, culture and other areas related to the quality of life add a new dimension to the cities of the developing countries.

Mass urbanisation opens a new era of changes in the quality of life. The issues related to the quality of life in urban settlements are complex, of course, and have several aspects. One consists of the socio-economic and psychological consequences of urban congestion, alienation and atomisation. Another concerns the problems of crime and the faster globalisation of crime in the urban environment. Here some important issues should be raised concerning the relations between democracy and the quality of urban life. Have dictatorial regimes handled urban "law and order" more effectively? Is the only way to handle crime in cities to condone a police state that murders street children, carries out summary executions of criminals, and fosters an atmosphere of terror? Are there not more democratic choices, such as activities by non-governmental organisations to protect neighbourhoods?

An Indian authority on urban affairs stated some time ago, "The efficiency of our cities will determine our economic growth,"[49] but what exactly is meant by the efficiency of a city? To use a simplified, conventional formula, it means the costs and benefits and sustainability of urban development. The problems, however, and the socio-economic indicators of efficiency are much broader than that. (1) How can access be provided to sources of income for the rapidly growing urban population? New strategic responses are needed. In this decade alone, more than 230 million new jobs must be created in the cities of the developing world. It is a crucially important issue. How the capabilities of the cities to deal with this problem can be reinforced? (2) Cost-effective management of cities, especially the financing of the infrastructure and housing needs, is a major issue for future study. The estimated requirements in the developing countries alone are around US $100–150 billion a year. These needs cannot be covered without major international efforts. (3) Another important task for global society that cannot be quantified is the anticipation and handling of the conflicts that emerge from urbanisation. Cities have been traditionally the centres of most of the social struggles. (The uprisings of the peasants were much less numerous.) In the past, they were related largely to the workplace, or communal relations, like ethnic, religious conflicts, segregation. In the new era, the "residential" issues, the large income gaps within the cities between rich and poor, the highly unequal access to urban services, including water, sanitation, health, education, became crucial sources of potential conflicts. They are often interrelated with the communal problems and social exclusions.

There are further socio-political conflicts of another nature. The political and economic transformation of the former socialist countries, for example, affected the status of certain cities and regions, as the hierarchy of the system was replaced by a more democratic structure. Decreasing centralisation of the political system and the economy meant that the national and international importance of provincial cities increased. In most countries, however, the capital, as a concentration of power, continues to dominate opportunities and wealth. This may also give rise to regional conflicts.

There are important environmental aspects and indicators of effectiveness in the area of environmental management, use of energy, electricity and water, handling air pollution and management of urban waste.

[49] *Far Eastern Economic Review,* August 17, 1995.

74

New urban-rural interactions

One important issue with global implications is the future of urban-rural interactions. These have many dimensions. In their social dimension, there are some fundamental questions to address. Will urbanisation radically reduce the rural population, creating a population void in rural areas? Or will technological development and economic growth tend to lessen or eliminate differences of income levels, quality of life and cultural opportunities of rural and urban societies? If they do, will progress at a given level of economic development be spread more evenly over rural and urban areas? The experiences of certain highly developed countries, such as Switzerland and the Netherlands, indicate that differences between the rural and urban areas may diminish, halting urban growth and perhaps resulting in a healthy lessening of decongestion. Most countries in the world, even industrialised ones, have a long way to go before they reach that stage. Meanwhile there are some immediate problems.

In political terms, the question of a bias towards urban areas has become an important question in the analysis for urban-rural interactions. The policies of developing countries especially tend to favour cities, notably the capital city, and neglect the rural areas in many ways, so that the gap between rural and urban increases. The public in many countries talks of exploitation of the rural areas by the urban in several ways.

In the context of urban-rural economic linkages, particularly in the developing countries, urbanisation influences directly and indirectly agricultural and non-agricultural production activities in rural areas, with implications for income and employment and consumption patterns. More research is required on the relative importance of production and consumption linkages between cities and rural areas, and on the influence of the income gap and production linkages on households, entrepreneurship and institutions. However, one issue of particular importance in the future, especially in developing countries, may be whether the urban centres can be fed by the rural areas. Historical experience has shown that cities did not come into existence until there was a sufficient surplus of agricultural production to support them. Political and economic settlements developed that were capable of encouraging or obliging the rural population to produce surplus food and supply it to the cities. Some cities supported themselves by extorting food from rural areas by violence. In the 20th century, there was forced urbanisation in some socialist countries, especially the Soviet Union, and drastic measures to extort food supplies from the countryside and make agriculture subservient to industrial and urban development. Technological development of agriculture in the industrial countries allowed production to grow, so that the cities represented a major, often lucrative market for farmers, which facilitated the "industrialisation" of agriculture. Inputs of industrial origin increased rapidly and so did output, which transformed the production, trading and transportation of food into an efficient agro-business. This process may eventually help rural transformation in many developing countries as well. At present, however, agriculture in most developing countries obviously cannot produce a sufficient food surplus to feed the cities.

At this stage, the weak performance of agriculture or structural problems with the output of cash crops mean that urbanisation increases the dependence of many developing countries on food imports. Productivity in agriculture does not improve and there are even cases of agricultural activity declining, due to urbanisation-related environmental events such as increased soil salinity, reduced land availability and increased water consumption.

There are also other important social issues related to urban-rural interactions. One relates to gender. Are the urban centres promoting gender equality? Do they tend to transform patriarchal societies or does urbanisation impede the liberation of women? The tentative answer so far seems to be that the urban environment has a positive effect on the liberation of women. Other questions of importance include the impact of urbanisation on fertility rates, the consequences of having a growing number of households headed by women, and the gender characteristics of employment in urban centres. Empirical evidence shows that cities bring extra problems, such as increased prostitution and the exploitation of women as sweatshop labour, but by and large, urbanisation opens greater opportunities for female labour, in income and in skills.

Another urban-rural issue of essential importance is the future ability of the cities to create more jobs. Their job-creating effects in developing countries are much below the effects found historically in the cities of the present industrial world. Economic development is slower and present-day technological changes mean that the modern industries of the developing world are less labour-intensive, so that they absorb only a small fraction of the immigrants from the countryside. The labour absorption of the industries is of course limited by technological developments. All these factors help to explain why immigrants into the cities congregate in the informal sector, to a greater extent than ever before. The urban informal sector plays a specific role as a source of jobs and income for the working poor. In many developing countries, it accounts for between a third and a half of the employment in major cities. No firm forecast of the trends in the coming years can be made, but it must be emphasised that the informal sector should not be idealised or considered an acceptable solution to employment problems. In fact, it reproduces poverty and destitution.

Migration from rural to urban areas is an other source of interactions. This process may lead to the depopulation or changing age and gender composition of the people in vast regions. It may be resulting in the urbanisation of poverty. Poverty, homelessness and slums are increasingly associated with urban growth. The process is mostly informal and unplanned, often resulting in people settling on unwanted and dangerous locations. Slums expand particularly in the developing world. There is an inadequate provision of land. The speculative investments increase tenure insecurity for the urban poor also in the informal settlements.

Most of the fifth of the world's population that lives in absolute poverty, without adequate shelter, food or clothing, still live in rural areas. However, the world's urban poor will outnumber the rural poor quite soon.

What features does urban poverty show, by comparison with rural poverty? For one thing, it is more conspicuous, so that it affects not just the urban infrastructure – housing and its environment – but the whole quality of urban life. One specific manifestation of urban poverty is the increasing number of homeless street children. This phenomenon is not only detrimental to balanced urban growth, but an important source of prostitution, drug abuse and criminal activities in the cities. Most countries are not equipped to deal with the problem of street children in a humane or future-oriented way.

Land distribution, as an essential question related to urbanisation, also emerges in the context of urban-rural interactions. Are the expanding cities creating problems for rural settlements, by redistributing land in favour of the cities? More complex is the question of land redistribution within the cities. The spread of slums onto public land and subsequent legalisation of the squatters has become an important source of land speculation in many countries.

Global linkages in urban transformation

The process of globalisation causes many national and international changes to become interrelated. Globalisation affects the urbanisation process in a number of ways. Cities are the main centres from which the impact of globalisation spreads through a country in various ways. (1) Most importantly, the food and energy supplies of the cities depend in many countries on imports, not the local hinterland. This lengthens the supply lines to the cities and may raise costs. (2) The cities are the focuses of the global standardisation of consumption and culture. (3) The transnational corporations base their activities in the big cities.

Will urbanisation in the developing countries accelerate the process of globalisation? Will international political and institutional co-operation among the cities comprise a new field of international relations? The answers to these questions are connected at least partly with the influence of the urbanisation process on growth and development in the developing countries. Co-operation and competition between cities has become an interesting and important global issue. There are opportunities for co-operation among cities in solving many problems. They can learn from each other, but there is also increasing competition between the main conurbations in the world, for instance for financing, investment, and employment and income-generating business ventures. In many countries, cities are striving to attract new investment by offering various incentives to transnationals and other entrepreneurs. These incentives, more often than not, are the source of special taxes levied on the population. So while certain segments of the population may gain, others are paying the costs of this. The various global changes related to such measures, such as structural adjustment, also influence the socio-economic position and scope of cities. They are especially exposed to the adverse consequences of austerity measures, through the reduction of financial resources for social services and the infrastructure, job cuts in the public sector, and the removal of subsidies from services such as transport, water and energy.

It must also be underlined that as with many other aspects of the globalisation process, there are both similarities and a great diversity of problems and adeptness in solving them. The main sources of the diversity include historical traditions, demographic patterns, ethnic characteristics, development levels, and geographical, ecological and institutional characteristics. These must be considered when dealing with the problems of urbanisation and urban settlements.

The question of whether the expected high level of urbanisation is increasing or diminishing the vulnerability of humanity and increasing or endangering global security is fundamental to the future and requires further research, so far no clear answer can be given. However, the process, at least for the time being, is irreversible, even if its effects on human security may be adverse, especially in poor countries. It also has to be understood that urbanisation may open unprecedented opportunities to deal with some of the major problems of misery, disease, backwardness and ignorance that have haunted the world recently and in the more distant past.

PART II

THE TECHNOLOGICAL AND ECONOMIC DIMENSIONS

5. HUMAN CONSEQUENCES
OF GLOBAL SCIENTIFIC AND TECHNOLOGICAL
TRANSFORMATION

Technological transformation has its quantitative and qualitative aspects in every society. Human beings are important and are influenced by both aspects of the transformation process. Humans are producers, disseminators and consumers of knowledge. Knowledge in turn, determines the effectiveness of human interactions with technology. Some of the most important factors, which are important and relevant in the process of technological progress from human point of view are the following:
- changes in occupations and changes in the distribution of wealth and income, influencing social stratification;
- education and training, which improve the quality of labour;
- public health and medical services, which contribute to the quality and effective performance of the population;
- changes in the living conditions and cultural amenities, which influence the values of the population;
- industrial relations, which influence a wide range of attitudes in the society;
- tensions and conflicts resulting from technological change and social innovations;
- deterioration or improvement in the ecosystem.
- major transformation in the info-sphere of the individuals and of the society, influencing communication, work, lifestyle and sometimes even the language.

Technology has always been two-sided. On the one hand it has promoted man's mastery over his physical environment and increased his ability to achieve certain human goals, such as improved diet, better shelter, more rapid transport and communication, prolongation of human life, on the other hand technologies produced or were accompanied by negative effects or unwanted side-effects. Technological change on our globe has always been a highly unequal, extremely differential process.

Technology is in constant interplay with economic and social structures and cultural values. New technologies energise and set off different socio-political forces, and interest groups. The social aspects of "creative destruction" comprise extremely difficult and complex issues. On one hand the process is an important condition of social progress, prosperity and welfare, on the other hand it is a source of conflicts and human suffering. It triggers and demands social, political and cultural changes. Long-term studies in many countries suggest that advances in technology have been responsible for at least half of long-term economic growth, through improvements in capital and labour productivity and the introduction of new processes, products and services.

At the beginning of the new century there are a number of key issues related to the global scientific and technological transformation. One is related to the character of the new technologies and their relations to science on one hand and to the societies on the other. Taking into account the pervasive impact of new technologies on people, social structures and institutions and on the ecosystem, the issue: to what extent did technological changes outrun adaptive capabilities is not any more a theoretical problem. The old concepts of social adaptive capability are out of date. It demands more profound human and institutional changes than in the past. An other important question is: to what extent became technology a part of the causes of the different crises in environment, population and in other areas or did it become an instrument for their solution?

At this new stage, one of the most important driving force behind the ongoing transformation processes is science. Its direct influence on global transformation and on the future of society is however through technology. The combined role of science and technology in global changes is more widespread, pervasive and multifarious than ever before in history. Science and technology have a major influence on global politics, economy and on the ecological changes. They influence population growth through family planning, health care and education. They influence the growth and patterns of employment, too. There are also new interactions between science and technology. This change is the background of a concept which is defined as "knowledge-based development".

An OECD document has defined knowledge-based economies as systems directly based on the production, distribution and application of knowledge and information. However, the role of knowledge has always been important. Since the earliest analysis of modern economic growth, knowledge and technology have been recognised as factors of key importance to it.

According to the concept developed by OECD experts, a knowledge-based economy embodies a fuller recognition of knowledge and technology in economic growth. Such an economy possesses a community of scholars, researchers, engineers, technicians, research institutes and firms engaged in high-technology production and service provision, forming innovation-production systems (OECD, 1996). Advanced-technology industries account for a high share of national production, foreign trade and investment. Thus, a modern knowledge-based economy brings a qualitative change in the assessment of knowledge as a factor.

- Science promotes a great number of innovations that improve living conditions through the production of goods, contribute to public health, provide energy and new information channels, and promote many other areas. The inventions resulting in new technologies are based on science, so that science is involved not only in the invention process, but in all phases of application and diffusion. The knowledge-based system is therefore impossible without a critical quantity of researchers and engineers. Science becomes an essential factor in shaping the competitive position of the country and its firms in the global economy.

- The impact of the changes in knowledge-based economies is not confined to the high-technology sectors of production and services. These changes pervade a variety of production processes, product groups and service activities. The application of knowledge-based technologies brings changes above all in the industrial world, in output and consumption patterns, skills, lifestyles and institutions, but it also has unprecedented consequences in regions. A new, knowledge-based international division of labour emerges, influencing the whole structure of international trade, production and consumption, including several traditional industries and the evolving "industrial agriculture".

- The diffusion of the new technologies, notably the spread of information, is in itself a major source for a more intensive internationalisation process. Science and technology have always been international, in the sense of employing a globally accumulated stock of knowledge for discoveries and inventions, and in the diffusion and consequences of these. However, R & D in all their dimensions have become more globally connected than ever in the new era.

- Information technology is the central component of knowledge-based development – an enabling technology that affects the whole economy. The demand for workers who can create, apply and use IT extends across manufacturing and services, transportation, health care, education and government.

In the context of the human dimension of science and technology a number of important questions have been raised in public debates. Is modern science a leading force of human progress or merely an instrument in the service of those who are in power in politics or in the economic life? How can scientific and technological development be better motivated for the solution of the great priority problems of humanity in an increasingly profit-oriented world? Are the relations between science and society up to the postulates of the 21st century, which has been declared as the era of "knowledge-based" development? How could science better contribute to a more equitable global development? How to make its benefits more readily available in less developed countries, as a way to fight poverty, disease and environmental degradation by diffusing scientific and technological capabilities?

Relations between science and society were the subjects of different studies practically since the ancient times. One of the focal points of the analysis was the relationship between science and political power. For a long period of human history "the science" was philosophy, which integrated beliefs, theories and knowledge. The "power" was the ruler, the king or the prince. The revolution, which separated science from philosophy opened up a new chapter in the relations between science and power. The essence of these new relations was expressed by Bacon's famous words: "knowledge is power". The era, which followed the Industrial Revolution made science and scientists increasingly important actors and indispensable for governments for military considerations and economic competitiveness. The states at the same time became the main sources for funding sciences. A more complex and qualitatively new chapter in the relations between science and the societies has been opened again by those changes, which have been brought about the new industrial and technological revolution and the globalisation process in the second half of the 20th century. Some of the main characteristics of science and its role in this era differ from the earlier periods.

1. There has been a historically unprecedented expansion of new knowledge about nature, materials, technology and about the societies. Science has become an extremely diverse new profession. It is very difficult to measure the expansion of human knowledge. There is a more or less general consensus among academics, that it has grown between 30 to 50 times as compared to the 1950s. The increase of the amount of knowledge has been highly unequal in different areas. Its growth depended on one hand on the "effective demand," which stimulated research, meaning first of all the demand of the sponsors and to a certain extent on the urgency of the problems, the solution of which required new discoveries and approaches. It has depended of course also on the capabilities of the researchers. National defence expenditures and the competition between the two main confronting blocs has been a crucial factor in the "effective demand" after the Second World War. The spatial spread of new knowledge has been also unequal, reflecting the high concentration of R&D expenditures and researchers in the developed industrial countries and in the former socialist states. It has depended also on the location of more than 500 thousands scientific journals in the world.

2. Qualitatively new interrelations developed (in fact became indispensable) between science, technology and the society. The role of science in the generation (or the acquisition) of new knowledge, in the fast efficient and multiple application of new technologies and in the adjustment process of

the society gained special importance. The critical mass, structure and quality of national sciences, the quality of the scientific and technological infrastructure including educational and research institutions and government agencies, became key factors in shaping output and consumption patterns, skills, lifestyles and institutions. Directly science-based sectors emerged and became crucially important in the restructuring and growth of the global economy. The global system of science and technology became directly associated with or organised by the transnational corporations. In those sectors both product and process innovations are directly linked to sciences. They provide both new products and production process innovations for other industries and the service sectors. New high-technology services emerged (like information services), which resulted in the network of integrated high-tech manufacturing service industries (like computers, biotechnology etc.) Major changes have been taking place in the traditional industries as the result of the new high-tech-based production processes. The new, highly productive service sector in itself became a vehicle of the changes in the traditional industries and in agriculture. The changes facilitated the rapid growth of small firms with highly specialised knowledge. The emergence of the three centres of science and technology: North America, Western Europe and Japan became fundamentally important factors both in international co-operation and global competition.

3. The internationalisation of science and the global interconnectedness of the universities and other centres of research increased very rapidly during the past five decades. Modern science is by definition has been national and international simultaneously. Even though the "mosaics" of national scientific communities are the building blocks in the global structure of modern science, there has been a growing strong interconnectedness, interaction and interdependence between the different academic institutions, universities and other centres of research. This process was a cause and at the same time the natural consequence of the expansion of knowledge. The fast increase of knowledge would not have been possible without rapid internationalisation of science. This process has been reflected by the great number of different channels, of formal and informal relationships, which have developed between scholars in the different disciplines also across national frontiers. The main organisations, initiating and undertaking such co-operation have been rather wide-spread. They included transnational corporations, professional organisations, universities, international intergovernmental research projects and the deliberate actions of certain intergovernmental global or regional organisations. At the beginning of the 21st century, these relations take different forms. In the system of the transnational corporations they may be deployed in different countries of the world, depending on the strategies and approaches of the given firm. In the non-business world, there are

research centres or projects on a given location comprised of academics from many countries, there are international networks of contacts and cooperation between scientific and academic institutions and scholars working on similar issues in different parts of the world.

The world at the beginning of the 21st century is in transition to a new technological era. This transition, which began in the late 1960s and early 1970s, is an important component of global change, also in human development.

A technological era can be defined primarily by the technologies, on which its system of social production is based. These are of prime importance in shaping the structure of output and consumption, and determining the increase of total factor productivity. Their "logic" and postulates influence skill and employment patterns, investment needs and international competition. The dominating technologies influence the style and quality of life, transform the system of organisation, infrastructure, information and entrepreneurship, and set the choices available to society. They bring about big pattern changes in the international division of labour and the functioning of global markets. They may have also major consequences for national security and influence military doctrines.

The present transition to a new technological era is taking place in a diverse and increasingly internationalised global economy with two tracks. One track is the industrial world and a small group of medium-level economies that have been facilitating, supporting and sustaining the process of technological transformation. The other track is the developing world. Most developing countries, struggling with social and economic problems, have failed to develop capabilities to sustain technical and economic progress. This has left them increasingly marginalised in the modern part of the global technical and economic system. There is of course an important source of knowledge in the practices of the traditional communities in these countries, which has been receiving increasing attention in recent years. It has been recognised that traditional knowledge plays a key role in the preservation of biodiversity. Besides, many activities and products based on traditional knowledge are important sources of income, food and health care for a large part of the population. Traditional knowledge and practices are also increasingly studied and integrated into modern technology in some areas, like pharmaceuticals, cosmetics and agriculture. In terms of their response to technology, the countries of the world can be divided into the three well-known groups: innovators, followers and technological deserts.[50]

[50] Jeffrey Sachs, director of the Centre for International Development at Harvard University, in a press article divided countries in a similar way, into technological innovators, adapters and excluded countries. He estimates that some 2 billion people live in the last (Sachs, 2000). According to my scheme, "technological desert" states are ones that lack the conditions for innovation and for importing and employing technology.

Previously outside the global market system, the former socialist countries had a peculiar technical and economic structure before the transition came and they began to reintegrate. The civilian sector of their economy was isolated from the mainstream of global technological transformation, while the heavy Soviet concentration on military technology resulted in a closed and very costly scientific and technological block, with little or no spillover to other sectors. Their entry into the new technological era has been slow, uneven and distorted by political-strategic and economic-systemic factors.

The transition to the new technological era on a global scale is under any circumstances and in any country a complex, uneven, long-term process. Countries and regions differ greatly in their technological capabilities. Such capabilities have several main components. (1) To what extent can a country or region contribute to generating new knowledge, inventions and innovations? (2) To what extent can it cover its technological needs with its own research and development? (3) To what extent is it a source of technology for others? (4) If it is dependent on technology imports, how efficiently can it absorb and use them? (4) How efficiently can it manage the socio-economic consequences of technological change?

The new era of technological transformation sets a relatively high "threshold" for the late-comers. It is costly and time-consuming to build the necessary technological infrastructure and national capacities, and develop the technical capabilities and skills to support of the modern industries and services dependent on the advanced technologies. Even developed countries face difficulties in adjusting to the rapidly changing requirements, especially in the scientific infrastructure and the educational system. The newly industrialised countries provide a characteristic example of the problems involved. They managed rapid progress by importing the advanced technologies to upgrade certain sectors in their economies. They were then able to develop export industries, using their cheap and relatively skilled labour force. However, they will have to make further great efforts in the coming years to upgrade their technological capabilities. Otherwise, they will not "graduate" into the group of developed industrial economies. (The dilemma they face is commonly styled the "third stage" of modernisation, which requires the upgrading of human capital and rapid progress in national R & D infrastructure and other supportive efforts in socio-economic life.)

The former socialist countries, despite relatively large numbers of university graduates in the labour force and quite well-developed scientific infrastructures, remain in a weaker position with their innovative capabilities and international technological and economic competitiveness. They also face major problems and dilemmas in creating the structural conditions for the greater competitiveness and efficiency they need in the process of world-market integration. Several shortcomings will have to be filled, notable qualities of entrepreneurship. The character of their relations with the main actors in the global technology markets, the transnationals, will have a major influence on the process. These relations will have a great bearing on the effective utilisation of the assets developed in past decades, which are important in some cases. Here, let me underline that it would be a big waste, for them and for the global community, if their human assets and R & D capabilities were lost or minimised amidst the difficulties of the transition. It is not just that relatively poor societies have paid a high price to build up the human capital. Given appropriate national policies, these capacities could help them to integrate faster and more efficiently into the global innovation system. Of course, there are major quantitative and qualitative differences among the former socialist countries in their human and other scientific and technological assets. In some countries, these are relatively compatible and closely tied intellectually to the industrial world than any other institutions in those former socialist countries. (That accounts for the danger of a brain drain.) In others, especially those isolated from the main scientific and technological centres for long decades, these assets are small and not able to give much help in the modernisation process. Unfortunately, the R & D sector in all these countries has been facing great difficulties due to shrinking government subsidies and declining orders and for other reasons. Many good researchers in Hungary, Poland and Russia, for example, have left scientific research for business (which in many cases has been useful, resulting in small and efficient high-technology private firms) or moved to foreign firms. Many have gone abroad, even to positions inferior to their qualifications. The R & D sector in those countries can still be saved by wise government policies and support, with internal restructuring and efficient participation in the global system of science and technology. This will have a major welfare effect in these countries and facilitate their participation in the evolving global international division of labour.

The new trajectories of science and technology and the human dimension of change

Changing technological capabilities and the spread of the new technologies have always had a stimulating effect on the patterns of the international division of labour, as well as on the patterns of production, consumption and employment. The present new technologies, which are partially replacing both labour and materials, have curbed strongly the comparative advantages of countries with high natural endowments or cheap labour. The decline of transportation and communication costs has reduced the importance of proximity advantages, based on being close to large markets. The distance factor in production location is confined to fewer goods. As the results of the new technologies spread and production and consumption structures are transformed, the global map of traditional and acquired comparative advantages changes radically. All these alterations have influenced the functioning of the global economy and the relative position of the actors in international economic relations. They have brought about new imperatives and patterns in competition and co-operation between the three global technological and economic centres. They have created a new environment, with constraints and opportunities for countries that are mainly or exclusively followers in the hierarchy of the technology markets. However, only a small group of countries have reduced the technological gaps to an extent that improves their competitive position in world markets and thereby facilitated the utilisation of their qualified manpower in their economy. (Increasing numbers of skilled people in many developing countries have resulted in under-utilisation of them and increasing pressures for a brain drain.)

The main changes have developed and diffused globally in different stages and in different clusters. Their cumulative effects brought major structural changes in world trade between 1970 and 1999. The share of manufactures in world exports increased from 60 to 69 per cent. Much of world trade is now in services. In world manufactures trading, there was a fast increase in the share of high-technology products. The new technologies, especially information, communication and transport technologies, have facilitated the division of labour through all stages of production and marketing, with value being added in several countries. Integrated production and service systems have emerged. These changes have influenced the functioning of the global economy and the relative position of the actors in international economic relations, bringing about new imperatives and patterns in competition and co-operation, especially between the three global technological and economic centres. There have also been major changes in the relative positions of countries, especially in high-technology products. The share of the developed countries in this product group declined from 97 per cent in 1970 to 85 per cent in the second half of the 1990s, while that of the developing countries increased from a little less than 3 per cent to almost 14 per cent. Some developing countries, including China, have been able to penetrate developed countries with exports in a large number of high- and medium-knowledge-intensive products. India has become a leading software exporter. In 1999, its software exports were worth US $3 billion and in 2000, they were set to surpass $5 billion. They could eventually reach one third of the country's exports (Smith, 2000).

There has been a global decrease in the share of raw materials and agricultural products in world trade. The declining material intensity of finished goods, the higher knowledge content, the development of the material sciences (to produce, for instance, cheaper and more efficient substitute materials and qualitatively better alloys), and the reduction of waste will reduce further the importance of the traditional global raw-material economy. The ratio of aggregate mineral and metal consumption to industrial output, according to my calculations based on UNCTAD data, declined by an average 1.9 per cent a year between 1970 and 1997. This has caused declining or slower growth in demand for raw materials and completely new demand patterns. The production of fuels and minerals has also become more capital- and knowledge-intensive, with the introduction of high-technology equipment.

Based on present trends and the pull and push effects of new technology, there are four main areas where major technological advances can be expected in the next 25–30 years: information technology, micro-electro-mechanics, biotechnology, and the energy sector, as well as combinations of these.

Progress in information technology (IT) is resulting in a steady increase in computing power. The decline per unit of value will continue and probably accelerate. IT will have an increasing interactive influence. Computers became capable of interacting more directly with human beings, through visual capabilities and voice simulation. Smarter software facilitates swifter responses to human needs, including advanced robotics and interactive, advanced multi-media systems. A large part of the globe is interconnected and different networks function, resulting in ubiquity, diversity and simplicity. A large number of people will carry customised information instruments, resulting in a specific new medium, an individualised info-sphere. This will make a vast amount of information instantly accessible. The vertical and horizontal growth of this personal info-sphere will facilitate simultaneous participation in different social activities and development of "virtual communities". It will connect people along different lines, reducing further the impact of physical boundaries. This also implies many problems. Individuals will have to live and cope with a higher level of complexity. This could also become a new framework of centralised control. There will be pressure from information overload and the demand for shorter reaction times will mount. To succeed in this environment will call for continual education and adjustment, particularly from those in the modern parts of the system. The system will also have its drop-outs, who cannot cope with the information society. There will probably be specific diseases associated with the information society, due to the stress and other still unpredictable consequences of the changes. The spread of IT will accelerate innovation by disseminating knowledge and simultaneously by its demonstration effects.

The consequences of progress in the field of micro-electro-mechanics must be conceived as a framework incorporating information technologies and biotechnology as well. It involves above all the miniaturisation of sensors, transmitters, receivers and actuators for mechanical devices, where progress has already been very fast. It may increase human safety, allowing faster travel and making space exploration more cost-effective. The devices are becoming especially important in developing sophisticated weapon systems.

Another trend in nanotechnology devices of increasing future importance will be the use of molecular fabrication techniques similar to those in the human body. The use of such biomimetic techniques that learn from nature is an interesting trend still at a very early stage. The potential innovations and their implications will have a fundamental influence on science, medicine, transportation, energy use, industry and agriculture.

The third area of scientific and technological change is biotechnology. Biotechnology shares several characteristics of science-based industries. Innovations rest on high cost and risky R & D activities, which have a multidisciplinary knowledge base. It has also wide applicability in many industries. The advent of molecular biology in the mid-1970s and what became known as the "new" biotechnology promised great opportunities for addressing major development problems. Improved health care, enhanced agricultural productivity, cleaner energy and environmental protection were among the goals of biotechnology. The markets for application are however more distinct than for example in information technology. The breakthroughs in genetics, genetic engineering and neurobiology may bring especially dramatic results for humanity, of more importance than those in any other science. They include such activities as transgenic research and development, where genetic material is moved between species and even between animals and plants. Further progress in this field and use of the knowledge already available in some areas depend largely on governments and the attitudes of lay society. Controversy surrounds genetic engineering of human beings, which in principle could already lead to cloning and modification of the traits in future generations. The potential consequences of genomics on the economy and the society are widely debated in the academic community and in government and religious circles. One more recent example is the new literature on the subject. L. M. Silver, a molecular biologist from Princeton University, in his book "Remaking Eden" argues that genetic engineering may lead to a two-class society. There will be the "GenRich" individuals whose parents can afford genetically engineered talented and healthy children and the "naturals" conceived the old way. An opposite view is expressed by G. Saint-Paul of Toulouse University in his paper on "Economics of Cloning". He argues that cloning will be resulting in a classless society because at the end the cloned people may have high ability genes. An other expert Prof. A. B. Krueger of Princeton University, in his provocative article (NY Times March 1, 2001) suggests that whatever impact of cloning, researchers are on the verge of learning much more about the genetic determinants of health and other life outcomes than their social and environmental determinants, and social science has to catch up with genetic science. There are strong social forces opposing genetic engineering, which may block the transformation of agriculture into a system that replicates genetically manipulated grain, fruits, vegetables and animals. In those areas where use of biotechnology has proved to be important, for instance, assisting in the pharmaceutic treatment of many ailments, by producing drugs that enhance the human immune responses against certain diseases the research work has been attacked and criticised much less vehemently.

The progress with new energy systems is harder to predict, since they require big investment and dependence on the traditional sources. Progress is stimulated and inhibited by the price of oil and by the dangers of the greenhouse effect. Petroleum, coal, hydropower, nuclear energy and wood will probably remain major sources of energy for the next 25–30 years. Breakthroughs are likely in achieving higher efficiency and limiting environmental effects. There is ongoing R & D, which may be important for the future, relating to hydrogen use in engines, high-density storage systems, photo-voltaic solar cells, solar heat absorption, wind power, biomass gasification, and geothermal energy. Nuclear fusion is still considered a potential alternative source of nuclear energy, but its effective containment and control is still unsolved.

A document at the June 1999 World Conference on Science, for example, stated, "The combined advances in computer technology and microelectronics seem likely to result in a decrease in the number of commercial outlets for products from less industrialised countries, because the latter will be less competitive. Automated manufacturing procedures bring the threat of unemployment to countries where there are adequate supplies of labour, but not of capital. Yet, these technologies also offer great benefits to those countries capable of exploiting them; for example, in data processing, communications, manufacturing, and quality control. Applied microbiology and biotechnology offer the possibility of producing a great number of substances and compounds essential to human life and prosperity. Improved fermentation processes with higher yields, improved fertilisation techniques, cheap production of biologically produced fuels for cooking and heating, and biotechnological production of foodstuffs all offer distinct benefits, especially to developing countries. Furthermore, biotechnology is particularly important for those regions that are rich in bio-diversity. If biological resources are not utilised locally, there is a risk that they will be exploited by foreign-owned or multinational corporations, which may not sufficiently compensate the local regions with economic benefits. Renewable forms of energy like sunlight, which are sometimes more effective and accessible than conventional forms, while at the same time environmentally less destructive, are especially attractive options because they promise savings on energy imports. More generally, humanity should be careful not to insist on making the same mistakes that were made by industrialised countries when they opted for unsustainable modes of production and consumption, and science can be a great partner in the effort to correct these mistakes. Although the neglect of sustainability may appear to produce quicker returns in some cases, in the longer run the consequences will be disastrous for everyone. But in some cases, pressing vital needs may require immediate attention at the expense of sustainability. The international community should assist them in compensating the costs of sustainable policies. The exploitation of scientific knowledge through the production of marketable goods requires an economic and industrial infrastructure, especially skilled labour, production facilities, and capital. These goods are in short supply in non-industrialised countries. In their quest to expand the manufacturing base and with their relative lack of capital for launching new industries, developing countries have to compete with each other when attracting capital through foreign investment. The availability of skilled workers is a major attraction in the competition for such investment. Thus again, education in general, and science education in particular, are of the utmost importance for industrial development" (Hoyningen-Huene et al., 1999).

There are no easy answers to questions about the speed of technological breakthroughs, how they will be implemented and what will be their influence on human development and other areas of economic and social change. Experience suggests it may depend on macro- and microeconomic and social factors: the rate and global spread of economic growth, the increase and distribution of incomes, the availability of skills, international investment and entrepreneurship, the character and factors of competition, and in some areas, moral factors.

The impact on the labour force is critical. The rapidly expanding market sectors of today tend to have a highly literate and skilled workforce. The most important members of the workforce in the information economy are the new "knowledge workers", working with their brains. To compete, today's workers must acquire "21st-century literacy": the ability to read, write and compute competently, think analytically, adapt to change, work in teams and imbibe new technology. The postulated degree of literacy in the 20th century was a basic threshold of reading, writing, and mathematical computing. This sufficed for the Industrial Age, but today's jobs require a higher level of academic, workplace and technical skills. The level of literacy required has risen decade after decade and continues to do so.

There are factors to indicate that the speed at which scientific discoveries translate into new technologies and enter commercial use will remain fast and may accelerate. There are also factors to suggest there will be more mod-

erate growth than in the past. Among the indicators of accelerated application of new technology are the spread of IT, sharp international competition
demanding rapid commercialisation, improving scientific and technological
capabilities in developed countries, the spread of technological capabilities in
the developing world, increasing market incentives and entrepreneurship in
former socialist countries, and continued growth and expansion of the global transnational sector. Constraints on this could be more limited and reluc-
tant state funding, due to the decline in defence spending, and slower economic growth. These may slow the entry of new products and processes. The
main innovative, developed countries may maintain a high rate of technological progress. Some developing countries, such as China, India and Brazil,
may manage to increase their innovative abilities in important areas,[51] while
others lag behind and the gaps between the groups of countries grow.

Corporate systems and knowledge-based international development

The transition to a knowledge-based economy is taking place in a period
when the transnational corporations play a fundamental role in controlling
the development, use and diffusion of knowledge, innovations, new products and processes. These are the main sources of competitive advantages.
Knowledge extends beyond the traditional R & D activities and includes
product design, process engineering, quality control, maintenance services,
marketing and management skills. The growing importance of knowledge
increases and intensifies the international linkages of R & D, through the
"global sourcing" policies of the transnationals. This international interconnection makes competition across national frontiers much greater than
before. Constant improvement in products, processes, management and marketing became vitally important. To exploit the knowledge base in different
countries, transnationals extend their R & D networks worldwide. The proportion of international R & D in this framework is already about 18–22 per
cent. The policies of the transnationals in R & D engender various interactions with national players, which influence the innovative performance of
almost all countries, including the transition economies. They also transform
knowledge produced by non-market institutions into products marketable
on a large scale. The international corporate system influences the "speciali-

[51] India, for example, has developed a big competitive advantage in software. It has 120,000
engineering graduates a year and over 3000 computer-training institutions. Among other
achievements, it has become the world's leading developer of business software for enterprise-
resource planning.

sation" of countries in the way that best suits it, which may or may not be optimal for the countries concerned.

A transnational's overall, globally integrated strategy relies on being able to locate R & D, procurement, production, administration, financing and inventories in the countries that promise the best profits, and to direct supplies to them. Such strategies cover several countries. They may be regional (for Europe, say, or North America) or global. It is becoming harder to describe the legal, economic and technical activity of these corporations in terms of a single country or branch, even if they developed from a particular national or branch base. However, the parent country as a base remains a major factor in the group's activity.

In the new era, the role that transnationals can play in a country's specialisation, based on scientific and technical development, depends on the competitive strategies they adopt and the technological capabilities and receptiveness of the host country. The strategies of the transnationals make a symbiosis of less and more developed countries feasible within their system, in a knowledge-based economy. Coupling the special competitive advantages of different levels of economic development can bring success in international business. It is not clear how the benefits of this could be shared more equally. There are also big differences in the knowledge intensity of the sectors that facilitate such a symbiosis. Foreign investment in the manufacturing of traditional consumer goods (textiles, textile garments, leatherwear and footwear, printing, wood) is concentrated mainly in countries with a lower level of development. Even in these countries, cheap labour can be combined with developed technology, which can multiply profits. Industries requiring economies of scale (vehicles, sections of electronics, metalworking, foodstuffs, parts of the chemical industry, glassmaking, building materials) are important to countries at a medium level of development and can serve highly developed markets in an internationally integrated production process. The organisation of internationally integrated production in the car industry reflects the profitability of the symbiosis. Even the knowledge-intensive sectors where scientific and technological capabilities are important (pharmaceuticals, biotechnology, some branches of electronics, aerospace, etc.) and which are concentrated in developed countries, tend increasingly to deploy some components of the value chain to countries at a lower level of development. In some cases, transnationals use the availability of highly skilled specialists in less developed countries, to provide special, high-technology services. India's software industry is an example.

Long-term studies on the sources of economic growth suggest that innovations have been responsible for at least half of long-term economic growth, through improvements in capital and labour productivity and the introduction of new processes, products and services. The fact that an increasing proportion of the new knowledge is concentrated in transnationals places limitations on its availability. Diffusion of it becomes subordinated to the profit motive for its possessor firms. National policies for the development of technological capabilities will become even more important in the future. The strategies focus on three complementary goals:

- Building industries that are competitive in both domestic and global markets;
- establishing business conditions attractive to technology-oriented investment, including foreign investment, technology transfer and managerial know-how;
- promoting public/private research and development partnerships to promote adaptation, commercialisation and spin-off of technologies.

Human development is a fundamentally important condition in building innovative capabilities and strengthening the competitive position of countries.

Human development policy in a competitive global system

Human history is the cemetery of cultures, which were not able or ready to adapt themselves to the changing conditions. The appropriate management of human dimension of change is a fundamental condition of adaptation and progress. Human development constitutes the central factor in the human dimension of change. What is human development? It is a multidimensional concept. Human welfare, health, fertility and mortality, the level of education, participation and liberty and many other "components" are part of this concept. It has a distributional dimension, an "empowerment" dimension, a relational dimension: related to the given level of development in the societies and to the individuals. The human dimension of change and development commands, directs, organises, plans, controls the utilisation of other factors and the quality of human resources both as an objective and an instrument determines its efficiency.

In the framework of the UN system UNDP, the United Nations Development Program started serious global dialogue and research work on the main issues, needs and priorities of human development during the 1970s. It has become a comprehensive project, out of which the annual Human Development Report was born. One of the outcomes of this report has been the effort to measure human development and compare the performance of the countries with the help of a Human Development Index. There are three main components of the Human Development Index: longevity, which reflects the quality of life, knowledge, reflecting the capacity of people and material welfare.

In the international community the first commitment related to human development was made for the very first time in 1948 in the Universal Declaration of Human Rights. Access to education, health, political participation and a decent standard of living were recognised as specific social and economic rights. Since than these rights and the measures for their implementation have been elaborated further. There was marked improvement in human development in a number of countries over much of the past half century. There was an important improvement in human health. The health transition is characterised by the process in which infectious diseases, which thrive people living in unsanitary conditions give way to degenerative diseases associated with longer life expectancy. Globally, average life expectancy at birth has risen to 65 years and the gap between the developed and developing countries more than halved over the past 50 years. Despite this progress there are still many serious, old and new health problems. Old diseases, like TBC re-emerged and new epidemics, like AIDS are still spreading.

Regardless of political ideologies and systemic factors, education is seen by people and governments as essential to human progress, economic and social development and international competitiveness. At the beginning of the 21st century the role of education and other forms of investments in human capital became particularly important sources of all other factors. They are helping the adaptation of societies, the modernisation of the economy and the society, also upgrading the quality of the individuals in order to adapt themselves to the changing technical and mental needs of an increasingly complex world. It helps the citizens to discharge their social and individual responsibilities better.

The average educational attainment of the working-age population increased dramatically, particularly during the second half of the 20th century. Literacy rates have risen almost everywhere in the developing countries. The population became more educated everywhere. Here comparable data are more readily available for the industrial countries. In the United States, for example, the median number of years of education per adult was 7.86 in 1913, 11.27 in 1950 and close to 14 in the 1990s. In Japan, it was 5.36 in 1913, 9.11 in 1950 and somewhat over 14 in the 1990s. In China, the median was 2.2 years in 1950 and close to 6 in 1990. In India, the number grew from 1.35 in 1950 to over 4 in the 1990s. In the former Soviet Union, it was 4.1 in 1950 and 12 in 1990.[52]

Several factors contributed to the improvements. One was the decolonisation process and the efforts of new countries to establish strong education-

---

[52] The historical data were calculated by Angus Maddison (1995). The data for the 1990s have been calculated by the author, using UNDP data.

al and professional foundations for national existence. Another factor has been the acceleration of technological progress and the much more qualified labour force it requires, which have contributed to changes in the skill and employment structures. A third factor has to do with new individual needs and attitudes towards social mobility. Education has become an important instrument of social mobility, all over the world.

Because of economic difficulties and constraints, and the shortage of qualified educators, there has been increasing variation in the quality of educational services – globally and within countries. This has meant that most pupils in many school systems hardly attain a level of functional literacy, while other school systems directly prepare students to enter the era of the information revolution, even to the extent of equipping them with computer literacy. By the end of the 1990s, the median years of schooling for the population over 25 years old was more than three times higher in the developed countries than in the developing countries.[53]

The countries of the world were spending about 4.8 per cent of global annual GDP on education in the second half of the 1990s, which was US $1.9 trillion at current purchasing-power parity. The proportion was 5 per cent in the developed countries and 3.8 per cent in the developing countries. In per capita terms, the global annual amount spent on education was US $316 – about US $1500 in the developed countries and US $47 in the developing countries. The comparable amount would be about US $120 in the former socialist countries.

At the beginning of the new century, the general global interest in education is motivated by a number of factors. The transition to a knowledge-based economy has upgraded the importance of education, as the main source of obtaining knowledge. Knowledge involves experience and learning and a definitive degree of awareness and consciousness. Education and training, more than any other initiative, have the capacity to foster development, awaken talents and empower people. It is the most important long-term instrument for governments to upgrade the human potentials of a country.[54]

There is a strong link between level of education, employment and income. Higher levels of educational attainment are associated with better labour-market integration. Education affects not only performance at work,

---

[53] Calculated on the basis of data in UNDP (2000).

[54] There are important postulates in the context of the educational sector, necessary to improve the quality of human capital. Educational standards must be high. Teaching must be a prestigious and valued profession. There must be a good practical orientation in the educational system. There must be high-quality forms of higher education available. Close links between educational institutions and employers and a high level of in-house training at firms are also important and useful factors.

but social behaviour such as hygiene, increased social and environmental consciousness, improved parenting, and higher levels of political participation.

Modern production and services have an increasing knowledge content and international competition is increasingly knowledge-based.

The development of education has also been a symbol of political prestige for many countries, especially higher education.

Due to its place and role in the different societies, education is exposed to the influence of most major demographic, political, social and economic changes within countries and in the global system. The various general and specific changes in societies that influence the importance, the character and the functioning of the educational system relate either to the system as a whole or to specific aspects of it. Some problems relate to participation in the educational process on different levels: enrolment and drop-out rates, and degree of access to higher-quality educational institutions. Other problems relate more to harmonisation of the educational system with social changes (such as family, migration and urbanisation) and with the changing socio-economic needs of modernisation and transformation. Changes relate to utilisation of the skills provided by the educational system, to qualitative improvement, to adjustment to or adaptation of new needs, and to the capabilities and readiness of countries to finance the sector's growing needs.

The global educational sector in all its dimensions is marked by major imbalances. These reflect global inequalities and problems and the attitudes of different societies and cultures.

About 75 per cent of global educational spending go on primary and secondary education. The development of primary education is still considered a top priority in most developing countries, since it is the source of functional literacy. Enrolment is high almost everywhere. The problem is not to get children into school, but to keep them there. Almost half of the children who enrol leave after less than the four years that is considered the minimum period of schooling for functional literacy.

According to UNICEF estimates, rapid progress in primary education is being jeopardised by spending cuts that leave educational strategy in the doldrums. Progress towards universal education is faltering.[55]

Secondary education has an important role to play in a number of areas. It prepares the foundation for university education. It provides the bulk of the knowledge and skills to the population, for vocational and technical insti-

---

[55] Over 90 per cent of the developing world's children start primary school. Due to high drop-out rates, there are globally about 120 million children aged 6 to 11 not in school, two-thirds of them girls. The target is a basic education for all children and completed primary schooling by at least 80 per cent. See Unicef (1999b).

tutions also belong in this category. Its role is especially important in the era of information revolution, building the foundations of computer literacy in many countries. The quality of secondary education is an essential determinant of the knowledge base in the development process. Between 1970 and 1997, secondary enrolment in the developing countries tripled, from under 20 per cent to over 60 per cent. The global secondary enrolment ratio was 65 per cent, with 88 per cent in the developed countries (UNDP, 2000, p. 197). This increase of the enrolment ratio was not matched by an improvement in the quality of education, training of teachers or management of schools. The gap widened between the relatively high-level private and the public institutions. In public secondary schools, budgetary constraints in many countries led to deterioration in the quality of education and equipment.

Higher education has received high priority almost everywhere in the world. It is recognised that without a good system of higher education, it is impossible to overcome the impediments that hinder socio-economic development. Higher education is crucial to teacher training, curriculum development and methodology for primary and secondary education.

The second half of the 20th century brought fundamental changes in the global spread of the university system, the socio-economic processes affecting enrolment, and the relevance and attitude to society, the state and the applied sciences. The various global changes influence the universities very strongly, because of the international connections of science and technology and the role of universities in training specialists, adapting countries to change and generating new knowledge. The universities, much more, and much faster than other educational institutions, are channelling the outcome of the globalisation processes into national cultures.

The author shares the views of a former director-general of UNESCO: "The universities are much more than centres of higher education: they represent the most qualified watchtower at the national level to ensure that the knowledge and lessons learned from the past will be applied for a better and freer future throughout the world" (Mayor, 1990). But I would add that they play a crucial role in the process of globalisation.

Many new universities were established in all countries during the decades that followed the Second World War, especially in the developing world. Huge numbers of qualified professionals were needed in various fields, such as education, medicine, the armed forces and business and funding for universities was greater increased. There was also a strong popular pressure for chances of a higher education, as a means of upward social mobility. The elitist philosophy of higher education has been giving way in many parts of the world to an approach of providing higher education on a mass scale.

There was a big expansion in the range of university faculties and in over-all enrolment. On a global level, the number of university students increased from 10 million in 1950 to over 90 million in 1999. University expansion in Europe, North America, the Soviet Union, Central and Eastern Europe, India and China was based largely on existing institutions, although many new universities had to be established and major reforms introduced. The existing traditions were much more limited in Africa, where the few establishments inherited from the colonial period had been institutionally subordinate to the system in the colonial power. Even after independence, staff from the former colonial power continued to predominate, and universities founded after independence largely replicated the European system in their curricula, organisation and values.

Greater personal mobility and easier access to the centres of modern science and scholarship, coupled with the new needs of developing countries, have encouraged the internationalisation of education. Transnational university networks have emerged, integrating institutes of higher education in several countries.

Curricula have changed in response to new political, socio-economic, scientific, technological and intellectual imperatives, as new disciplines emerge and so on. The importance of the postgraduate education has increased substantially in realising the scientific potentials of countries. There has also been an increasing demand for continuing, further education and adult education in many countries. In some parts of the world, "research universities" have emerged, concentrating on major scientific capabilities. Qualitatively new relationships have developed between universities, business and government, in research, financing, and the training of specialist staff.

Between 1980 and 1997, the tertiary enrolment ratio increased in the developed countries from 30.8 to 37.9 per cent and in the developing countries from 15.6 to 16.4 per cent. The global number of highly skilled people has been growing. A world total of about 90 million people had university and other higher educational qualifications by the end of the 1990s, which was more than double the number 30 years earlier. More than two-thirds of these lived and worked in the developed countries or in Central and Eastern Europe, but quite high concentrations of the highly skilled appeared in certain developing countries, due to national policies of increasing the number of university graduates. South Korea, China, India, Egypt, Thailand and Indonesia, for instance, have seen the number of graduates reach the threshold required for creating and sustaining modern industries and efficient research centres. These improvements have been beneficial, of course, but in many developing countries, more graduates have been produced than the labour market can absorb, adding a new redundant or under-utilised segment of the population. This group is the main target of brain drain.

The development of human resources or human capital in a national framework will have a major influence on the changes in the former socialist countries. The region had developed an educational system closer, in many respects, to the standards of the industrial world than its economy was. The transition to the market system and the increasing inequalities have had an adverse effect on the educational sector in almost all countries, although attempts have been made to maintain the proportion of GDP represented by education spending. There is a danger that earlier educational achievements may be jeopardised by funding problems, lost public support for schools, underpayment of teachers, and a widening gap between private and public, mass schools and universities.

Modernisation of society calls for more and better-educated people. Appropriate utilisation of them can also become a difficult social problem in a society where economic development is slow and the modern sectors are too small to absorb them. The issues of work and employment are however much broader and much more complex at the beginning of the new century, than the job opportunities in the modern sector of the developing countries. The global transformations, particularly in population dynamics, technology and education and the globalisation process are sources of major changes in the world of work. The nature of work is changing. There are a number of other factors, like the changing age composition of the population, the fast increase of the people in working age, the growing participation of women, technological shifts, urbanisation, etc. put the problems of employment, unemployment into the centre of national policies. It has become one of the most important global issues.

6. GLOBALISATION OF EMPLOYMENT AND INTERNATIONALISATION OF LABOUR MARKETS

The systemic models and the labour markets

All societies, regardless of political ideology, systemic factors or cultural differences, see employment as fundamental to defining the sources of social problems and conflicts or achieving social harmony. Employment, unemployment, jobs, workplaces and workforce are concepts born of the mass wage employment of the industrial world. Work has changed in many ways in the last 200–250 years. Most of the occupations in the industrial world today did not exist three centuries ago, and even the ones that did are pursued now under the influence of new technological, social and economic forces. Global forces also have a major influence on work in the developing countries, where the categories of the industrial world are confined to the modern sectors.

Some analysts have sought a common denominator for the different categories in the concept of livelihood, which is thought by its advocates to encompass the complex realities of the world more effectively (Chambers, 1995). Livelihood is certainly a concept that corresponds better to the realities of the poor, whose survival strategies may embrace begging or marginal street vending in the informal or black economy, part-time employment, black employment, prostitution, bonded labour or small-scale farming. Employment implies a single, relatively secure, more or less predictable and sustainable source of income based on a job. In a global market system, it is the labour market that reflects the employment situation, working best where demand roughly matches supply. Here such concepts as full employment, unemployment, under-employment, flexibility, rigidity, and "reserve army of unemployed" reflect distinct market situations. Labour markets are linked to the overall market situation, particularly the rate, conditions and patterns of economic growth. Some theoretical economists have developed concepts for defining interrelations. The most famous is the "non-accelerating inflation rate of employment" (NAIRU), also known as the natural rate of unemployment, which has also been used by monetary authorities in some industrial countries. It corresponds to the rate when labour demand equals labour supply and there is no tendency for real wages to change. The full employment rate has been defined on this basis, so that 6–7 per cent unemployment has been seen as "full" employment. Full employment and unemployment, however, are complex, dynamic categories, related to the rate and patterns of economic growth, as well as being affected by demographic factors. The celebrated Beveridge Report, submitted by the British academic Sir William Beveridge in 1942, usefully defined the level of full employment as a situation in which there are more vacant jobs than unemployed.

The economic history of the post-war period indicated that markets alone could not produce such outcomes on a long-term basis. Full employment in the developed countries and the former socialist countries resulted not only from favourable growth conditions, but from deliberate policies designed to foster growth and social welfare.

At the last stage of the 20th century major problems have emerged however in all the countries.

The following main problems are considered as more or less globally important at the beginning of the 21st century:

- continuation of the structural changes, declining employment in agriculture, manufacturing industries, mining and slower growth of employment in the service sector;
- shrinking employment in the public sector and slow growth in the private sector, mainly in smaller firms;
- the growing importance of the informal sector in employment;
- rapidly changing occupational structure with growing skill requirements, increasing demand for computer literacy and higher skills;
- lower level of job stability and job security, more part-time, short-term employment, increase in structural and long-term unemployment;
- growing international polarisation of the labour markets.

These general trends may have different consequences and implications in the diverse conditions of the labour markets. The national and regional differences derive from different achieved levels of development and sets of historical socio-economic conditions for economic growth and institutional changes.

The labour markets of the industrial countries differ in the role of institutions and have more specific characteristics in general, compared with other markets. Labour markets are shaped by the different systemic models of the market economies. They are necessarily a scene of conflicting interests (as are other markets), but those interests are often exceptional in the strength with which they are articulated and the institutional protection they receive. Moral and political factors play a much greater role in labour markets than in other markets and the character of information in them is a specific issue.

Many countries collect large amounts of data on labour-related matters, without managing to reflect adequately all the dimensions of their employment problems, or even determine the number of people inside and outside the regular labour force. The same applies to unemployment statistics. The proportion of concealed unemployment may be very large in some countries.

The American model of a pluralist market economy has probably had the most influence on the global economy for many years, due to the great power of the United States. Although this model has undergone several changes, it maintains several basic characteristics. These include a basis in flexible, risk-taking entrepreneurship, symbiosis of small, medium-sized and large firms, a sophisticated, competitive money market, a flexible labour market based on complex economic opportunities, and a large area, promoting labour mobility between firms and regions. The American model has proved especially efficient where strong demand factors are generated either by growth of income or income redistribution through the budget. However, too strong a reliance on the market as the main instrument of adjustment has exposed a large segment of the population to the uncertainties and risks of the market place. The predominantly short-term view of the main players has made economic performance increasingly vulnerable in areas where long-term strategies, actions and commitments are required. Some vulnerable points include long-term adverse changes in savings-investment ratios, deterioration of some parts of the physical infrastructure, the implications of the defence budget on competitiveness, long-term declines in productivity, and stagnation and decline in the performance of the educational system. The United States destroys jobs and creates new ones at a rapid pace. The 500 largest US corporations shed about 4.7 million jobs between 1980 and 1992, about one quarter of their workforce (Walker, 1995). The population of the US grew by about 80 per cent between 1950 and 1999, but the increase in the labour force was 124 per cent and in the growth of civilian employment was 129 per cent. The number of non-farm jobs grew by an average of 2.2 per cent a year over the same period (USGPO, 2000). Since the early 1980s, most new jobs have been created by the entry of new firms. Two-thirds have been created by firms employing less than 25 people, and most of these in firms employing less than 10 people. The annual failure rate of these firms has been 16 per cent. According to data from individual manufacturing plants, 10.3 per cent of jobs disappeared in a typical 12-month period and another 9.1 per cent were created. These were the fastest job-cutting and job-creating rates in the industrial world, caused by technical and economic changes accompanied, especially since the early 1970s, by slowing wage growth and widening inequality.

The American patterns may be interesting and important to other regions of the industrial world. The structural shifts towards the service sector, especially its low-productivity branches, the increasing demand for highly qualified staff and the steady devaluation of low skills and unskilled labour have contributed in general to a decline, stagnation or decreased growth of real wages. These have an even greater influence on labour in a slow-growing economy, which undermines the traditional flexibility and job-creating capacity of the economic system. In a competitive market economy, the rate of economic growth is the fundamental condition for employment creation. The increasing importance of international trade in a developed economy, where the sources of competitiveness are decreasingly to be found in low wages, accelerates the process of substituting less-skilled labour with a more highly qualified workforce. The declining power of the trade unions reduces the bargaining power of workers and increases wage inequalities. The relatively short period covered by unemployment insurance forces many unemployed to accept lower-quality jobs more readily than their counterparts do in Europe.

The socio-economic model in Western Europe can be characterised as a variant of a social market economy, combined with what remains of the postwar welfare state. This model grew out of the European political tradition of representative democracy. In all its variants it presupposes intensive interaction between social groups and the state, in a delicate, difficult and pragmatic balance of market forces and state interests. Within this model, certain countries have proved very efficient in maintaining or restoring socio-political equilibrium and co-ordinating national policies in such areas as savings and investment, research and education, and improvements in the quality of government. Other countries, with a more problematic domestic political balance, have greater difficulties and less success.

The Western European model has a strong inherent characteristic of protecting firms and citizens from the major shocks of the adjustment process. In recent decades, the rises and falls in employment have been related more to cyclical than to structural factors. Upturns in output were followed within six months or so by an increase in employment, while downturns caused similar unemployment increases. However, the recession of the early 1990s and the patterns of recovery from it revealed the increasingly structural sources of unemployment (European Commission, 1999). Unemployment rates rose and the number of long-term unemployed also increased, so that the social costs of unemployment became much higher. The annual costs of unemployment in the EU in the 1990s, including income losses, exceeded US $200 billion, of which about two-thirds went on providing unemployment benefits. The concept of a social market assumes market deficiencies and imperfections, governmental responsibility for correcting them, and provision of various public services. Such services have been interpreted and applied differently in each country, but job security has always been an essential policy component.

The major dilemma facing the Western European countries is how to harmonise the sustainability of their social commitments with increased flexibility on the labour markets. A competitive global environment applies strong pressure to lower labour costs. This brought major restructuring to many European firms after the late 1980s and a substantial rise in unemployment. The conflicting tasks of how to sustain growth and create employment, was formulated by the US secretary of labour in the mid-1990s in plastic way.[56]

There is another vital issue, relating to the welfare-state patterns in the integration framework. An economically integrated Europe will inevitably face problems concerning national priorities and institutional and policy differences. These issues will certainly influence the process of internationalisation of the labour markets within the region and naturally, international migration. One of the most difficult aspects of the integration process will be implementing the concept of a "Social Europe". The main social-security structure sustained (in one form or another) by political forces in many parts of Europe is the welfare state, based on the principle of compensating the disadvantaged section of the population. However, the welfare state is only able to function effectively within national boundaries, safeguarded by the domestic balance of social forces. In this context, in fact, it is an anti-international system. Social legislation, enacted by governments as a means of securing support from their electorates and sustaining political stability, effectively places upper limits on comparative labour costs, which hampers the creation of a competitive Europe-wide labour market. If national welfare systems are to be prevented from harming competitiveness by becoming European, answers must be found to some practical questions. Which country should set the norms of a social market system on a European level, and which socio-politico-economic structures should apply?

The Japanese model of economic development differs in many ways from that of other advanced industrial countries. Some of its characteristics are rooted in Japan's history, while others have recent origins. In a world of severe changes and problems, the long-term orientation of the Japanese model has been recognised as an essential element in Japan's success. The Japanese have long understood that the true dynamism of a market econo-

---

[56] Robert Reich, speaking as US secretary of labour at a conference of advanced industrial countries on employment issues, asked in 1994, "Are the citizens of advanced economies condemned to choose between, on the one hand, more jobs which pay less and less, or good jobs but high levels of unemployment accompanying those good jobs? I think there is a third choice, and that third choice may be to combine the kind of investments in education and training and apprenticeship that we find in Europe with the dynamic labour mobility and flexibility we find in the US, all encased within macroeconomic policies which encourage growth and jobs." Cited by the *Financial Times*, March 14, 1994, p. 4.

my, in a world of strong competitors, is not created by textbook competition between many independent producers, but by application of the most up-to-date technology, by firms with immense market power. In the Japanese view, modern competition is a comprehensive battle, in which education, technical development, resource accumulation, competitive pricing, quality manufacturing and market penetration are all important instruments in a long-term game. (Long-term perspectives and planning have become an important factor in the development of the Asian newly industrialised countries as well, especially South Korea.) In Japan, government and non-governmental players in the economy have consistently taken a long-term view emphasising the need to concentrate on economic growth and technological development.

This perspective has been manifest in Japan's approach to many issues affecting economic development and social change, such as education, technology and production. Measures taken in these areas have reduced ecological and external economic vulnerability and enabled the simultaneous concentration and diversification of global sourcing and marketing activities. The long-term approach has facilitated strategic integration of co-operation and competition at corporate level. It has allowed special relationships to arise between the main firms, in risk sharing and access to capital and technology, while avoiding what is perceived as excessive competition. Another advantage of the corporate model is its multidimensional, co-operative approach, uniting the government and business sector on all-important issues so that each can rely on the other in global competition or realisation of national goals. This includes flexible co-ordination of macro- and micro-economic policies, facilitated by a system of constant consultations on various committees and other groups, with the Ministry of International Trade and Industry at the centre, aiming at a consensus on a wide range of industrial and trade-policy issues.

One special component of the Japanese model, reflecting national traditions, has been the sustained cohesion and corporate loyalty of workers and employees. This emerges out of guaranteed life-long employment and other management instruments, such as advocacy of a "common destiny" among those in the firm, which inculcates a normative attitude based on highly philosophical, almost religious overtones of togetherness.[57] Other manage-

---

[57] Employees had a high degree of job security, unprecedented in other industrial countries, until the financial crisis of the 1990s, while management could count on worker loyalty and devotion. Japanese companies, even in difficult situations, did their utmost to maintain employment. They were rather more flexible over working hours instead, curbing overtime, cutting bonuses, etc. in lean times. Small firms were seldom able to offer the same job security as large. They paid less than large companies (about 60–80 per cent for equivalent work). The changes in the 1990s precluded continuity of lifelong employment in the old way, although job security remains greater in Japan than in Europe or the United States.

ment instruments include the role of individual participation in different circles ranging from quality control to mutual instruction, the wide use of both material and non-material incentives, and the widespread and respected seniority system, to mention a few. Unemployment in Japan has remained the lowest among major industrial countries. Lifetime employment had a number of advantages, but also many disadvantages. It tended to sustain low productivity and internationally uncompetitive industries. It blocked labour mobility and sustained a seniority system in earnings, with the under-utilisation of the younger talents. The disadvantages became especially strong in a slow-growing economy, making structural adjustment very difficult. International competition during the 1990s forced Japan to change this system and restructure employment patterns. It has created major psychological and social problems. This however may take place only gradually, due to the deeply rooted character of the system, and the mentality of the people. The character and patterns of the labour market of Japan is influenced by a number of other factors. As it has been already mentioned, ageing, the growing participation of women, the acceleration of technological changes are some of the main factors, which will play a greater role in the future.

The labour markets of the developing countries are characterised by a high proportion of workers in the rural sector, a relatively narrow, formal group of modern waged labour, the high concentration of labour in the low-productivity informal sector and the absence of adequate safety nets. The role of women in the labour market of these countries has also specific characteristics. Their role as bread winners is much greater in agriculture.

A few countries have been able to strengthen the employment-sustaining abilities of rural areas, as a way of stemming migration to the cities. In China, for example, increases in agricultural efficiency forced more than 150 million rural labourers off the land. The increase in the population of working age has added millions more to those searching for jobs. So far, about 80 million people have migrated to large cities, despite the success of the village industrialisation programme. The majority of migrants to cities in most developing countries have found employment in the informal sector, in the absence of sufficient job openings in the formal sector. Several surveys have indicated that the informal sector (in the employed and the self-employed categories) makes up more than 40 per cent of the total urban employment. The various tasks include improving the capacity of rural areas to sustain and create jobs, encouraging small-scale industrial and service ventures, improving urban employment opportunities, and giving special assistance to migrant families in urban slums.

Modern employment is expanding rapidly, especially in the fast-growing regions of Asia, but the quality of the new jobs is often very poor.

Sweatshops, bad working conditions, compulsory overtime, child labour, and industrial hazards and accidents are more or less general. In the context of Asia, there are a number of important and interesting aspects of the fast growth, related to labour-market situations. It has become increasingly evident, for example, that the high rate of economic growth and the rapidly expanding local market has had a double effect on the informal sector in most countries. On the one hand, the informal sector has become more dynamic and tended increasingly to graduate to the formal sector. However, this small-scale sector on the frontiers of the formal and informal sectors still invests little in technology, training and labour safety, and pays low wages to unskilled labour. The close to 250 million working children aged between 4 and 14 are an easy source of cheap unskilled labour in many countries. Nonetheless, it is an important step forward from the informal sector, which offers even worse conditions. On the other hand, an increasing part of the informal sector's activities have been exposed to competition from the small-scale formal sector. Informal sector activities have become even more confined to serving the poorest sections of the population, who cannot afford the services of the formal sector. The employment-creating potentials of the informal sector have not changed in a meaningful way. It has remained as a last resort for many who cannot find employment in the formal sector, even in a fast-growing economy. The Asian experiences may be relevant to other parts of the developing world.

The share of public-sector employment is still high in many developing countries. In some cases, it is the only source of modern jobs in the formal sector. About 40 per cent of all employment in China is still in large, state-owned enterprises. Their share in total employment has been declining during the 1990s. One of the social functions of the public sector has been to increase employment opportunities. This is also one reason why public institutions and state-owned firms have been overstaffed. Job opportunities in the public sector are now diminishing in almost all developing countries, due to liberalisation and privatisation, or inevitable rationalisation of the state sector. In some cases, the decline is substantial: from 30–40 per cent to 20–25 per cent of modern employment. Economic growth in many countries, especially in Africa, is too slow and the private sector too weak to generate new jobs in sufficient numbers and quality. Job creation is not considered a priority in the private sector. Case studies on Nigeria, India and Indonesia point to the tasks of strengthening the job-creating capacity of the private sector. They also stress that this depends above all on economic growth and market opportunities. Tax breaks or special supports for training and upgrading the labour force could also help.

The development of the labour markets in the former socialist countries of Europe was an important proof of the influence of social and institutional factors. The socialist ideology did not consider labour as a commodity in the system. In the earlier years of central planning, the plan dealing with human resources included the allocation of labour, the patterns of education, the number of participants in the educational system, wages, etc. It offered job security, essential benefits were guaranteed through employment, workers were involved in enterprise matters, and labour force participation was high.[58] While the central allocation of labour was abolished in most countries even before the systemic changes, important consequences of it survived in the rigidities of wage policies, allowing narrow differentials and little open unemployment. Labour hoarding was encouraged by the system, resulting in a highly inefficient use of labour. In a number of countries skilled workers earned more than engineers, and in a number of cases, semi-skilled workers earned more than skilled workers. Labour mobility was restricted by legal measures and socio-economic outcomes of the functioning of the system. Employment offices have existed mainly for the distribution of labour among enterprises.

The establishment of a labour market, so it could support sophisticated employment services, increase the mobility of labour, facilitate a market-oriented wage determination, was an important task in all the countries. They had to build up institutions for both the active and passive labour market policies, like job offices, institutions for the management of the unemployment problem, introduce unemployment benefits, retraining institutions, job counselling.

The development of the labour market in the Central and Eastern European countries has been unequal with weak institutional framework. The region had a relatively well-educated labour force, which facilitated the adjustment process for the majority. In some of the transition economies the high educational level, and the relatively low wages facilitated for the majority of the labour force to adapt to new market conditions and to meet the demand for labour. The components of the demand changed as the results of the changes in ownership structures due to privatisation process, foreign direct investments, dismantling many large state enterprises, the low level of new domestic investment. Occupational patterns have changed reflecting the specific demand.

Full employment which was artificially maintained by huge state-financed investments in the labour-extensive sectors of the economy has come to an end. Unemployment, due to the declining output, the obsolescence of skills and the changing structure of labour demand created almost

[58] Nicholas Barr (ed.) *Labour Markets and Social Policy in Central and Eastern Europe. The transition and Beyond.* (Oxford: Oxford University Press, 1994), pp. 122–123.

insurmountable problems. The evolving labour markets were also influenced by the sluggish development of an appropriate legal and institutional framework and by the factors shaping the bargaining power of the main players in the economy. There was a marked decline in trade union membership. ·

In industry, one of the main sources of the changes has been the collapse of the Eastern markets, the decline in defence industries and the shrinking domestic demand. The privatisation process was an other source of unemployment. The influence of the privatisation process on employment has not been analysed deeply enough. However, there was much evidence that large-scale privatisation released workers faster than it has created new job opportunities. Since overstuffing in the socialist economy was significant, this was more or less inevitable. Besides, the increasing labour mobility commonly takes the form of job-to-job movements, and few of the unemployed have benefited from new ownership patterns. In all of the Central and Eastern European countries, the employment rate in the large-scale firms has declined more than in the case of the smaller establishments. The patterns of new private initiatives in entrepreneurship contributed to the increase of employment in the black economy, the share of which is very large in almost all the countries of the region. The "unofficial economy," in these countries, is not quite the same as the informal sector in the developing countries but there is a resemblance in the sense that it functions outside the systems of taxation, registration, social security and the law. In most former socialist countries, at least 25 per cent of the labour force is employed full- or part-time in the unofficial sector.

The politics and economics of employment in the new century

The dynamics of employment are the most important issues related to the functioning of the labour markets. The world at the beginning of the 21st century faces serious employment problems that could become major barriers to globalisation and undermine international security, if not managed and eliminated.

The problems can be measured with two main sets of indicators, which may also shed light on the future trends in global development. One set consists of the size and proportion of unemployment and the factors behind it. The other concerns the change (increase or decline) in the number and composition of those actually in the active labour force. The first set reflects wastage of human creative energies and the second the job-creating capacity of a country or region or of the whole world, and the kind of jobs available. Unemployment statistics are the less certain. Despite the standards set by the ILO, they exclude many people without jobs, who are no longer recorded in

112

national statistics, for various reasons (systematically discouraged from job-seeking, serving a jail sentence, etc.) Employment statistics are more realistic and comparable.

There are two often-contrasting vantage points for looking at employment issues. The more political view derives from economic and social rights and commitments to full employment. The other, more pragmatic view looks at employment issues in terms of the capacities and performance of markets.

There has been a well-known and important international commitment by all nations (or at least of all members of the United Nations) that relates directly, not only to employment issues, but to general human welfare.[59] The full-employment pledge of the UN member-states turned employment and the development of human resources into global issues for the first time. Article 55 of the UN Charter states, "With a view to the creation of conditions of stability and well-being, which is necessary for peaceful and friendly relations among nations, based on respect for the principle of equal rights and self-determination of peoples, the United Nations shall promote: (a) higher standards of living, full employment, and conditions of economic and social progress and development..." In 1948, this commitment was reiterated in the Universal Declaration of Human Rights. The International Covenant on Economic, Social, and Cultural Rights, adopted by the UN General Assembly in 1966 and in force since 1976, gave the right to employment a central place among economic and social rights. As mentioned earlier, the commitment to full employment was reconfirmed at the Copenhagen Social Summit of 1995. The basic document of the Copenhagen follow-up, the UN General Assembly special session of June 2000, reported that progress had been slow and uneven (UN, 2000e). This statement was contradicted by another in the same document – "Employment promotion has increasingly been put at the centre of socio-economic development, in recognition of the central importance of employment to poverty eradication and social integration" – unless it referred to the less than satisfactory results of efforts by governments. The tasks are enormous and in many ways unprecedented. Employment problems may well pose the greatest challenge in the human dimension of global change.

Issues of employment and unemployment have major political and economic importance. There is a well-documented link between unemployment,

---

[59] The "full employment" commitments are rooted in the initiatives of US President Franklin D. Roosevelt and Sir William Beveridge. Many feared that the Second World War, like the first, would be followed by a deep depression and mass unemployment. Roosevelt proposed a post-war economic bill of rights based on the fundamental right to a job and fair wages. Beveridge proposed full employment as the basic post-war goal for Britain. Both proposals were criticised by major political and business groups and aroused major debate.

poverty, hunger and deprivation. The European turmoil between the two world wars proved that socio-economic conflicts caused largely by unemployment could destabilise and even destroy democratic regimes. At the same time, economic co-operation had collapsed, the world market had dissolved into rival blocs, and relations between nations had turned hostile and unmanageable. These days, despite advances in social policies, humanity still faces the kind of intractable social problems that have caused extremism, war and social disintegration in the past.

The human-security implications and politics of employment issues are linked in some ways with the global, regional and national political changes since the end of the Cold War. The Cold War and the arms race had played a significant role in many countries in creating and sustaining employment, through defence orders and the needs of large armies. The armies themselves absorbed a proportion of the population of working age. Demobilisation and reductions in defence spending likewise have effects on the level and patterns of employment in many countries. Nonetheless, the world has to find more humane, rational and sustainable ways of creating employment than to increase defence spending.

Policy approaches and market perspectives often conflict in employment problems. There are also conflicting policy perspectives. The policy recommendations relating to adjustment programmes often exacerbate unemployment and create unsustainable social problems in developing and transition countries.

The market view of employment and unemployment problems construes the labour force as a production factor, linked to supply and demand. On the supply side, the growth and pattern of employment are affected by population growth, labour-force participation rates, migration and the development of education and skills. On the demand side, expansion of output generally remains the main employment creator, but it is also influenced by the labour intensity of technology, productivity increases, structural factors and the way available work is distributed.

The conflict between the policy and the market approaches increases in the context of the globalisation process. The main problems arise from the divergent interests of the social groups, firms and countries involved, the differences in the economic philosophies of the governments, and the trends and patterns of linkage with the global economy.

There is general agreement that wasting human resources through unemployment and underemployment causes a major loss to the global community and especially to certain countries. Most governments and international organisations, including the EU, have been dealing with the problems of unemployment and employment creation, but there is still no serious, realistic answer to the problem of how to provide gainful occupations for hundreds of millions during the early decades of the 21st century.

A high level of employment, close to full employment, had been achieved in the Western industrial countries by the 1960s and lasted for about two decades. Full employment was achieved in the socialist countries through relatively large-scale underemployment "within the factory gates". Full employment there ended with the change of political system after 1989. The developing countries have never managed to approach full employment.

The rise in unemployment and underemployment in the 1990s signalled a number of structural problems and policy deficiencies in the world economy. The inconsistencies between world economic growth and human development result from a complex set of global, regional and country-specific factors.

On the supply side, there are two important issues: longer-term consequences of population growth in countries where the economy is growing slowly or shrinking, and changing age and skill structures.

It is estimated, based on the UN population data, that the world labour force in 2000 consisted of 3 billion people, having increased from 1.2 billion in 1950. Of this huge reservoir of labour, the number not productively employed was close to 1 billion, about 33 per cent. The number of registered unemployed was 140 million (about a quarter of them in the industrial world). Over 800 million were underemployed. More than 75 per cent of the global labour force worked in the developing countries. While the rise in industrial employment has been quite rapid in the developing countries (about 4.0–4.5 per cent during the past 25 years, albeit with large regional differences), it was able to absorb only 22–24 per cent of those of working age. The proportion of people of working age increased on a global level from 57 per cent in 1970, to 62 per cent in 1990 and 64 per cent in 2000. If population projections remain on their current trajectory, the global labour force will increase from 3 billion to about 4.5 billion by 2050. According to projections by the ILO and the United Nations, only 4.7 per cent of the increment in the working-age group will come from the developed world and over 95 per cent from developing countries. The potential labour force in the world's 50 poorest countries will increase by 235 per cent between 2000 and 2050. In the developing regions, the rate of increase of people in working-age groups will be most rapid in the Middle East, South and Central America, and certain African countries. Their already double-digit unemployment rates may double by 2050. The largest numerical increments will be in South Asia and China. According to estimates that take into account the increase in the working-age population, the level of unemployment and the increasing participation of women, about 1600 million new jobs will be needed to achieve full employment in the next 2–3 decades. This is a historically unprecedented task.

There is growing pressure from both rural and urban unemployment. Historically, the growing rural population was able to bring surplus land into cultivation to generate income. The frontiers of agricultural expansion today are extremely limited. Global arable land per capita has fallen by 50 per cent since 1950. Migration to the cities, as discussed earlier, fuels already high urban unemployment. The demand for new jobs is growing very fast in the cities of developing countries. Job creation in urban areas requires major investment in the infrastructure, industry and the services. Between 2000 and 2015, about two-thirds of the new demand for jobs in developing countries will arise in urban areas. While the people of the world have become more educated and experienced over recent decades, as the result of the urbanisation process, the supply of unskilled labour in cities has grown everywhere, creating big problems by increasing unemployment and social tensions.

Another important factor on the supply side is the rising participation rate of women, which is already much higher than ever before.[60] In many developed countries in earlier decades, women were "secondary participants" in the labour force, often with the aim of increasing household income. At the beginning of the new century, many working women are "primary participants," as heads of households or independent persons. In the developed countries, the proportion of women in the labour force increased from 23 per cent in 1900 to almost 50 per cent by the end of the century.[61]

[60] Recent decades have seen some significant breakthroughs and improvements in the status of women worldwide. Changes in the status of women in the 20th century resulted from a combination of three main sets of factors. (1) There has been change in the global macro level processes, such as industrialisation, the growth of the service sector, globalisation, urbanisation, technological changes and employment. (2) The situation has been affected by various domestic collective actions, social movements, revolutions and reforms. (3) International factors have included the role of international intergovernmental organisations, above all the UN system and the international NGO movements. The UN Convention on the Elimination of All Forms of Discrimination against Women, ratified by over 150 states, has laid the foundation for an international women's law of human rights that transcends the bounds of national, religious and customary law. The convention sets out the rights of every woman to health, education, political participation, credit facilities, and her right to marry, found a family and divorce on an equal basis with men.

[61] The EU employment rate for women in 1998 was 51 per cent – almost a quarter lower than in the 67 per cent rate in the United States. This cannot be explained wholly by cultural differences, since the three best-performing EU member-states had employment rates for women similar or superior to that in the American one. Various factors may contribute to the low rates in most EU countries and provide pointers to the kinds of policy action that may be taken to address them. For instance, welfare systems in Europe may not be providing the right incentives for women to participate in the labour market. Adequate childcare facilities for working mothers may be lacking. The nature of the jobs available and the wages offered may not be good enough to attract women back into employment after bringing up children. Many women work in jobs well below their potential as measured by their level of educational attainment.

The share of women in the labour force in the more developed part of the developing world was about 8 per cent in the early years of the 20th century. The end-century data for the developing region as a whole were about 35 per cent. It is extending beyond the sectors, such as the informal sector, where the share of women has been traditionally high. The increasing participation of women is fuelled by a number of factors. The educational level of women has risen, which boosts their productivity. Lower fertility rates have increased the amount of time women have for activities outside the home. Urbanisation has moved many women from the rural informal sector to the labour market. There is also an income imperative for many women to find jobs. In export-processing zones, for example, 70–90 per cent of the labour force is female. More and more women work part-time. The majority of working women in several countries are clustered in lower-paid public-sector jobs such as teaching and nursing. There are many specific problems, particularly in countries where the population is ageing.[62] The future of work in Europe depends, in general, largely on the participation of women.[63] The working age population is shrinking, in some countries quite fast. This means there will be fewer taxpayers to support the welfare net. European women, especially mothers, are taking jobs in record numbers. They accounted for over 42.5 per cent of the EU labour force in 1996 and the proportion was increasing by about one percentage point a year, although it remains lower than in the United States. In the prime employment years between the ages of 25 and 54, 72 per cent of American women work, compared with 61.5 per cent of women in the EU. But in the second half of the 1990s, 75 per cent of the net additional jobs went to women, with 700,000 European women entering the workforce every year.

While more women work, the type of work they do outside the home has not changed much over the years. According to ILO figures, the proportion of women managers and entrepreneurs has remained at around 16–17 per cent over the last 20 years. Women are in a majority in the lowest category of routine work, holding about three-quarters of such jobs. Large numbers of women work only part-time, which penalises them strongly in an earnings-related pension system. The rapid growth of the female labour force has coincided with the increase in the service sector. Women hold most of the new service jobs, which are low-paid and low-skilled. In China and many South-East Asian countries, sweatshops have emerged in export-oriented indus-

---

[62] Job growth in Europe in the late 1990s was close to the 1 per cent rate in the United States, but it had eased every year since 1991. On the other hand, it was much higher than in Japan, where employment fell during the 1990s recession, for the first time since the first oil crisis in 1974. Still, Europe's employment rate remains far below the Japanese and US rates of about 75 per cent.

[63] *Wall Street Journal,* January 19, 1999.

tries. Electronics sweatshops emerge in many parts of the developed world. In both cases, the employees are predominantly females.

However, another notable trend is the increasing knowledge content of the new occupations creating opportunities for the educated elite. Furthermore, the ratio of women to men among higher-education graduates in the EU is 11 to 10. Over the last ten years, 85.8 per cent of new jobs in the United States have been for knowledge workers, including scientific and technical workers and corporate managers, and over half of these have gone to women.[64]

On the demand side, slowing global economic growth and structural changes in output have been the main factors affecting the employment problems. Most studies dealing with the economics of employment and unemployment emphasise the role of cyclical and structural factors. In Europe, for example, employment growth correlates closely with overall GDP growth, with the former lagging about six months behind the latter. However, GDP has to grow at least as fast as productivity to maintain the employment level.[65]

Both cyclical and structural factors will remain important in the future, although their relative roles may change. The cyclical factors consist of the direct macroeconomic linkages between the growth or decline of GDP and employment. The deceleration of global economic growth since the 1960s, accompanied by increasing regional differences in growth rates, in volume and per capita terms, has had important consequences for employment and the growth and distribution of incomes. Growth rates in most industrial countries and the majority of developing countries were too low to produce substantial reductions in unemployment and underemployment. In Japan in the early 1990s, 4 per cent annual GDP growth was considered by experts as the least that could help to sustain the socio-economic balance. In the developed European countries, about 5 per cent annual growth over at least five years was needed in 1994 to reduce unemployment to 5 per cent by the end of the 1990s (OECD, 1994). In the United States, where the greatest number of jobs were created in the 1990s, the quality of the jobs deteriorated for many during the long boom of the 1990s. The decline of GDP in the transition economies was greater than the ones experienced by the United States or

[64] *Newsweek*, May 18, 1998, pp. 14–15.

[65] The EU in its *1999 Report on Employment* (EU, 1999) draws two important conclusions from experience gained in the 1990s, which may be relevant to other countries. (1) Relatively high GDP growth appears to be needed to achieve a relatively high rate of net job creation. (2) High GDP growth in itself is not a sufficient condition for attaining employment objectives. The success of countries in translating output growth into more jobs varies widely, but the higher is the output growth, the greater is the chance of success.

Table 2
The macrostructure of world employment 1965–95, percent of total

	Agriculture		Industry		Services	
	1965	1995	1965	1995	1965	1995
World	57	46	19	18	24	36
Industrial countries	22	6	37	25	41	69
Developing countries	72	58	11	16	17	36

Source: ILO.

Germany during the Great Depression. It brought a big rise in unemployment and impoverishment for tens of millions. The important lesson from the history of Europe that slow growth, stagnation or decline gives new life to nationalism and protectionism, undermining and weakening social cohesion, rests mainly on cyclical factors.

The cyclical factors also have structural consequences that may result in a deceleration or stagnation of growth.[66] The recession in the early 1990s, for example, accentuated and deepened certain long-term structural problems present in the labour markets of the industrial countries for some time. The demand for labour generated by the economic activities that were expanding was smaller than the demand generated by the ones that were contracting. Both occupational and regional mobility became harder in environments of stagnation or slow growth in many industrial countries. It was also more difficult to implement the necessary structural changes. However, by the end of the 20th century, the structural changes that accompanied the diverse trends in growth rates had become greater sources of increased unemployment and shifts in employment trends and patterns than the cyclical factors were.

Some of the structural issues relate to longer-term shifts in output and demand, while others derive from technological changes. Longer-term structural changes in output and demand caused major shifts in employment between the main sectors of the economy: agriculture, industry and services. The macroclassification of global employment patterns shown in *Table 2* illustrates the structural employment changes in the main traditional sectors.

[66] There is no simple way to explain why some countries achieve higher rates of employment creation than others, and why there are significant differences in this respect between economies with apparently similar features. Institutional and structural characteristics seem to have an important influence. The main difference in employment between the United States and Europe, for example, is not in agriculture or manufacturing, where employment rates are broadly similar, but in the services, where the overall gap in employment rates is 14 percentage points. Services have been the main area of job growth in both economies. Jobs also expanded in the rest of the American economy, but in Europe, the rise in services was offset by major job losses elsewhere. See EU (1999).

The global trends have brought a substantial decline in agricultural employment and a smaller decrease in the proportion of employment in manufacturing, coupled with growth in employment in the services. However, it would be a simplification to look at these three sectors in a traditional or isolated way. The process must be understood in an interactive framework of countries operating in the three main sectors of the global economy, taking into account the fact that certain manufacturing activities have simply been reclassified as services. The structure must also be broken down into the developed and developing world.

The relative and absolute decline in the number employed in agriculture has been viewed for many decades as a basic consequence of economic development and modernisation. Fewer and fewer countries treat agriculture in a way that isolates it from the general framework of rural development. This is particularly important in countries where agriculture remains the chief source of livelihood. Some arguments relate to the patterns of the modernisation process. Contrary to popular perceptions, a properly modernised agriculture that combines modern technology and labour in a rational way can still offer important potentials for sustainable livelihoods for much of the rural population. There are other arguments for saying that it is neither possible nor desirable to copy the course taken by the industrial countries. One of them rests on the difficulties in creating urban employment and the high costs of urbanisation. Another relates to the concern about depopulation of rural areas. The search for alternative rural development strategies has become a priority for poor countries that are densely populated and land-scarce, like India and China, and for those with reserves of uncultivated land and low rural population densities. In practical terms, however, few countries have been able to boost the employment-sustaining capabilities of their rural areas and thereby slow migration to the cities.

It is far from simple or easy to address the broader question of how to strengthen the factors that can improve the capacity of the rural economy to provide hundreds of millions of people with livelihoods and improved living conditions. It calls first for a substantial increase in agricultural productivity, to sustain a growing rural service economy, infrastructure and trade. Another important potential source of employment is the development of rural industry. This requires other, supporting measures, such as improved rural education and training, special marketing organisations, concessionary sources of finance and the availability of appropriate technology. Private-sector activities and local and national government policies need to be better harmonised. The impact of the globalisation process and the related technological and economic transformation of the agricultural sector must also be taken into account. It is not entirely true that the globalisation process has avoided agriculture. The modern agricultural revolution has resulted radical increase in the productivity of agricultural workers of the industrial countries and of several limited sectors in the developing countries. The ratio of productivity between the traditional manual agriculture and the industrial agriculture is now 1 to 500. Traditional agriculture is essential to the survival of a large fraction of the population in the developing countries. Agriculture in the rich countries uses very little labour, particularly the corporate-driven "industrial agriculture" (including plantations in many developing countries), where it provides strong production, R & D potentials and marketing power. The labour input into agriculture has been reduced also by the green revolution, but it has increased somewhat the rural employment opportunities in activities designed to serve agriculture.

Export-oriented agriculture and often the producers for the domestic market in developing countries have to compete with the high-input, industrial agriculture of the developed countries. However, government subsidies play an important part in the profitability of agriculture and to some extent its ability to provide employment. Aggregate subsidies by the OECD countries averaged US $350 billion in 1996–98, which was double the value of aggregate agricultural exports by the developing countries (Unctad, 1999a). Concentration is occurring in agriculture, with reductions in the number of farms and increases in their average size and output. The concentration is even stronger in inputs and trade. A handful of transnationals dominate the production and distribution of such strategic inputs as fertilisers, agricultural chemicals, machinery and seeds. In international trade, the five largest commodity traders now control 75 per cent of the grain market. Concentration is also increasing in such sectors as fruits and vegetables. At local distribution level, the top five retail chains in some European countries, such as France, Germany and Britain, control over 50 per cent of the food sales. The role of supermarkets and hypermarkets is also increasing in the developing world.

The tens of millions of farmers pushed out of agriculture by technological and economic change will remain the main source of urban migration in the developing countries, unless rural development becomes more widespread. All too few countries have succeeded in strengthening the employment-sustaining capabilities of rural areas and slowing migration to the cities.

The trends in manufacturing employment in the developing and developed countries are diverging. In the industrialised countries, manufacturing output has declined in relative and absolute terms. In the 12 relatively industrialised developing countries, on the other hand, the manufacturing labour force has grown. There have been some important shifts in the branch structure of the manufacturing sector. On a global level, the sharpest increase have been in the share of industrial chemicals and pharmaceuticals, followed by engineering and electrical engineering, electronics, precision engineering, machine tools and office equipment. The sharpest relative declines have been in textiles, wood, iron and steel.

However, the relative decline of industry as a proportion of GDP in the industrial countries is less than as a proportion of employment or in the absolute number employed in manufacturing. Manufacturing is still the most important sector of the global economy in productivity. Manufacturing output per employee in the OECD countries increased by an average of 3.7 per cent a year in 1965–95, as opposed to 1.6 per cent in the services. The structural changes on a global level were closely related to the process of technological transformation and the redeployment of some industrial activities from the developed countries to developing and former socialist countries. Modern industrial employment in the developing countries was dominated by the public sector until the 1990s. Privatisation has resulted in a decline of manufacturing employment, amounting in some countries to almost a third of the industrial workforce. This process has also encompassed structural changes in the workforce. A similar trend, on a much larger scale, has marked the transition process in the former socialist countries. The new structural problems in the former socialist countries are not due exclusively to the privatisation process, of course. There was no real market for labour under the previous system. Job security was combined with low wages and a high degree of egalitarianism. Unemployment or underemployment "within the factory gates" has been a major impediment to structural change. The transformation process in the labour market has been marked by short- and medium-term emergency measures. The inevitable structural changes have been slow, even in countries that have suffered less severe socio-economic problems during the transition.

Certain qualifications are necessary when discussing service employment. The distinction between manufacturing and the services can be artificial. Many jobs in manufacturing are actually of a non-manufacturing, service type, such as engineering, design, sales, marketing and distribution. These service activities account for over 50 per cent of the costs of the manufacturing process. In more or less the same way, service functions are accompanied by manufacturing processes and industrial processes account for a large part of the agricultural system. This mutual infiltration is reflected in the macro-structure of employment. However, many new service fields in which employment is increasing fast, particularly in the industrial countries, are not related directly to other sectors. A common trend across the developed countries is a shift towards more highly skilled occupations and a decline in the number of manual workers employed. The structural shift towards a service economy is clear from the list of fastest-growing branches. These (commercial activities, health and social work, hotels and restaurants, education, recreational and computer-related activities) are all service activities, while the declining branches are almost all in agriculture and manufacturing.

As for the occupation structures in the modern sections of the economy, almost all countries show a strong converging tendency in broad categories of jobs and skills. Labour demand is rising in professional, technical, administrative and managerial occupations, especially in jobs related to information technology. All these require high skills. Demand for low-skill, low-paid occupations will not disappear, however. Demand is buoyant especially in personal services, where there will be a marked increase in jobs in high-income countries. However, there are several trends specific to certain regions or countries. Most developed countries will have problems in the 21st century connected with the changing demographic composition of the workforce, increasing polarisation of qualifications and payment, and increasing ethnic diversity in the workforce. These will require a number of adjustment measures from the institutions of society and in the public mentality.

The role and the integration of the informal sector – the grey or black economy – will remain an important employment issue, chiefly in the developing and former socialist countries. However, the longer-term role, growth potentials and upgrading of the informal sector will remain a very difficult task, mainly for the developing countries.

Surveys in the developing countries indicated that the share of the informal sector in total urban employment in the 1990s (including self-employment) was more than 40 per cent.[67] The concept of informal sector or informal economy was introduced a few decades ago in order to characterise and analyse the realities of the developing world. This sector is made of unregistered, untaxed activities. In Africa, for instance, the modern sector provides only about 10 per cent of employment, while the informal sector accounts for more than half the employment in urban areas and about a quarter of the total employment. In India only about 10 per cent of the total workforce is employed in the formal public and private sector. In the former Soviet Union and Central and Eastern Europe, the unofficial economic activity is close to 25 per cent. It has been estimated that the informal sector, including the world's shadow, black or underground economies produced about US $9 trillion a year in the 1990s.[68] It provides a livelihood for 40–45 per cent of the developing world's population. On the average, workers in the informal sector earn half of the amount paid in the formal sector.

The structural problems of employment on a microlevel derive mainly from the new relations that have developed between demand patterns, com-

[67] See the *Human Development Reports* (UNDP, 1991–2000).
[68] *The Economist*, August 28, 1999.

petition, production, employment and technological change.[69] The function of technological progress in this network of relations is still not well understood. The employment effects of new technologies, for example, include many diverse, heterogeneous processes in the industrial and the developing countries, including influences on the kinds of jobs available now and in the future in technical, managerial and new administrative occupations calling for high-technology qualifications. These spring from two trends: job creation in the new high-technology industries and services, and the creation of high-technology jobs in traditional industries and services.

The patterns of the 1990s reflect to some extent the new interactions between the factors mentioned already. (1) The technologies involved are more labour-saving than earlier technologies. (2) The technological transformation includes all sectors, not just industry. Computer-based and telecommunications-related processes have revolutionised the services as well, which in the past absorbed much of the labour released by industry. (3) The process is spreading to the developing countries, mainly through the transnationals. Their investments create fewer new jobs than earlier, when the availability of cheap, semi-skilled labour was an important attraction for their investments. Low-wage competition involves increasingly skilled, low-wage labour working with highly productive technology. Two other areas of technological transformation do not receive sufficient attention at present, but have an increasing influence on global employment. (4) One factor, which concerns the global material sectors, is efficient use of metals, minerals, fuels, etc. and further growth of the "knowledge" or information content of GDP. (5) The other is the increasing role of biotechnology in agriculture. Technological progress is bringing employment changes to agriculture and rural-urban linkages (especially in production and consumption). Agriculture still employs the bulk of the world's labour force, so that the spread of bio-genetic plants may have a big influence on future agricultural employment.

Seeking solutions

It has been generally recognised that the search for solutions to employment problems has to start in a national framework, but international cooperation is also indispensable. It requires, above all, an understanding of the

---

[69] The terms *jobless recovery* or *jobless growth* have become current among experts and in the press, to denote a trend in relations between growth and employment in the industrial world. Although not new, the gap between GDP growth and employment increase has been widening fast in some countries, reflecting structural changes in output and labour-market rigidity.

potential size and quality of the labour force and of the longer-term needs of the economy in each country. A national economy is a complex formation, defined by the size of the market, level of economic development, structure, growth, and the systemic model in which economic institutions function. These are all factors relevant to employment and related policies, whose relative importance differs strongly between countries. Labour markets differ in kind from goods or capital markets. Social and political interests are in general more strongly articulated and they are given greater institutional protection, so that moral and political factors play a much greater role in labour markets.

The character of information on labour markets is an issue of general importance. Many countries collect large amounts of statistical data about labour matters, but it cannot adequately reflect all dimensions of their employment problems. This applies especially to countries with a large informal sector, where a high proportion of people do not fit the traditional "labour force" concept, since they are both inside and outside the regular labour force. The same applies to unemployment statistics. Some countries may have an extremely high proportion of concealed unemployment.

Goals such as job creation and improvement of job quality and security are conditioned by complex, long-term socio-economic processes that are undergoing major changes at the beginning of the 21st century. These changes have a big influence on the rate and patterns of economic growth and the efficiency of markets, as well as the quality of national governance and the policies of the institutions shaping labour legislation. The supply and demand patterns in education and training and the mobility of people are in transition. The political importance of these processes underlines the need for political commitments and initiatives in all these problem areas, including relevant policies and practical programmes in action aimed at stimulating the economy and developing new sources of employment and a new labour-related policy framework.

There are some important issues on which there is at least an intellectual consensus and some convergence of policies worldwide. They include the need to promote quality employment that meets the labour standards defined by the ILO and international agreements, including bans on forced labour and child labour, and guaranteed rights of association and collective bargaining. There is also consensus on non-discrimination in employment. This is especially important for some vulnerable groups, which may need special attention through active employment-oriented growth and labour-market policies. On a global level, there is fairly general agreement among governments about some actions to reduce and eliminate unemployment and upgrade the workforce.

125

The most important instrument is support for employment-oriented economic policies and various national and international "pro-employment" development measures. The condition for such policies and the type of measures taken depend largely on the domestic socio-economic environment. The three main economic models – the American model, the European social market model, and the Japanese corporate model – represent specific patterns of development, with resultant differences in innovation capacities, production and consumption structures, international competitiveness and attitudes to social problems, including employment.

Since the 1980s, the increasing global interconnection of economies, along with market forces and increasing competitive pressures, have caused some convergence in organisational forms and policies. More research is needed on the extent to which the historical, cultural, social, and institutional environment of a country still influences its attitudes to labour, employment and labour-market policies, in terms of these models. However, as a general conclusion, based on the experiences of these countries, sustained employment-oriented growth depends on increasing productivity, as the prime source of income growth. This means more investment in R & D and plant and equipment. It calls for skills that promote wider applicability and better adaptation to rapid technological change, and improvements in the quality and appropriateness of the education system. Labour markets can adjust under the economic conditions of slower growth. The required structural adjustment is always painful, and those most affected are seldom reasonably compensated.

Here Europe will probably face more difficult, long-term problems than the United States, with its more flexible labour market and the greater territorial mobility of the population. In the United States, a less-regulated labour market offers employees a variety of combinations of working conditions, fringe benefits and wages. Of course, there are several drawbacks as well, since they have less job security and fewer mandatory social services. However, excessive regulation can be an extremely costly way of preserving employment and sustaining traditional work patterns, leading to the conservation of structural patterns that lose their competitive position and comparative advantages. The lifelong employment commitment in Japan has been undermined by the economic realities of the 1990s.

In Europe, where unemployment during the 1990s has been around 10 per cent, a medium-term European employment strategy has been adopted and is being implemented to meet the employment challenges. The centrepiece is the definition and implementation of annual employment guidelines. These are adopted by EU countries on the proposal of the European Commission and involving a country surveillance procedure, based on national action plans and annual implementation reports, examined by the Commission and the Council. (The first such guidelines were agreed by the Special European Council in Luxembourg in 1997.) The European Employment Strategy extends over a number of years. It emphasises that employment has top priority for the Union, as the best way of providing real opportunities for people and combating poverty and exclusion effectively, as the basis for the European social model. The Cologne meeting of the European Council called for the development of a European Employment Pact, aimed at a sustainable reduction in unemployment. There are three main elements that add up to a policy response to the employment challenges facing the Union. Emphasis is placed on a macroeconomic policy based on growth, stability and employment. It calls for improvement in the efficiency of labour markets and for structural reforms in goods, services and capital markets. It deems structural reforms essential for improving competitiveness and market functioning.

In the developing countries, the pro-employment policies of states are in principle more important, but in fact, there are much more limited policy means and instruments applied. In addition, the marketisation process has resulted in the replacement of the earlier comprehensive labour-force policies with more moderate and confined goals, often focussing on how to keep the unemployed off the streets of the main cities. Few countries have detailed programmes for the training and employment of youth or for rural industrialisation. The problems of employment-oriented growth are extremely complex and difficult, even in the developing countries that have such programmes.

Modern employment is expanding rapidly, especially in the fast-growing regions of Asia. The quality of the new jobs is often very bad. Sweatshop-like working conditions, forced overtime, underage (child) labour, industrial hazards and accidents are more or less general. In Asia, there are some important and interesting aspects of fast growth, related to labour-market situations. It has become increasingly evident, for example, that the high rate of economic growth and rapidly expanding local market have had a double effect on the informal sector in most countries. On the one hand, the informal sector has become more dynamic, with strong flows into the formal sector. The small-scale sector, functioning on the frontiers of the formal and informal sectors, still invests very little in technology, training or labour safety, and pays low wages to unskilled labour. Its aggregate labour force includes almost 200 million children between the ages of 4 and 14. Informal-sector activities have become even more confined to serving the poorest sections of the population, who cannot afford the services of the formal sector. The job-creating potentials of the informal sector have not changed in a meaningful way. It has also remained a last resort for many who are unable to find employment in the formal sector, even in a fast-growing economy.

127

The Asian experiences may also be relevant to other parts of the developing world. The growth of the modern formal sector in the developing countries, with the development of modern industries and services and modernisation of agriculture, are firm guarantees for the generation of stable employment. The informal sector may be considered an important supplementary source, but not a substitute for modern employment opportunities.

It is also difficult to implement pro-employment economic policies in most former socialist countries. Employment in all the transition countries has fallen substantially since the changes began. The growth in employment in some countries since 1994 has not been nearly enough to compensate for the losses in the early 1990s. The number in work at the end of the 1990s was still 10–40 per cent lower than in 1989. In the second half of the decade, a number of active programmes were adopted, including targeting policy toward specific categories of unemployed, retraining, credits for small entrepreneurs, public works, subsidised employment, special programmes for youth, etc. These were relatively successful only in countries where economic growth accelerated and favourable structural changes promoted more competitive activities. Even in the most successful countries, there have been constraints caused by institutional weaknesses and shortages of funds. The potentials of the small- and medium-size firms are considered by the authorities as important sources of employment growth. The quality of jobs in this sector are however often inferior: with lower wages and bad working conditions.

Education and improving human capabilities are important conditions for gainful employment, especially in an era of fast and widespread technological changes and intense global competition. Educational policies also have to be conceived as integral parts of employment-oriented economic and social policies. The relations between educational and economic policies are especially important in four areas. There has to be improved enrolment and reduced drop-out rates. The need to improve public access to higher-quality education is also important to promoting functional literacy (especially among young females). Better harmonisation of the educational system with the changing socio-economic needs and with job-training measures is indispensable to greater convertibility and efficient utilisation of skills, to employment creation, and to upgrading the workforce. (In the industrial countries, rising interest in skills has encouraged "competency and outcome"-based approaches.)

In view of the main trends that will characterise labour supply and demand in the coming decades, it is crucially important all over the world to decide how to deal with the unemployed or underemployed. This group differs in size and composition from country to country, and in the average period spent without a job. There are differences, of course, in the statistical coverage, but it is generally agreed that the developing countries have the highest proportions of underemployed and unemployed among the economically active population. The experiences with "active" and "passive" labour-market policies indicate that industrial countries are much better equipped to deal with the problems of unemployment than they were. Still, they find chronic unemployment hard to handle or to deal with such groups as young people or the unskilled. In many developing and former socialist countries, governments have no policies or institutional capacity to deal with the problems of the unemployed. There are no benefits, or very limited ones, and few retraining institutions. Public charity is also limited. Public works are not widespread and not too popular as a solution. Emigration, as an instrument of reducing unemployment, has an extremely limited impact.

The role of the private sector in creating new jobs is crucially important in the era of privatisation, but the results have been mixed. It has been already mentioned that the small- and medium-sized firms employing a large number of people offer very limited, if any social security and training. Increasing competitiveness and reducing costs are important considerations for the private sector, and in most cases, this implies trimming the labour force. Nonetheless, there is a consensus that the private sector has an important role to play everywhere in creating jobs, not least in the developing countries. The job-creating and sustaining capabilities of the private sector should be supported by governments and international financial institutions, particularly in poorer developing countries.

Also important is the job-creating role of the transnationals, the largest and strongest players in the private sector. Transnationals seldom consider the employment problems of the countries in which they locate or help them with job creation. However, they have a better record with upgrading employment, through their training and retraining activities.

The role of the state in promoting pro-employment policies depends on a number of factors. The ability of the economy to create jobs is a complex institutional and structural question, as mentioned earlier. The tasks of the state includes defining and improving the efficiency of labour-market policies and actions and introducing comprehensive policies on human resources. The practical approaches to employment problems in a national framework have been determined primarily by the nature of the political authorities in each country and the strength of the national groups and organisations that take job creation and full employment to be priority issues.

Another big factor is the country's level of economic development. Where markets are backward or undeveloped, or entrepreneurship and the private sector small, government needs to be active in industrial development and employment generation. Vigorous labour-market policies, such as increasing the labour content of public works, training, retraining, skills upgrading and employment services, are also functions of government. The state can act against marginalisation of the unemployed by providing "workfare" or subsidised employment. It can reduce the mismatch between supply from the education system and demand from the employment system by making schools more diversified and responsive to labour-market needs. Emergency measures by the state can include rural public works and housing construction. Another important government task is to improve and enforce labour standards, rather than lowering them. Other provisions may include affordable childcare facilities for women workers and investments in female human-resource development. Finally, government can initiate involvement by civil organisations.

Unemployment benefits may be contingent on community service or other forms of voluntary activity, such as hospital work, caring for the elderly, caring for young people with special needs, park maintenance, and so on. These unpaid jobs are to be seen as transitional to re-entry into employment, so that people do not feel resentful at not being paid for jobs while others are. To prevent the psychological side-effects of unemployment, especially where people are not engaged in training or retraining, they should be encouraged to take educational courses in computing, accounting, upgrading computer skills, foreign languages, child development, and so on.

In the long term, sustainable pro-employment policies also call for better international co-operation. One of the hardest problems here has been to define the scope and content of the resultant policies. Employment issues are still a neglected area of international cooperation, despite the international implications of national employment policies. In a liberalising global economy, national protectionist policies, freedom of international trade and foreign direct investments become very closely related to national employment levels and patterns. Workers and their unions seek to protect their jobs, wages and working conditions. Globalisation and liberalisation have always been subjects of employment-related political struggles. These may become more intense. The international bonds between labour markets may create serious problems and tensions unless they are backed by efficient forms of co-operation, agreements on labour standards, growth, and employment-oriented harmonisation of national policies. The pressure is rising in various parts of the world to increase human security. It is not enough to re-emphasise the moral commitment of countries to promote welfare and full employment, as laid down in the UN Charter. The Charter, of course, offers a significant global guideline for national policies and future international co-operation, but specific action is also needed, to strengthen the global foundations of human-centred development.

Issues and mechanisms in internationalising the labour markets

The internationalisation of a market, as a process, is usually defined by the degree to which the international mobility of the factor or commodity concerned is liberalised and by actual movements across frontiers. The degree of internationalisation of labour markets depends first on the degree to which the international mobility of people is liberalised, especially that of people of working age. It is also influenced by the international convergence in labour legislation and the increasing internationalisation of labour standards. Furthermore, it is affected by growing similarities in skill requirements and occupational, educational and training patterns, caused by the postulates of the new technologies and the internationally integrated production of the transnationals. The consequences of internationalising labour markets are assumed to include a better international balance of supply and demand for labour and convergence in its costs.

Preparing the workforce for the 21st century in practically all countries, but notably in Europe, where the integration process is most developed, involves preparing them for the increasingly integrated global markets of an ever more globalised world.

One of the human consequences of globalisation mentioned most often is its reduction of barriers and distances. The concept of a shrinking world includes not just freer, easier, cheaper and faster movements of people, but emergence of a global culture among them as well. This global culture is not just superimposed. It becomes mixed with national cultural identities through the workings of various media, such as the Internet, television, music, films, books, and even drugs and crime.[70] This culture includes a new, globally acceptable type of functional literacy, human skills that are universally applicable, and knowledge of foreign languages, all of which enhance the mobility of people.

Another great influence on labour markets and the trends and patterns of employment, including skills, wages, and labour standards, is the growing global interconnectedness. This applies despite the fact that the vast majority of the world's 3 billion employed (and unemployed) operate within national economic frameworks. In other words, governments formulate and implement their employment policies in response to domestic political, social and economic pressures and conditions. Within countries, employment has its specific demographic, technological, macro- and microeconomic, political

---

[70] According to the UNDP Human Development Report (see UNDP, 1997, p. 83), there are more than 1.2 billion television sets in the world. The United States exports over 120,000 hours of television programming a year to Europe alone.

and institutional dimensions. A macroeconomic category based on a definition of full employment or a "natural rate" of unemployment (the subject of much controversy in any case) makes no sense on a global level. Full globalisation of the labour market would imply that employees could take jobs anywhere in the world, without institutional constraints, while the employers would be free to "fish" from a global pool of job seekers. It would simultaneously imply that labour and capital were mobile to the same degree. This is still not the case, of course. Labour is far from free from territorial constraints, even within the EU, where gradual development of European citizenship is an official objective.

Labour markets at the beginning of the new millennium are the least internationalised of the three main types of market (for goods and services, money and capital, and labour). Nonetheless, there are many international aspects to employment problems. National employment in an interdependent world is related directly to changes in the external conditions of demand and supply and to international competition, especially in countries heavily dependent on foreign trade or strongly involved in FDI, as sources and hosts. Employment problems in turn influence the character of international trading regimes, through national attitudes toward international trade policies and agreements. Here the capacity to adjust has become a pertinent variable, since the labour markets of different countries have become connected more directly with a relatively liberal international trading system, through transnational corporations and their marketing and distribution operations. This connectedness influences the changes in employment supply and demand and in occupational structures. The trend is also enhanced by erosion of national labour-market regulations and welfare systems.

The future and sustainability of the present, relatively liberal international trading system depends largely on how successfully new employment opportunities are developed. Will the interconnectedness and internationalisation of national labour markets bring about an increase in employment opportunities and improve the efficiency of national policies in human resource development?

The internationalisation of national labour markets will probably occur faster in regional frameworks, through deepening international co-operation between countries in them. So far, the process has been important only in Europe, within the European Union. Its character and speed remain uncertain and dependent on several political, social and economic factors, such as migration pressures, public attitudes toward foreigners, social peace, and the readiness of national groups to accept Europeanisation of social policies, future patterns of economic growth, etc.

Why do labour markets remain less internationalised than the markets for goods or capital? First, the international mobility of people is a complex issue influenced by many political, economic, social, and cultural factors, including development levels and the role of "fixities" in the lives of groups. There are also much bigger constraints on the international movement of people than on that of capital or goods. Only a limited part of the labour force can be considered internationally mobile. The institutions that could promote mobility (including those related to flows of information on demand, for example, such as temporary or longer-term labour shortages in certain countries), and the supplies of mobile labour are highly specific and less developed, for instance, than is the case with capital movements.

Secondly, labour markets are strongly influenced by national, historical, socio-political, and institutional factors, and notably by the political process. It remains a political act even when individuals cross international frontiers for reasons that have little or nothing to do with politics. Labour markets are diverse structures, behind which hard economic realities lie, such as wide differences of development level, productivity and income. Specific issues relating to the internationalisation of labour markets differ in nature in Europe, North America or the developing regions of the world. The functioning of labour markets depends on institutions that are often at odds with one another. Some advanced industrial countries are highly unionised, while in others, the role of trade unions is limited. Looking at the industrial countries, union coverage of bargaining is about 18 per cent in the US and 95 per cent in Sweden. The role of government regulations in labour markets also differs widely, as do labour conditions and incentives. In some countries, a high proportion of pay derives from the bonus system, while in others, wages are predominant. There is also variety in unemployment benefit programmes, training and retraining mechanisms, and immigration regulations.

The main policy goal when liberalising labour markets is not "globalisation" or international mobility, but flexibility. Increasing flexibility involves the following main efforts:

1. Expose labour markets to the laws of supply and demand, use labour when needed, and reduce employment whenever demand is low due to cyclical factors or technological changes. Immigrant workers can be important in adjusting supply.

2. Use working time in a flexible way, including part-time employment, and working hours set according to the needs of employers, allowing fixed-term contracts, employment of temporary workers, and hiring from employment agencies.

3. As part of the general efforts to reduce costs and increase profits, cut the costs of labour by using wage differentials and employing workers with lower or non-existent social-benefit entitlements. This may include certain types of immigrant worker.

4. Reduce collective bargaining as far as possible, since this tends to curb redundancies and may result in "wage rigidities". This also implies that the powers of the trade unions have to be limited.

In some of the countries, which became independent states after the disintegration of the Soviet Union, there is even a process of de-internationalisation of the labour markets. This is the result of ethnic strife and the preferences given to the members of the ruling nation. There is also an emigration, or expulsion of the "new" minorities from some countries.

International migration in the process of the internationalisation of the labour markets has been also playing a certain but limited role.

The realities and prospects of international migration

The Japanese once executed foreigners for entering their islands. Japan remained probably the least open country for immigrants even therafter. Immigrants on the other hand were officially welcomed in some countries. A number of Latin American countries, Australia, Canada and particularly the US had been the main targets of emigration. United States is still the largest host country for international migrants.

According to neo-classical concepts, international migration is one of the main instruments for internationalising labour markets. However, cross-border movements of labour and migration in general are influenced by a combination of factors, not just the simple supply and demand for human resources. The issue embraces both voluntary and involuntary movements of people and the movement of refugees, and has economic, social, cultural, political, human-rights and ethnic dimensions. Its consequences may be demographic, economic, social and political, and positive or negative for the migrants and the host and home countries. The discussion here focusses mainly on economically motivated migration, which is related to the internationalisation of the labour markets.

According to UN estimates, the number of people living in a country in which they were not born is 50–80 million.[71] Other estimates put the number higher, at about 140 million. This almost negligible proportion of the world population is smaller than the proportions found in the late 19th and early 20th centuries.

The modern history of international migration can be divided into four periods. (1) Migration patterns between the 16th and 19th centuries were connected with the process of colonisation and mercantilist economic growth in

---

[71] Calculated from data in UNDP (1992), pp. 54–55 and UNWPP (1998), pp. 16–20.

Europe, which was based increasingly on raw materials obtained from colonies. (2) The period beginning after the Napoleonic Wars saw massive flows of people from Europe to North America, certain Latin American countries, Australia and New Zealand. By the eve of the First World War, the proportion of the population born abroad was 22 per cent in Canada, 15 per cent in the United States (white population only), 30 per cent in Argentina, 16 per cent in Australia and 26 per cent in New Zealand (Kuznets, 1966, p. 297). Economically motivated migration was an important means of easing the pressure of overpopulation in Europe, which exported 10–15 per cent of its labour force to the Americas and Oceania between 1850 and 1914. (3) International migration then became extremely limited between the two world wars, as restrictions were introduced in all the traditional receiving countries. However, the Second World War brought massive redeployments as slave labour, followed by huge numbers of displaced persons. (4) The period since the Second World War has seen an increasing globalisation of international migration. In the early part of the period, most of the big population shifts resulted from political changes. Since 1947, when India and Pakistan became independent, more than 40 million people have moved across the frontiers between them. There were also big movements of people to and from Palestine, related to the establishment of Israel. However, wars, revolutions, and upheavals have given rise to tens of millions of temporary international refugees or permanent migrants in all continents. During the 1960s and 1970s, there has also been a big worldwide increase in economically motivated migration, producing a transnational workforce in a number of countries that have not been traditional destinations. Britain, France, Germany, Sweden, Switzerland and the Netherlands became important target countries in Europe. Saudi Arabia, Kuwait and the United Arab Emirates also received millions of immigrant workers. In Africa, the Ivory Coast, Nigeria and South Africa became magnets for immigrants. As an indication of the role immigrants have played, it is worth noting that in the early 1990s, the proportion of those born abroad was 16 per cent in Canada, 6.2 per cent in the United States, 20.6 per cent in Australia, 16.7 per cent in Switzerland, 11 per cent in France, more than 7 per cent in Germany, 6.3 per cent in the United Kingdom, 64 per cent in the United Arab Emirates, 42 per cent in Israel and in Kuwait, and 22 per cent in Ivory Coast.

It is now possible to speak of the beginnings of a fifth period of international migration, since the end of the Cold War. An interesting characteristic of the period has been an increase in the flows of people from and among the former socialist countries.

Predicting the future trends in international migration is difficult. As mentioned in Chapter 4, migration relates on the one hand to demographic pressures, which are predictable in certain parts of the world, and on the other to expected economic opportunities, especially employment. On the demand side, it will be increasingly specific and selective. A new factor in the global migration trends of coming decades could be an increase in Europe's importance as a host. Immigration is one possible solution to the labour shortages in Europe that will be caused by ageing of the population. According to some forecasts, there will be a need for 50–75 million immigrants into Europe over the next half century.[72] Europe needs highly skilled specialist and cheap unskilled labour. Europe was a major source of emigration at the beginning of the 20th century. Now the developed parts of the continent face a reversal of this trend in the early 21st century, but the vast majority of Western Europeans are not prepared for it politically or psychologically. The problems are especially difficult for non-European immigrants into Europe. The "Economist" in its survey on the European immigration rightly stated "Many ordinary Europeans have not faced up to these changes. A wave of anti-immigrant sentiment is washing across the continent over asylum seekers in Britain, foreign workers in Germany, immigrants in general in Austria. These new arrivals are popularly perceived as welfare-scroungers, job-snatchers and threats to stability. Such views are fanned by politicians chasing the nationalist vote. And much of this can be blamed on the popular confusion who today's immigrants are."[73] Immigration will probably remain relatively high in the traditional receiving countries (the United States, Canada and Australia). The annual flow in the 1990s was about 800,000 into the United States, about 600,000 into Germany and 220,000 into Britain. Illegal immigration into the United States is estimated at a quite high 500,000–600,000 a year. Some 400,000–500,000 illegal immigrants enter the EU countries each year, in addition to the legal immigrants.[74]

Refugees fleeing persecution, civil unrest or natural disaster form an important category of migrants. The largest numbers of refugees at present come from sub-Saharan Africa and Asia. Most migrate to neighbouring countries and leaving the home region is rare. The intention is normally to return to their home country once conditions permit. However, this is not necessarily the case with refugees in Western Europe, many of whom have come from former Yugoslavia. The number of asylum applicants in the EU countries rose from 200,000 in 1988 to almost 700,000 during the Bosnian War, and then ran at almost 400,000 during the Kosovo crisis. An increasing number of these asylum seekers are economic migrants. The EU still has no common policy on applicants for refugee status. Increasingly, applicants are being

---

[72] *The Economist,* August 5, 2000.
[73] *The Economist* May 6, 2000, p. 21.
[74] *The Economist,* May 6, 2000.

rejected as "economic refugees" not covered by the Geneva Convention. The large number of asylum seekers perceived as "false" decreases the public tolerance for genuine refugees. The "golden age" for Gastarbeiter in Western Europe is over. The changes in Eastern Europe have altered the list of countries from which political refugees are accepted. The climate of opinion is likely to bring stricter immigration criteria, including tighter quotas and harder conditions for obtaining citizenship or acquiring education and property. An important area of concern is the political and cultural identity of the immigrants. The spread of Islam in Europe, for instance, is already a source of discomfiture in some circles. Increasing public hostility may be as important in curbing immigration as restrictive legislative measures.

Countries with mass emigration face a different set of problems. Emigration in past decades was a palliative for unemployment in some Southern European countries, but it cannot mitigate such problems in the developing countries in a similar way, where the historical experiences of Europe in this respect are irrelevant. Most migrants from European countries entered a cultural environment not dissimilar from their own. More importantly, the numbers were of a different order. The demographic conditions in the developing countries today make emigration pressures much greater than they ever were in Europe. On the other hand, the demand in the receiving countries is more limited, due to the technological and structural changes that have occurred and the increasingly knowledge-intensive character of the modern economy. In the immediate post-war years, for example, the Asian countries managed to export less than 0.1 per cent of their labour-force increment. Considering the current and projected disparities of economic development and the likelihood that economic inequalities will increase, the pressure for international migration in different forms seems certain to become an important problem in all parts of the world, especially between developing and developed countries, and between Central and Eastern Europe and Western Europe. Another factor, which facilitates international migration, is the greater availability of modern transport and telecommunications systems, at least for some segments of the population.

International migration may well become a big source of international and national conflicts and social violence. There is an increasing concern for example in the European Union that due to the large wage differences, there will be a mass exodus from Central and Eastern European countries, which are on the waiting list of membership. The different proposals for temporary restriction on the free movement of labour from these countries are reflecting these concerns. Central and Eastern Europe is not the only source of potential immigration. Europe became an important target of the legal and illegal emigrants from the Southern belt of the Mediterranian, from the Middle East and even from the Far East. There is a probability that the old Iron Curtain across Europe will be replaced by a "golden curtain" between North and South and to a certain extent between East and West. Seen in one light, this will be an important, controversial human rights and humanitarian issue, since the right to move and emigrate can be seen as a universal human right. Refugees will certainly have to be helped and will be helped. The definition of refugees however may change such a way, which will allow the refusal of refuge in those cases where the persecution "for reason of race, religion, nationality, membership of a particular social group or political opinion" cannot be clearly proved. Economic asylum seekers will have to face increasingly with measures protecting the labour markets from foreigners.

The economic importance of migration as a factor that internationalises labour markets must be also analysed as something that tends to reduce economic disparities and wage differentials between countries, helps to increase productivity, and stimulates demand for goods and services (through consumption by immigrants and through their remittances to their countries of origin). Both "push" and "pull" factors are important in the process. Internal migration may also have important international consequences, especially movement from rural to urban areas, which according to the empirical evidence, increases the push factors.

Cost-benefit analyses of migration have often been limited to movements of the highly skilled. Historically, many developed nations have benefited from immigration by highly skilled professionals. However, the brain drain from poorer to richer countries is a special problem. Its causes include poor working conditions, low wages, lack of resources, scarcity of appropriate jobs, unstable institutional and governmental support for science and technology, and lack of incentives for scientists and science students. The countries exporting scientists to richer countries may be precisely the ones with fewer scientists relative to their population and a bad need to increase their numbers. The brain drain, which affects some developing countries severely, can only be reversed by ameliorating the causes mentioned. Of course, international co-operation may help to counteract or mitigate the drawbacks. The brain drain of the early 21st century is connected with the growing need for people with special skills, in evolving areas such as information technology, where there was a worldwide shortage in 2000 of over 1.5 million specialists (about 850,000 in the United States and 600,000 in Europe).[75] There are also shortages in Japan and a number of other countries, including some developing countries. Many developed countries relaxed their rules concerning employment of foreigners to promote the immigration of IT specialists.

There are experts, who consider the brain drain as in part a favourable process for the sending countries, in view of its influence on the income lev-

[75] *Financial Times*, August 12/13, 2000, p. 6.

138

els of those who remain and work at home. According to abstract macroeconomic theory, wages are determined, in a well-functioning labour market, by the balance of labour supply and demand. If there is a relative scarcity of workers in one market, wages will be high, while in the case of relative abundance in another market, wages will be low. Migration in principle represents an equilibrating mechanism. The consequences of the process should therefore not only be increasing international equalisation of labour compensation, but elimination of the relative advantages employees gain from labour-cost differences between countries. Ultimately, according to this argument, international differences in labour costs (as incentives for FDI, for instance) will disappear. However, wage differences in themselves do not provide sufficient justification for international migration or the only incentive for it. Furthermore, an exodus of the highly skilled may reduce the income-generating capacity of those who remain. According to several analyses of the consequences of migration, it has not raised the wage level of those remaining at home, although it has created competition on the labour market.

Another interesting observation is that the majority of the immigrants to a number of countries have not been unskilled, although they often compete with the lowest skill segment of the workforce in their destination countries, and had certain comparative advantages in doing so. The influence of immigrants on the labour market of receiving countries was more to do with the availability of labour in some jobs not favoured by native workers, than with downward pressure on wage levels. In a number of cases, local trade unions managed to defend wage levels in jobs favoured by immigrants and thereby influenced the immigrants' earnings as well.

Remittances by migrants raise an important set of problems. The service is provided in some parts of the world by a special profession, by remittance brokers. The volume of the remittances back to some countries, such as Turkey, Greece, Pakistan and Egypt, make them a major source of finance for local development, through purchases of housing, land and small businesses. They also stimulate local consumption and contribute to the repayment of personal debts.

The role of transnational corporations in internationalising labour markets

Transnational corporations have been important actors in the process of internationalising the markets for goods and capital. Their role has been more limited in the internationalisation of the labour markets and also in global employment and employment creation. They have been playing however a stimulating role in the international convergence of labour legislations.

According to UN estimates in 1998, transnationals were employing about 90 million people worldwide, included the corporations' countries of origin. Of these, 17 million people were employed in the affiliates located in developed countries and 19 million in developing countries (UNCTAD, 1999b). This is a very small percentage of global employment. Of course, they also have major indirect effects on employment, through subcontracting and other forms of sourcing. Indirect employment effects in many countries can be larger than direct effects.

Cheap, skilled labour has long been cited as one of the incentives for foreign investment, as a potential source of profit. There are three factors (beyond the direct and indirect costs of labour) important for transnationals in this respect. (1) The quality of the educational system and the availability and development of skills in the destination country. They decide the availability of researchers, engineers and other qualified technical staff and the quality and availability of apprenticeship schemes. (2) Transnationals look for transparency and flexibility in labour markets, in connection with labour legislation, unemployment insurance and retraining facilities. (They are often criticised by trade unions for disregarding union rights and the national bargaining process and shifting operations from country to country at short notice.) (3) The degree of freedom of movement for the labour force to enter and leave the country is important for mobility of labour within the international system of a transnational.

Wage levels alone no longer bestow much advantage on a country in its dealings with transnationals. There is a wide choice of low-wage countries, including China, Vietnam and the ex-socialist countries of Europe. However, the attraction of lower wages is still important when combined with relatively high levels of skills, qualifications, discipline and morale, and when other operating requirements of foreign companies are met.

The global development of information services and education has made it easier for transnationals to combine the effective and efficient technologies they develop in their base countries with cheap and relatively skilled labour elsewhere. This cuts their production costs and raises productivity considerably.

Transnationals have a greater influence on the international demand for and career expectations of a number of professional groups than on those of unskilled or semi-skilled labour. They also have direct and indirect influences on changes in the global patterns of occupations.

The transnationals have proved more important globally in upgrading the labour force within their system than in promoting international migration of the workers. Their concentration in high-technology sectors requiring higher skills means that they will probably continue to play an essential role in disseminating new skill requirements, and thereby, internationalising skill and educational standards. They are efficient instruments for passing on skills to local staff, through personal contacts, on-the-job training, organised visits to other operations in their international system, and formal training courses. In most cases, firms owned by transnational corporations have higher skill levels among their employees than domestically owned firms or the public sector. This also means they have higher pay levels. It is not in the interest of transnationals to introduce converging compensation levels in their international system, because of the benefits they enjoy from lower wages. However, they usually pay better than their local counterparts, because their skill requirements are higher and they are more demanding with discipline and productivity. They often offer better working conditions as well, because of their greater visibility.

An important global issue concerning transnationals is their role in labour relations and the global restructuring of worker representation and rights. Their policy of considering the company as the focus of worker loyalty directly or indirectly undermines the traditional notion of workers' representation, in a number of ways. (1) Labour relations, the rights of workers' participation, company information and other forms of industrial democracy are so constructed that workers are incorporated into the global structure according to an agenda that gives priority to the company's interests. This may become an important source of conflict in the future. (2) The organisation of work, with such techniques as team-working, team briefings and direct communication with employees, coupled with the establishment of works councils instead of unions, may undermine the traditional union-management regulation of work and demand exclusive loyalty from workers. (3) Decentralised, informal relations are gaining ground particularly in countries where neither traditional union practices, nor labour legislation influence worker-management relations. This is the case in many transition economies and in certain developing countries.

The strategies of the transnational corporations in the framework of the integration groups resulting in the redeployment and restructuring their production and sales operations have also important influence on the labour markets. These strategies are also influenced by the policies of the integration groups.

Regional integration and internationalisation of labour markets

Regional integration groups have formulated programmes for employment, migration and migration policies in almost all parts of the world, but these are mostly rudimentary and in most cases recommend national action. The EU is the only regional organisation to start creating supra-national labour-market institutions, through its concept of "Social Europe" and some other initiatives, which promote deregulation and harmonisation.

The task of establishing a European labour market has proved more difficult and complex than with goods, services or capital. In a Union with 15 "official" languages and substantial diversity of culture, customs, attitudes to work, hierarchies and industrial relations (including trade-union roles), free movement of labour or pay disparities between countries are only parts of the problem. Another complex task has been to combine the abolition of discrimination of workers on nationality grounds with a national framework of treatment for foreign workers.

The free movement of the workers has been anticipated, including full aggregation of the national social security and national health care systems. National labour markets, however, are heavily regulated, which influences entry in a number of ways. Countries are keen to protect their labour market regulations, which not only sustains but also hardens the national fragmentation.

Four important areas have caused difficulties in labour-market integration: approximation of national labour-market regulations, mutual recognition of qualifications (skills and diplomas), access to social security elsewhere in the Union, and the treatment of barriers to migrant workers.

The most important is approximation of labour-market regulations. The parameters of the labour-market regulations applicable to all member-states are wider than those of national governments or national bargaining systems. EU law increasingly covers areas that cannot be reached by domestic law, such as equal opportunities throughout the Union. The processes of constructing the EU have often increased the diversity among players in national labour markets, particularly in areas affecting the flexibility of the labour market (minimum wages in one country, working time or bargaining practices in another). There are still great differences in such areas as legislation on minimum wages, collective contracting, the rules on hiring and firing, flexibility of work contracts, and the length of the working week. Mutual recognition of skills and diplomas remains a difficult and controversial issue, despite legislation and some progress. National regulations determine, for example, what can be considered as the "public interest" when rejecting an application for recognition.

These differences move beyond technical or institutional developments and become value laden. Approximation or convergence of labour regulations basically concerns the social structure, with macro- and microsocial aspects. The model of convergence as a process of increasing uniformity of political and legal processes produces very different results than those produced by the microactors of labour markets: trade unions, works councils, corporations or employers associations. These may also diverge strongly between countries, for instance between those with a long history of industrial democracy and those with corporatist traditions. As a result, migrant workers enter national labour markets almost entirely on the terms of regulations set by the host countries. Support measures for migrant workers, such as low-cost housing, are extremely limited. Health insurance beyond national frontiers can still be an important barrier, unless there is a mutual acceptance commitment among insurers. The EU labour market remains in many ways a collection of national labour markets and cross-border movements of labour are still very small. Foreign workers from other countries in the Union comprise a small minority of the total workforce, about 2–3 per cent, of which about half are from Greece, Spain, Portugal and Ireland. Non-EU migrants far outnumber migrants from within the Union.

Despite some converging trends in the long-term movement of labour costs, the differences in wage levels and social-security benefits remain wide. The extent to which these differences will level off and what mechanisms will cause this form an important issue for future research. The integration process could contribute to internationalising the labour market, through common co-ordinated policies to increase the quality of the labour force, including educational and vocational skill levels and structure, and its ability to adjust in a flexible, disciplined fashion to changes in demand and technology.

Certain trends in the early 21st century suggest that in spite of the constraints and differences between countries, labour markets are becoming more internationalised, thanks to various direct and indirect factors. There are however important problems. The present level of internationalisation already calls for more extensive international co-operation in such issues as the rights of the migrant workers, labour standards, working conditions, safety and health, remittances, freedom of associations, settling disputes, abolition of child labour, elimination of forced labour. Most of the debate over the internationalisation of labour markets concentrates on migration, which has become an increasingly important global issue. In Europe, there is rising public feeling against foreigners and the push effect of economic difficulties in the evolving market economies. On the American continent, there is concern over a new explosion of migration, with increasing volume and changing patterns, not only to the United States, but to Argentina, Brazil and Venezuela. In Africa, civil wars and instability contribute to mass flows of refugees. The flows in the Middle East have been increased by the consequences of the Gulf War and the shrinking revenues of the oil-exporting countries. In Asia, the opportunities for foreign workers created by fast economic growth have brought the migration issue to the forefront. Ethnic conflicts, created by influxes of foreign workers, and new political and economic aspects of migration call for a comprehensive approach to analysing the process that goes beyond its economic causes and effects. The basic neo-classical model that concentrates on "expected higher income" is inadequate to explain or even to study the process in an appropriate framework. Much more relevant to studying its determinants and consequences, including return flows and options for re-migration, is a structural approach of looking at demographic, political, institutional, socio-economic, gender, urban, rural and international interactions. There will be a number of problems related to future internationalisation of the labour market that go beyond international migration. One such issue is "social dumping" and another the future of labour standards. The process of demographic polarisation of the globe will also be an important source of problems. In a world, where labour is influenced by a great number of political, demographic, social, economic and technological factors, there will be growing pressure for adjustment. New and more flexible forms and mechanisms of international co-operation must be established by governments, to strengthen social cohesion and solidarity and avoid the evolving dangers of the new century, which was characterised by a recent publication of the Dag Hammarskjöld Foundation as the century of erosion, technology and concentration.[76] Erosion according to this concept influences a number of areas: cultures, human health, equitable relations but first and foremost the environment. Past experiences proved that centuries were more complex than the different catchwords attached to them. One may share however the concern about the erosion of the global ecosystem, which includes the genetic erosion, erosion of species, soils and the atmosphere.

[76] *The ETC century. Erosion, Technological Transformation and Corporate Concentration in the 21st Century.* (Stockholm: Dag Hammerskjöld Foundation, 2001.)

7. ENVIRONMENTAL CHALLENGES
AND THE HUMAN ASPECTS OF DEVELOPMENT:
THE SEARCH FOR SUSTAINABLE FUTURE

The future of human development depends ultimately on the *life-sustaining capacity* of the Earth. Environmental degradation is a global problem that directly or indirectly affects the life and development of different communities and of the individuals. Global environmental change is vitally important for human development. Human survival requires that various bio-geo-chemical parameters of the global ecosystem, of the "media" in which human development takes place, should be sustained. Thus environmental sustainability is the bedrock of human economic and social development. The improvement of the life sustaining capacity of earth will be the result of different societal actions. Education, health, employment, regional and local development, natural resource management, infrastructure and the eradication of poverty will be particularly important. The poor countries are in many cases victims of environmental degradation, before becoming the sources of it.

In an ideal world, all ecosystems would be self-sustaining, so that scarcities would not develop into imbalances that destabilise and threaten living things. The notion of life-sustaining or carrying capacity is drawn from biology. It implies that a certain area can only support a certain population of a certain species. In terms of sustainable development, this concept suggests that there is a saturation point for the human population, beyond which the yield of ecological resources will start to decline. The growth of population and of consumption suggests that competition for the resources of the Earth will become more intense in the future. Environmental problems will become major constraints of human development without appropriate policies and measures in management practices, institutional arrangements and enforcement of international agreements.

Environmental policy may be defined as the sum of goals and measures designed to regulate the interactions of the given society with the environment or the ecological system. These policies can be focussing only limited measures or can be comprehensive. They may comprise aspects of rehabilitation, conservation and structural changes in consumption, production and trade.

145

Most serious environmental problems in the past were localised in scale. A provocative article by Garrett Hardin more than a quarter of a century ago compared the countries of the world with a collection of lifeboats adrift at sea after a shipwreck. The developed countries were portrayed as lifeboats with room for a limited number of additional people, the poor countries as help-lessly overcrowded lifeboats, a source of swimmers seeking access to the places in the lifeboats of the rich. Hardin's lifeboat analogy suggested that the underpopulated lifeboats should deny access to the desperate swimmers from the overcrowded boats. At the beginning of the new millennium, the environmental crisis that confronts humanity is far more complex than this analogy, however. "Local", "regional" and "global" have become intercon-nected. The world has become one huge lifeboat. The specific problems of certain regions, relating to size of population, settlement character, accumu-lated damage caused by development patterns, and effectiveness of policies on environmental issues have made the global life-support system complex and hard to manage. Weather catastrophes have increased for example by a factor of 14 between the 1960s and the 1990s. The economic costs of natural disasters is rising at about 12% annually, four times faster than the global GDP growth. Another important challenge comes from the big differences in the environmental culture of the population. This applies particularly to the former socialist countries of Europe, which have built up serious environ-mental problems through negligence and the consequences of industrialisa-tion patterns, urbanisation, unwisely massive use of chemicals in agriculture, and often lack of expertise.

Ecological problems are closely tied to various other dimensions of human development. The environmental aspects of demographic challenges, global population growth and urbanisation are the most direct linkages. Agenda 21 adapted at the Rio Conference in 1992 and the Programme of Action of the International Conference on Population and Development (1994) recommended actions to ensure the integration of policies concerning population and the environment, addressing the environmental implications of demographic dynamics.[77] The spatial aspects of sustainability are also important, including the patterns of human settlement. The process of *urban-isation* is one of the biggest and hardest challenges to the ecological system and opens new issues for the sustainability of global development as well. Cities face serious environmental challenges even in developed countries.

[77] Computer models and tools have been developed to better understand and address pop-ulation/poverty/environment linkages. Two models that have received United Nations sup-

These, however, are dwarfed by the environmental problems of cities in the developing world. Future environmental sustainability depends largely on future capabilities to manage environmental problems. Urbanisation has had major influence on the environment not only of cities, but of neighbouring settlements. The concentration of population and related consumption patterns produce much more waste. Waste disposal is crucial question all over the world. Waste production rates in both developed and developing countries are increasing at unprecedented rates. Municipal authorities often spend between 20 and 30 per cent of their budget on cleaning and waste disposal. The vast majority of this expenditure, around 70 per cent, is related to transportation costs. The cost increases are further exacerbated by poor collection efficiency due to poor vehicle routing and planning and inadequate maintenance. Increasing land prices and availability in or around the urban centres make waste disposal increasingly difficult and costly. Finding a suitable site that offers an economically sound disposal option is becoming increasingly difficult. City dwellers and industrial establishments concentrated in cities increase the use of energy and do it in a highly concentrated way, which has much greater impact on nature. Excessive use of this energy and its sources, particularly fossil fuels, could also cause major environmental danger. The relation of urbanisation and water supplies is another important and difficult issue. Water use in cities brings a faster increase in total water consumption and greater and more concentrated sources of water pol-

port for application in developing countries are the Population Development Environment (PDE) model, developed by the International Institute for Applied Systems Analysis, and the Threshold 21 model of the Millennium Institute. Among the useful tools for integrating population and environmental factors into development planning are geographic information systems (GIS) which combine mapping data, ecosystem carrying-capacity assessments and ecological risk analysis, together with economic, social and administrative information, to support integrated development analysis and planning. Participatory action research tools have been designed to help communities assess natural resource management, population dynamics, health status of the population and gender-related factors. Resource limitations in many countries have constrained the efforts of Governments to address population and environmental concerns. In many countries, conflicts, crises, natural disasters and economic, social and political instability have also limited the ability of Governments to implement Agenda 21 and other global conference results. Breakdowns in governance, inadequate infrastructure and competing financial priorities have reduced access to a range of basic social services, particularly quality health care and reproductive health services. While national sustainable development strategies, including population policies, have been formulated in many countries, much remains to be done in terms of implementation due to the lack of a cross-sectoral conceptual framework based on the complex interrelationships between population, environment and sustainable development, lack of suitable and accurate data; and lack of financial and human resources to implement policies and programmes.

lution. The super-urbanisation of the coming years will demand new approaches to water management.[78]

Both mass poverty and the wasteful consumption patterns of affluent societies are important factors in the human dimensions of sustainability. In the case of *poverty*, there is a double pressure of environmental degradation. The essential issue for the poor and hungry is bare survival. They often destroy their immediate environment to increase the available land, or over-graze grasslands, resulting in desertification, unsustainable farming conditions, and deteriorating bio-diversity. Then they move to already crowded cities to find employment, becoming even more vulnerable to natural and manmade disasters. About 60 per cent of the poor in the developing world – some 600 million people – live in vulnerable areas: on arid or semi-arid lands, steep slopes, or poorly serviced urban areas. The rural poor generally suffer from bad health, due to under-nutrition, malnutrition, or various forms of pollution, especially water pollution, indoor air pollution and direct exposure to agricultural chemicals. The health of the urban poor suffers from water pollution, air pollution, poor sanitation and exposure to toxic wastes.

Affluence is also a major cause of environmental degradation. Most people want to get richer and possess and use more things. About 10 per cent of the world population currently consume some 75 per cent of the world's resource production. In 1998, the top 20 per cent of the world population, in the highest-income countries, accounted for 86 per cent of total spending on individual consumption, while the poorest 20 per cent accounted for only 1.3 per cent.[79] The affluent are major producers of household garbage and indus-

[78] Urban growth poses a number of institutional, economic and environmental challenges for maintaining and extending services and for maintaining and improving water quality, especially sewage water treatment. In terms of water supply and sanitation, some progress has been made in the past decade. From 1990 to 2000 the percentage of the total population in developing countries with access to safe water increased from 72 to 78, whereas for sanitation it increased from 42 to 52. In most urban water systems in developing countries, water that is unaccounted for amounts to as much as 50 per cent of total withdrawals. To achieve the international targets of reducing by half the proportion of people without access to water and adequate sanitation, it is estimated that more than 1 billion people will need to be served with a water supply and almost 1.1 billion people served with adequate sanitation in urban areas. Even though urban areas are expected to accommodate more people than rural areas, there will be a steady increase in the absolute number of the world's rural population over the next 20 years. The overall growth in population, coupled with the demographic transition to urban areas, will have several socio-economic implications and will further intensify competition both within the urban and rural settings and between urban and rural water uses. (UN Division of Sustainable Development, 2001)

[79] UNDP (1998). These figures are based on country averages. Based on per capita consumption rates, irrespective of country, the difference between the wealthiest and the poorest quintiles is far greater.

trial toxic waste. They use more chemicals in agriculture and are the sources of massive automotive exhaust fumes. They also use much more water and energy. Their relative contribution to global warming is much greater.

Ecological problems joined with the spread of knowledge about them have increased public concern and mobilised millions of people in many countries. The Rio conference in 1992 introduced the "major group" approach, which is spreading also in other international organisations. There is a special consideration for the attitude, interests and problems of these groups, which promotes better the dialogue with them but also between them. The groups are women, children and youth, indigenous people, non-governmental organisations, local authorities, workers and trade unions, business and industry, scientific and technological communities and farmers. In spite of the positive approach to environmental issues by people and governments and support for common international action from a broad coalition of non-governmental organisations, real progress towards a global or even a regional environmental policy is very slow.[80] This is due to differing and sometimes diverging interests among those concerned, concerning priorities and the specific measures to be taken. The divisions over priorities occur not necessarily between the groups but mainly between *North and South*. The developed countries generate about 80 per cent of all the global pollution. Developing countries often argue that they cannot be expected to sacrifice their development to prevent environmental damage and mitigate problems caused by the developed countries. Radical experts or political figures in the South accuse the North of environmental imperialism, insisting that environmental issues cannot be dealt with in isolation from overall global socio-economic inequalities.

The North is heterogeneous in its area, scope and character, and in its willingness to assume responsibility or pay for environmental safeguards in such areas as CO_2 or CFC emissions. The process that led up to the Montreal Protocol on issues pertaining to CFC is an important case study of how micro- and macrointerests on a national level can influence disputes and how

---

[80] According to the information from the Division on Sustainable Development, the participation of major groups over the past 10 years has been largely ad hoc, lacking clear and formalised mechanisms for their full engagement in making decisions and implementing them. This constraint particularly affects the local and national major groups that feel marginalised, in terms of sustainability issues, in their communities and countries. Similarly, at the international level major group participation is still largely limited to a passive exchange of information. Sustainable development processes at all levels need to expand the available participation mechanisms so as to allow more meaningful contributions from major groups, including their participation in making decisions that affect their communities.

149

they are resolved. The disputes on CO_2 emissions and other sources of global warming are more complex. There are strong, diverging interests connected with the traditional sources of energy. The stumbling blocks to co-operation and common policies include information uncertainties, difficulties with monitoring compliance, and reluctance to embark on unilateral measures and costs, which would increase production costs and divert funds from other investment. For the developed countries, the costs of environmental measures and their influence on competitiveness has been an important source of disagreement. The diversity of interests is aggravated by systemic factors, since the diversity of national economic models still makes enacting multilateral measures difficult, even to implement various international agreements concluded in the past.[81] Various agreements to protect the environment signed, for example, under the auspices of the UN Economic Commission for Europe, remain only partially implemented.

Some lessons for the future emerge from the *history of environmental management* in a number of developed countries. Analysis of the environmental policies of major industrial countries reveals a three-stage development process that has followed similar patterns in several countries (Wiedner, 1991). (1) There is a phase of environmental inaction or negligence (preceded by ecological ignorance): the bureaucracy remains passive in spite of the proven damages to health and nature. Relevant information is ignored and social protest disregarded or suppressed. (2) There comes an era of symbolic activity, when environmental strategies are formulated and programmes and bills issued, but implementation of these is at best marginal. (3) Active technocratic environmental management begins in a piecemeal, selective fashion, but the measures become increasingly efficient. (Piecemeal management is here defined as measures that ignore the interdependence of an ecosystem's component parts when implemented.)

The transition from one stage to the next requires greater education among policymakers, heightened research and increased interaction among experts, parliamentarians and government officials. It also calls for changes in public priorities and attitudes, and in the particular level of international co-operation and its operational efficiency. The reintegration of the former

---

[81] By the end of 1990s, 18 important intergovernmental organisations and over 5000 international NGOs were dealing with the management of the ecosystem and co-operation on environmental issues. The UN General Assembly had adopted 15 main detailed resolutions, while ten other important resolutions initiating specific programmes had been adopted by various UN bodies, the OECD, the EU and other regional organisations with multilateral frameworks. Fifteen major multilateral intergovernmental declarations, 174 multilateral conventions, agreements, and protocols and dozens of bilateral agreements currently cover a variety of areas for environmental co-operation and joint action.

socialist countries into the global economy and global ecological system implies also new forms and models for participation in global environmental management.

The framework for this was defined by the Rio Conference on Environment and Development in 1992, based on two main pillars. One was the report of the World Commission on Environment and Development, known as the *Brundtland Report*, which emphasised the need to secure sustainable global development and called for an integrated set of policies to maximise human welfare within an inter-temporal framework. The report defined sustainable development as "development that meets the needs of the present without compromising the ability of future generations to meet their own needs" (WCED, 1987, p. 43). This definition serves as a basis for a normative approach to the environment by stressing environmental "needs" indispensable to society. It raises the issue of intergenerational equity: the development conditions for the next generation should be similar to the ones available to the present generation. It also sees preservation of the ecosystem as a global task equally important to all countries. The global dialogue on the *concept of sustainable development* is far from being over. According to a recent document from the UN World Institute of Social Research, the term sustainable development has become popular to some extent because it can be used in a neutral way, implying little more than a vague sense of purposeful improvement in the economic, social and environmental domains. Even so, the document recognises that the term serves a useful purpose by reminding the international community of some fundamental issues: development demands more than economic growth; some features of modernisation have unacceptable social and environmental costs; this calls for different economic policies, development strategies and approaches to planning.

The second pillar of the Rio recommendations was the work of the UN on environmental-security issues, as important components of comprehensive, global human security. This work had been going on for some time, with active participation by governments and the academic community. In the debate on environmental security, a number of definitions were formulated and proposed before and after the Rio conference. The common element in these was an effort to establish linkages between environmental conditions and human security.

Although competing notions of *environmental security* abound, they generally fall into three sets of claims: (1) States and non-state actors should guard against environmental degradation for the same reason as they guard against organised violence. Both threaten human, material and natural resources on a large and disruptive scale. (2) Local and regional environmental degradation and resource scarcities (exacerbated by population growth, inequitable wealth distribution and global environmental changes) are important contributors to sub-national political instability and violent conflict. (3) Military and security institutions (including intelligence agencies) can and should play a bigger role in environmental protection. The rising popularity of environmental-security slogans has accompanied increasingly prominent calls for new definitions of security to replace Cold War concepts, predominantly rooted in realism.[82]

In the different definitions the term environmental security refers to a range of concerns that can be organised into three general categories. The adverse impact of human activities on the environment, through different forms of pollution, results in further degradation, water scarcity, air pollution, global warming, and so on. The use of non-renewable resources continues to grow. Per capita energy consumption in developed countries is still increasing, but not as rapidly as economic growth. Energy intensity per unit value added is decreasing at about 2 per cent a year. In many countries, material consumption (expressed in kg) per unit value added is declining for steel (which peaked in 1918), cement (1926), paper (1972), aluminium (1976), chlorine (1971) and ammonia (1980). Consumption of petrochemicals, carbon fibre and silicon, on the other hand, is increasing in terms of kg/unit value added. There is shrinking diversity of the biosphere.

The governments of the world took a historically important step in global environmental governance by adopting Agenda 21, a global, comprehensive programme of action for sustainable development, and the *Rio Declaration*, defining the rights and responsibilities of states. As with any multilateral action, leadership was needed to press the cause of environmental protection and adopt norms for doing so. Not many countries showed interest in undertaking this leading role in implementing the Agenda. International financing was also needed for countries without the funds to implement required environmental policies. The total annual funding requirements for achieving the goals set forward at the Rio "Earth Summit" of 1992 has been estimated at US $125 billion. Only a small fraction of this was supposed to be available from external sources. Most of the funds had to be raised and spent within national frameworks. There were also important technical assistance requirements that could be met in a bilateral or multilateral framework. The machinery required for overseeing institutional environmental work, aided perhaps by sanctions against nations that ignore international agreements, was partially established. The setting up of a Global Commission on Sustainable Development, as proposed at the Rio Conference, was an important step towards establishing such a global structure, but the body lacked power and resources.

---

[82] A comprehensive analysis of the issues related to the concepts and operational use of environmental security appears in Bonser, (ed.) (2000).

The post-Rio years proved how difficult globally harmonised environmental governance was. Poverty, lack of domestic resources and insufficient international commitments to support countries without the requisite national capabilities and resources placed major constraints on the South. In the North, growing affluence was not necessarily resulting in improvements either. There are strong alliances and closed policy networks in energy, transport, agro-business and other areas in every country. These have the power to ignore environmental imperatives. *Ex post* economic and market instruments have not been strong enough in the implementation of policies. The establishment of national commissions on sustainable development in over 100 countries disguised in many cases a formal step, without influence on environmental policies. The harmonisation of international actions and co-ordination of work by different intergovernmental organisations proved more difficult than expected. Still, Rio marked a turning point in global environmental governance, whose results will probably materialise fully in the 21st century. It also opened new means of co-operation among voluntary associations.

During the 1990s, much work was done in formulating and clarifying the *concept of sustainable development* and its implications for theoretical issues and research on economic growth. The concept implied greater emphasis on the quality of economic growth than on its quantity, in the economic and social dimensions of welfare. The social dimensions of sustainability, in their broader formulation, cover the need to eradicate poverty, provide employment, improve health conditions, develop education, manage demographic problems, reduce inequalities, and increase participation in effective decision-making. Global health issues have been particularly important in this context. They are related most directly to environmental and social hazards.[83]

[83] Over the past decade, average life expectancy has increased, infant and child mortality rates have declined. In developing countries, the percentage of people with life expectancy at birth below 60 declined from 38 per cent to 19 per cent between 1990 and 1999. The proportion of people without access to improved water supply fell from 21 per cent to 18 per cent over the past decade. Many infectious diseases have receded, owing to improved sanitation, nutrition, drugs and vaccines. Despite undoubted health advances in many areas, poor health continues to be a constraint on development efforts. In some cases the process of development itself is creating conditions where, as a result of economic, political and social upheaval, environmental degradation, and uneven development or increasing inequities, human health suffers. Major setbacks in health gains occurred in Eastern Europe and the former Soviet Union, where the political and economic transition has been accompanied by decreases in life expectancy of five years for males. In the poorest countries of the world, one in five children still fails to reach his or her fifth birthday, mainly owing to infectious diseases related to the environment. The child mortality rate in the least developed countries in 1999 was 156 per 1,000 live births, compared to 81 in all developing countries and 11 in developed countries. Six major diseases currently

The interaction between the environmental and social dimensions proved extremely complex and in practical terms difficult to manage. Designing and stimulating effective decision-making and planning became important new tasks. Through information technology, decision-support systems have been developed to reflect and allow for the interactions of different issues and areas.

However, in a number of areas, measures and changes depend less on government decisions than on complex interactions of social norms and attitudes with various forces and factors affecting the functioning of markets. Balancing economic, environmental and social objectives in a sustainable development framework would be facilitated by valuing environmental and social resources in monetary terms, as economic resources are. Attaching a price to the availability of a natural resource is difficult, given imperfect information and competing priorities. Since market prices often do not reflect the values of environmental services and "willingness to pay" for such services is not always observable, non-observable values may have to be estimated. The Kyoto Protocol, for example, is expected to lead to an international market for greenhouse gas-emission credits. The volume of this can be 40–50 billion dollars. There may be many controversies and conflicts over

cause 90 per cent of the deaths from communicable diseases: AIDS, malaria, tuberculosis, pneumonia, diarrhoeal diseases, and measles. In addition, several parasitic conditions continue to cause considerable morbidity and disability: schistosomiasis (over 200 million people infected), lymphatic filariasis (120 million people affected), trachoma (over 150 million infected), trypanosomiasis, or sleeping sickness (over 55 million people threatened), and Chagas disease (up to 18 million people infected in Latin America). About 36 million adults and children are now living with HIV/AIDS, 95 per cent of them in developing countries. Several hundred million people continue to be infected annually with malaria, which results in almost 300 million clinical cases worldwide each year, and over 1 million deaths. The scale of the problem is increasing in many countries. Despite considerable progress in tuberculosis control in the 1990s, about 8 million people develop active tuberculosis every year, and the disease kills over 1.5 million people per year. Poverty is an important reason that babies are not vaccinated, clean water and sanitation are not provided, drugs and other treatments are unavailable, and mothers die in childbirth. A disproportionate burden of disease will continue to be borne by disadvantaged or marginalised women, especially those living in environmentally degraded or ecologically vulnerable areas, in zones of conflict or violence, or compelled to migrate for economic or other reasons. The feminisation of poverty is a major threat to social and economic development. Many health problems will continue to be exacerbated by pollution, noise, crowding, inadequate water and sanitation, improper waste disposal, chemical contamination, poisonings and physical hazards associated with the growth of densely populated cities. Badly managed urban settlements and overcrowded housing make it easier for infectious diseases to spread and for illicit drugs and violence to take hold. Urban growth has outstripped the capacity of many municipal and local governments to provide even basic health services. (UN Commission on Sustainable Development. E. CN. 17/2001/PC/6) evaluations and in general on how the market should function. All this implies difficulties in applying the theoretical concept of sustainable development. Some difficulties have been analysed in a recent OECD report.[84]

Applying the concept of *intergenerational equity* is even more difficult. There are two essential determinants of the potential to satisfy the needs of the present and next generation: availability of capital and population growth. Capital, seen in terms of sustainable development, includes natural capital (both natural resources and environmental assets), man-made capital (both physical capital and financial assets) and human capital (including health and education). Social capital, a concept encompassing social institutions, networks and norms, may also be included in this representation, although in practice, investment, depreciation and rates of returns on social capital are difficult to identify. Here a condition for sustainability is that the total stock of capital should not decline.

There are two main questions about the process. One is the extent to which the various components of wealth can substitute for each other. The other concerns technological progress. For some types of capital, there is no substitute and degradation will cause a loss to future generations. This is the case with non-renewable resources (bio-diversity) and with renewable resources exploited beyond their capacity to recover (such as fish stocks). With most resources, however, substitutes are likely to be found, at least for marginal changes. The OECD report also emphasises that assessing the degree of substitutability in the different components of the capital stock depends ultimately on value judgements, but these two approaches also inform different perspectives on measurement (see Chapter 6 of the report).

Technological progress is important because it offers opportunities for subsequent generations to increase the productivity of these assets. The process of global technological transformation and diffusion of new technologies is one of the main sources of concerns and opportunities in the management of the global ecosystem. Technology has always been a two-sided phenomenon.[85]

The ecological problems connected with new technologies are complex and subject to various influences. One problem concerns the direct environmental damage caused by using certain new technologies. Most new technologies, however, facilitate reduction of the energy and material-intensity of global production and consumption. They are therefore more "friendly" from the ecological point of view than earlier technological generations. They

---

[84] OECD (1999) offers a detailed analysis of these difficulties.

[85] An interesting historical analysis and overview of the characteristics of technology appears in Rosenberg (1976), pp. 213–280.

embody important potential help in resolving the many global problems concerned directly with people's lives: family planning, food production, restructuring the global energy economy, technology-based pollution regulation, etc. Solving a few important ecological issues depends strongly on the use of new technologies: reduction and proper management of industrial, especially chemical and nuclear waste, protection of the ozone layer, and reversal of the global warming process. The last depends on technological progress in the global energy economy, whose problems may serve at the same time as instructive examples of how difficult it will be in practice to introduce new technologies that are able to reduce and eliminate the adverse environmental effects. The technological scope for major changes are available in most areas. The investment required to replace the existing technologies and make the required organisational and institutional changes depends on fulfilling some complex internal and external conditions. These include acceptable prices for the technology, conditions for its international transfer, the ability to adapt technologies to different systems, capacities for assimilating technology, including enhancement of technological skills, and international mechanisms for addressing these needs. Some of these may be easily attained, but others are more difficult to develop, requiring further research and a broad consensus of attitudes and actions by the main players and international co-operation regimes, offering appropriate global policies.

All these factors indicate that sustainability offers humanity the chance to change the path of development more on a social than an individual level. One important question that remains open is how free and ready is a heterogeneous human society, constrained by social, cultural, political and economic factors, to alter its pattern of development in a desirable direction. Will the real and potential dangers, often presented in apocalyptic terms, be perceived strongly enough to enforce such changes? Will scientific rationalism, often guided more by disagreements than agreements on major dangers, be convincing enough to change lifestyles, production, consumption and distribution patterns? Will political decision-makers interpret the pace, depth and source of changes uniformly? Will global governance become effective enough to develop the global regime of international co-operation indispensable for sustaining the process, harmonising interests, and balancing costs and benefits? Answers to these and other questions may emerge from the follow-up to the Rio Conference in 2002.

The Secretary General of the UN in his Report to the Millennium Assembly in 2000 emphasised the following priorities:

- Coping with climate change: reducing the threat of global warming requires a 60 per cent reduction in emissions of carbon and other "greenhouse gases". This can be achieved by promoting energy efficiency and relying more on renewable energy sources. Implementing the 1997 Kyoto Protocol would be a first step.

– Confronting the water crisis calls for cutting by half the proportion of people without access to safe and affordable water before 2015. Starting a "Blue Revolution" would increase agricultural productivity per unit of water, while improving management of watersheds and flood plains.

– Defending the soil: according to the report, the best hope of feeding a growing world population from shrinking agricultural land may lie in biotechnology. Its safety and environmental impact are hotly debated, however. The secretary-general is planning to convene a global policy network to try to resolve these controversies, so that the poor and hungry do not lose out.

– Preserving forests, fisheries, and bio-diversity: in all these areas, conservation is vital. Governments and the private sector must work together to support it.

– Building a new ethic of stewardship: here the secretary-general recommended four priorities – education of the public, "green accounting" to integrate the environment into economic policy, regulations and incentives, and more accurate scientific information and data.

The problems of information became particularly important for collective actions. Sustainable development requires new ways of making public policy decisions. It requires a more integrated approach to economic, social and environmental problems and effects. The different initiatives which have been launched to improve environmental observations and data collection, like ozone monitoring under the Montreal Protocol or on the three Global Observing Systems are badly under-funded relative to the needs. The System of integrated Environmental and Economic Accounting (SEEA) developed by the United Nations Statistics Division of the Department of Economic and Social Affairs of the United Nations Secretariat is still not complete. The harmonisation and rationalisation of reporting is hampered by the slow progress on the standardisation of data. There is also a critical lack of basic statistical data on national level.

PART III

GLOBAL GOVERNANCE AND THE CIVIL SOCIETY

8. GLOBAL GOVERNANCE
OF HUMAN CHANGE AND CIVIL SOCIETY

Governance and changing communities in an evolving global system

The life and roles of individuals, including their rights and obligations, are still largely defined by different communities. The closest community is the family, the structure and economic foundations of which have been changing everywhere. The family as a fundamental unit of society and the traditional source of support has undergone particularly profound transformation over the last two generations. The extended family, which was still the dominating form in the developing world in the middle of the last century has been replaced by the "nuclear" family. The long-term changes in the economy and in the societies transformed the size, the nature and functions of the families. New types of families emerged: the migrant family, the single-parent family, with one wage earner, mainly headed by women. The other type of communities related to education and work, schools, firms and other organisations have always been much looser and amorphous formations than the families. They have been also exposed to the different forces of transformations. In the context of the global governance process the larger communities, like settlements, neighbourhoods, towns and nations were influenced by the forces, which transformed the families and also by those forces and factors, which governed the world community. New formations, like associations that join people, religious groups, professional organisations and interest groups emerged. The civil society, the institutionalised collective action of the citizens on the level of the smaller communities, countries or on global level became an important source of influence on the states, which however still occupy a central position in the governance process. Their membership is universal and they have a monopoly of force. Many people feel they owe a special loyalty to their country. Loyalties to the world community, on the other hand, are less strong. Humanity is also universal, but obligations to it are much weaker.

Governance as a concept relates to human beings in their communities. It is based on a variety of interests, on a set of values, policies and institutions by which the society harmonises economic, political and social processes at different levels: local, national, regional or global. The state has been the central institution of governance since the Treaty of Westphalia in 1648.

Governance comprises the mechanisms and processes by which different communities articulate and mediate their often diverging interests. It is a framework of rules, institutions and practices that set limits and provide outlets for the different groups. The globalisation process that promoted global integration globalised also the institutional framework of governance. I use the *concept* of global governance as the entirety of the actions shaping the collective capacity of states to deal with the global sources of risks and influencing the process of changes in the international environment, thereby avoiding major crises. In principle, global governance would imply a global framework for participants or actors in the international system, and also, in an optimal democratic framework, offer an increasingly universal set of principles, such as equity, participation, sustainability, transparency, effectiveness and the rule of law.[86]

Global governance however will have to deal with the other processes of international life: disintegration, fragmentation and localisation. It should be a consultative and communicative process for the resolution of disputes, for building consensus. It should be able to accommodate different cultures.

Global governance is gaining importance for several reasons. One of the most important is the declining ability of states to manage their domestic problems in many respects. Even issues such as unemployment, financial crises, environmental degradation, terrorism, crime, urban decay and drug abuse involve crucial external sources and factors. Another important incentive for global governance is the ethnic factor in politics, which is often connected with religious divisions. Another factor calling for global governance is the existence of mounting global problems. The sustainability of the system relies increasingly on the ability of countries to bind the world together with global governance in some form and structure.

Despite innovations and reforms, the *machinery* of global governance remains based on a past legal and institutional framework, not new, efficient collective-risk management procedures and responsible global visions and actions. Expectations aroused by earlier rhetorics about a new post-Cold War global order have not been met. Many earlier problems on the international agenda remain unresolved: old and new North-South issues of multilateral co-operation and diverging goals among forces advocating globalisation, multilateralism, unilateralism, neo-isolationism, neo-nationalism, bilateralism or regionalism. These influence and often impede progress in global governance.

---

[86] For an approach to this, see UNDP (1997), for example.

The mechanisms of global governance include large global inter-governmental conferences initiated and organised by the United Nations, mentioned earlier. They have been dealing with the common actions and with the management of vital issues such as the relations between the environment and development, the future of human settlements, the role and equality of women, the social conditions of human development, the future of children, and so on. The multilateral system of international intergovernmental organisations is also an important side of global governance. International agencies and co-operation regimes create an intricate framework for states, adding up to more than the aggregate of the work that states earlier performed individually. The various multilateral agencies and institutions comprise a loose, extensive and largely autonomous network, in which many of them represent some sectoral or functional constituency. Importantly, they develop an "enabling" environment for states to deal jointly and efficiently with socio-economic and other problems, by raising awareness, exchanging information and experience, conducting policy dialogue in areas of special or emerging concern, and devising norms, standards and other international instruments. The activity includes setting international and national targets and identifying areas for co-operation and direct support. They also play an integrating role in functional aspects of the main tasks. In social development, the global-governance role of multilateral institutions includes assessing such problems as future population trends, world poverty, the human dimensions of environmental issues, and management of the aftermath of man-made or natural disasters. The process is influenced by the fact that member-states have both converging and conflicting interests and different capacities and resources. The UN system, as the central component of the global multilateral system with a diverse, complex mandate, has made much progress over the decades in some areas. However, there are important, and in some cases increasing gaps between the needs of humanity and the capacities of the multilateral system.

Particularly in the context of the human dimensions of global development, the interests, values and *principles of national governance* are indispensable for global-governance structures and processes. The role of national governance in the global governance process has been emphasised in international political literature mainly in relation to the progress and sustainability of the democratisation process and its relative power and influence on the global system. Democracy cannot be treated in isolation from other social or economic processes and democratisation must be viewed in global-governance terms, as a universal international or global process, closely related to the global socio-political changes, especially the international and universal character of human rights. One of the most delicate sets of conditions for the success and sustainability of democracy concern the socio-economic problems already discussed. History has shown that sustaining democracy calls for a degree of justice, participation and equitable distribution of welfare. It cannot be sustained where the distribution of the national cake is a zero-sum game and there is large-scale exclusion. It must include the world's macro- and microprocesses: the character of inter-state relations, and the commitments of the great powers to building and sustaining a democratic world.

Some states have more influence on global processes than the UN or other international agencies in some areas, notably the United States as a hegemonic power. Most governments have no such direct influence on the main global trends and processes and contribute to collective decision-making through the multilateral framework. The influence of some countries is also greater on human-development issues, including poverty eradication, labour standards, gender equality and employment.

The future of the state system

There are two critical future issues in the context of the state system. One is related to the number of states the other is to the role of states. The *growth in the number of states* in the 20th century mainly came about through the disintegration of great empires. The current number of states is greater by far than at any other time in modern history and still increasing.

Fragmentation of political and economic units also creates new problems. The breakdown can occur without creating viable alternatives for the smaller countries, so that it leads to political and economic marginalisation. Some small states have insufficient political capacity to manage their domestic problems. Somalia has already provided an example of a state within the international system existing without a government. The increasing number of small states in the ruins of the Soviet sphere of influence may become a new source of lasting instability in Europe and Central Asia.

The growing number of states has important consequences for the sustainability of global and regional security. In terms of the global power structure, the present stage of the post-Cold War era has often been described simply as the end of bipolarity and the beginning of multi-polarity. (Some experts speak of uni-polarity, which makes describing the changing global power structure even more complex.) In reality, regional power centres are emerging and may at a later stage be interested in creating a network of client states around themselves. It is still a very open question how this process will develop. However, it is apparent that as the number of states grows, so does the diversity of the global political system, in terms of interests, values, intentions and political, military and economic potentials. Multi-polarity as a category in the evolving global power relations does not reflect sufficiently the

164

complexity of relations among the global and economic superpowers, medium-sized powers and small, even tiny states that coexist with them. It does not reflect sufficiently the fact that the increasing number of states and changing character of their relations have become a major source of uncertainty, for the 1990s and beyond.

Uni-polarity and multi-polarity may have different implications for what one might call "small state-ism" in global politics. The French statesman George Clemenceau is said to have remarked that small states are quite as bad as big ones, except that they cannot afford to be bad on so grand a scale. Indeed, the history of many small states in various parts of the world gives plentiful examples of the abuse of power. In the second half of the 20th century, when the majority of states were small, several have become sources of global risk, through domestic instability or regional belligerence.

One issue related to disintegration and fragmentation is the future of *conflicts* in the 21st century. Human history was full of factors that led to disintegration and animosity. Wars in the 20th century were especially violent and encompassed whole societies, so that it became the most militarised century in history. The heritage of militarisation, with the technological development and global spread of weapons of horrible destructive power will remain an important concern in the 21st century. Violence within and between states could reach unprecedented scale. Research on peace and security issues faces new tasks in a world where the new sources and the nature of conflicts will be more of an internal nature – civil wars of unprecedented intensity.

The other main trend, the *integrating* role of the globalisation process, also presents multiple challenges. First, it is difficult to harmonise the processes of disintegration and integration in the global system. Such traditional categories as national interests, national economic space, and full authority over the people and resources within a country's territory do not correspond any more with the earlier patterns and realities in a world economy that is more transnational than ever. A new and much heightened degree of internationalisation has brought about many new opportunities for investment, trade and migration, changing the character and mechanisms of international political and economic relations and processes. The postulates for sustaining simultaneously competitive and co-operative relations between the main global centres made capabilities for creating multi-dimensional sources of power, a key factor in shaping global political processes. Parallel to the globalisation process and often as a reaction to it, the role of regionalism is growing. Regional institutions are emerging in various parts of the globe, although none of them are as powerful as the EU. Politically and technically, it is crucially important for the future to know to what extent the processes of globalisation and regionalisation can be harmonised. What will be the role of states and their governments in this process?

The early 21st century is a critical period for states: Will they, or will they not be able to function effectively on behalf of their national interests in domestic and international arenas? The modern state system represents a concentration of power, which in theory exercises full authority over the people and resources within its territory with different degree of social control. Today, however, the traditional means of domestic social control are fastly becoming incapable of dealing effectively with crime, drug abuse, and the many other social problems that are damaging to societal norms and cohesiveness. Internationally, these states may be facing an unfamiliar "post-Westphalian" world where secular and unitary states are no longer dominant. Certainly, the role of the state is changing. Domestically, relations between governments and their civil societies are going through important transformations, and the role of non-governmental structures is growing. Internationally, the changes are even greater. The boundaries between international and domestic domains are being erased in many areas. Although great differences exist in the character and intensity of these changes vis-à-vis the state, one way or another even the strongest states are constrained, whether in real or in normative terms. In some areas – international capital and information flows, for example – states are either losing control altogether or imposing greater and often unsustainable burdens on their resources for retaining control.

States are exposed to all major social, political and economic changes and as institutions cannot and will not remain static either. There are three main cracks that may be widening. States are eroding from above by many different multinational organisations and co-operation regimes and by various social microoperators below, grouped in the broad category of the civil society. They are also eroding at the sides, through growing international interdependence and interaction among countries, which will set many new problems for institutions and governments. Governments are ever less able to manage their domestic problems without taking heed of these eroding factors.

The factors that have brought about *changes in the role of government* must be analysed in a comprehensive framework. Their consequences must be viewed empirically, not just in abstract terms.

The starting point for the analysis should be neither the Peace of Westphalia nor the Cold War era, but the 19th century. The growing role of the state in the 19th- and 20th-century industrial world derived from factors that included colonial conquests, wars and preparations for them, revolutions of various natures, and efforts to increase national competitive power. The Cold War also sustained the "strong state" in external relations in spite of the different forces of globalisation and transnationalisation. International discord and sources of conflicts did not disappear from the system after the disappearance of the political-ideological division between the two Cold-War opponents. New sources of conflicts will inevitably emerge. National security interests will remain important factors in sustaining the state system. The "developmental state" in the Third World and the role of governments in national competitiveness have been important sources in sustaining and strengthening the role of the state system.

However, a number of the factors behind the "strong state" were diminishing by the end of the 20th century. This does not mean that the state will disappear as an institution. It is evolving new functions that may become vitally important in the 21st century. As a consequence of globalisation, it will be vital to protect the country from the adverse consequences of the process, while promoting its potential benefits. The main challenge for the future is not the task of creating a "strong state". (Most states that are weak and dependent could not sustain the strong state as an instrument of their policies for a number of international or domestic reasons in any case.) The question is how to create and sustain a flexible state able to manage the new tasks. Underlying these tasks is always an assumption that governments are capable of setting compatible, realistic objectives, selecting and using efficient, effective instruments, minimising the costs of their policies and maintaining control on the political, economic and social environment and constraints in which their policies operate.

There is, of course, continuity in the role and tasks of governments. In the evolving *market system* of the 21st century, governments cannot disregard such general aims as efficient resource allocation for the provision of public goods or macroeconomic stabilisation of variables like production levels, prices, employment, exchange rates and indebtedness. They have to strive for social and environmental sustainability of national development, which includes tasks like adjusting income distribution, improving the quality of life, and providing the public with well-functioning health and education systems. The role of the state in education, research, the development of infrastructure and social protection differs from country to country. These have been recognised however everywhere necessary and important areas for public involvement.

Globalisation also creates new needs and conditions for protecting the economy and society from outside shocks.

Table 3 compares government revenues and spending as a proportion of GDP, in some major countries. The data do not suggest any decline in the relative role of government in redistributing income, even in the most globalised countries. Taxes and government spending have risen everywhere, not just in the leading states. The proportion of government spending to GDP in the industrial countries was 9 per cent in 1914 and 44 per cent in 1998.

Table 3
Government spending as a proportion of GDP, %

Country	Government spending		Tax revenues	
	1960	1998	1960	1998
United States	26.8	32.8	26.5	28.5
Japan	17.5	36.9	18.2	28.4
Germany	32.4*	46.9	31.3*	37.5
Britain	32.2	40.2	28.5	35.3
France	34.6	54.3	46.1	46.2
Sweden	31.0	60.8	27.2	53.3

Source: *The Economist*, July 31, 1999.
Note: *West Germany.

Globalisation has not reduced government spending. Both winners and losers by it face tasks and problems, internal and external, that require government action. The groups in society whose position is weakened and undermined by the changes seek protective measures, but governments have responsibility not only for protecting people from external shocks, but for helping them to seize external opportunities. Although their role has weakened in many areas, states and their governments representing specific territorial, national, ethnic, economic and social structures, interests, power positions, and weaknesses will remain the key actors.

Because the world will have to accommodate a much greater number of states than any time since the beginnings of modern history, improvement in relations will only come slowly. The increase in the number of states is becoming a source of increasing diversity in the intentions, interests, and actions of states. There will, correspondingly, be major and increasing differences between the traditions, international experiences, roles, and the political, military, and economic potentials of states in the international system. Global and economic superpowers, middle powers, and small, even tiny, states will have to coexist on the planet. The majority of states will remain the "price takers" of global politics and economics.

The main powers in the international political system of the early 21st century will be the United States, Japan, Russia, China and maybe Germany. The outcome of the integration process that may result in the "United States of Europe" is still highly uncertain, but even in the event of faster progress towards a politically united Europe, its impact on world politics will not be decisively felt in the first decades of the century. India an other large, fast-growing and populous country of the world, may also be very important power with major regional, and increasingly global role.

The future role of the state system will also depend on the effectiveness of the instruments of global and regional collective security. In a future hierarchical multipolar system, with a larger number of global and regional actors having a greater diversity of interests, the management and resolution of conflicts will require different structural forms and machinery, and new institutional safeguards. Under Cold War bipolarism, the two superpowers played a moderating role in conflicts and imposed certain constraints (to varying degrees of success) on the policies and actions of regional powers, especially in those cases when it was disadvantageous to superpower interests. In the future, this element will be absent.

While in a more peaceful world, there may be no need for discipline of a Cold-War nature. Certainly, new initiatives and more democratic mechanisms will in the future be required to substitute for those stabilising forces, which were conditioned by common strategic interests in the Cold War. These initiatives would, in part, constitute global political risk management, and would be of special significance to Europe. The danger of the increasing technological sophistication of the arsenals of smaller countries, the foment caused by policies towards different ethnic minorities, and the problem of international terrorist groups, have also become more serious risk factors requiring special global attention.

Civil society in global governance

The future role of the state system in a more democratic world will be increasingly influenced by the direct actions of the citizens through social movements. The *civil society* is becoming both within national framework and on international level an influential force in the governance process. The concept of the civil society requires clarification. Civil society actions evolve through local organisations, representing the micro level of national politics. The civil society concept is certainly not a substantiation of the concepts of the early anarchists.[87] Citizens of different countries gain special capabilities and information through education, the media and other forms of communication, and show concern for a variety of global issues with which they can identify themselves, apart from those of earlier decades. Earlier, citizens mainly in the developed countries established organisations devoted mainly

[87] Pyotr Alexeyevich Kropotkin, an ideological father of the anarchist movements, suggested in 1910 that human activities could substitute for the state. Various voluntary social groups could come to represent a network composed of an infinite variety of groups and federations – local, regional, national and international, temporary or more or less permanent. See Kropotkin (1910), p. 914.

to defined causes such as class or ethnic-group interests, religion, regional concerns, schools or military units. The only important exceptions were the peace movements. International civil society, dealing with global issues, is a growing trend, seen by most authors as the entirety of the international world of non-governmental organisations (NGOs). Some exclude movements that are fighting for independence and statehood. The NGO world in the past was also looked upon as an international forum, through which to advocate specific issues and influence policies, offering some visibility to them. Many organisations had consultative status in the different UN agencies or with ECOSOC as NGOs, allowing them to participate directly in the debates of governments. In any case, they comprised a much more diverse group than the states did. Their global nature is expressed in international strategic linkages, political strategies and convergence on a number of global issues, so that they share a global-participation ethic. Their orientation is often more global than that of governments. It is of course an interesting and important issue, what is the relationship between the movements of the civil society and the governments. The history of the past 40–50 years witnessed different types of relations. Some of the NGOs were in fact established by governments, ruling political parties, and/or served directly their policies. Relations in many cases are more co-operative than hostile. This is particularly true in a number of developing countries where governments do not allow the work of critical NGOs.

The civil society concept implies that the different groups and their activities are outside the "official" structure of government. Civil Society Organisations would be better and more relevant therefore than NGO concept developed and used by the UN system. Some scholars prefer the use of "grassroots" or the micro-sphere of international politics. James Rosenau, an American political scientist characterised the process in the following way: "the dynamics of the post-industrial era have led to the reorientation of citizens and have catapulted them to the center of the global stage. The confluence of conflicting role demand on their priorities and commitments has brought them into an arena in which the cascading process of turbulence florish. In effect, individuals have become, both as group members and as citizens, a major battleground on which states, governments, subnational groups, international organisations, regimes and transnational associations compete for their support and loyalties, thereby posing for them choices that cannot be easily ignored and that serve as both a measure of global change and a challenge to global stability"[88]. Non-governmental organisations real-

---

[88] James N. Rosenau: *Turbulence in World Politics.* (Princeton University Press, 1990), p. 213.

ly operate on every level: on the grassroots, regions, nations and on the level of the global system. They want to raise human quality, capacity and responsibility. Their advocacy role may be focussing on the conservation of traditions or on new ideas and approaches. The influence of these groups varies but may extend to local, national and global governance. Some of them are focussing on the information and education of the public, others are more action oriented. The social actions may include humanitarian assistance, lobbying or violent demonstrations. The main issues of the dialogue in the international NGO world have been human rights, gender equality, environment and development, the problems of global peace and security, poverty and social justice, freedom and identity. The globalisation process and the different social problems attributed to it, started a new wave of protests and stimulated the activities of the organisations of the civil society. Some authors are using the concept of "international" or "global civil society". Turner, an American political scientist writes: "Civil society is increasingly global not only because groups are establishing strategic linkages across national borders, but also because of the nature of issues NGOs and other social movements converge"[89].

A UN Report on global governance in 1995 suggested that nearly 29,000 international NGOs existed. Their number increased since then. The number of national NGOs have grown even faster. There are more than 2 million in America alone. In Russia where only a few existed before the collapse of the regime there are at least 65,000.[90]

At the beginning of the 21st century there are four main types of NGOs active in international life. The oldest are the traditional movements often with religious roots or advocates of international co-operation with strong ethical philosophies. They are involved in emergency relief and aid transfers. The second type could be characterised as social groups or political alliances lobbying for the more effective management or solution of some important global problems like environment, human rights or gender equality. The third group is questioning the established order in one or an other area often with violent actions. They may have different political, ideological and religious orientation. These groups became particularly active in the anti-globalisation movements of the late 1990s, early 2000s. There is also a fourth group, which is related to the unresolved ethnic minority issues.

Are churches parts of the civil society or not? There is no easy answer to this simple question. Church members, priests and church workers are usu-

[89] Turner, Scott: Global Civil Society, Anarchy and Governance: Assessing an Emerging Paradigm. *Journal of Peace Research.* London 1998. vol. 35 no. 1, p. 32.
[90] *The Economist,* January 29, 2000.

ally active in different civil society organisations. The role of churches is generally recognised as advocates of tradition, sources of cultural and ethical values often shared with states. They support and sustain different movements and organisations. They may be parts of the civil society and of the "official" structures. The issue concerning their role in the society in global dimension has been raised particularly in the context of two churches. Both are important in influencing the civil society and the governance process: the Catholic Church and Islam. The number of their followers has been more or less the same around the end of the 20th century: about 1 billion of each. The Catholic proportion of the population has stayed basically the same in all continents of the world except in Africa, the only major source of conversion. The Catholic Church is probably the most powerful global institution of cultural transmission. It is ideologically and institutionally transcendent of states. The church with its 2000-year-old hierarchies and tradition is facing major challenges in the 21st century. There are two extremes: the fundamentalists, heavily loaded with the past and the modernisers. The secularisation and the democratisation of the societies, the surge of evangelical Protestant groups and the spread of Islam had major influence on the policies, role and influence of the Vatican itself and the Catholic groups. Politically the Catholic church inspires extremely diverse social thinking and actions: humanitarian, anti-abortion, anti-death penalty. Some of the NGOs with Catholic ethical orientation are anti-capitalists, anti-globalisationists. Other groups have strong ties with the conservative Christian political parties.

The rapidly increasing number of the followers made Islam a growing force also in the civil society. There are many Islam-oriented NGOs in the world, in different areas of social actions. Some scholars consider Islam as the concluding chapter of the religious history of the world. Islam as a force in the civil society has many peculiarities. Most of the Islam NGOs are communal movements. The movements characterised as Islamists are radical and often violent groups. At the beginning of the 21st century, Islam is probably the most influential ideology in resisting Western cultural values. The Qur'aranic concept of umma wahida, or a single community of Muslims also transcends state frontiers. It considers all other divisions, including ethnic, racial or national as secondary. Statehood in Islam has been recognised more recently and the Organisation of Islamic Conference as an international instrument is also a more recent creation. The value system of Islam in shaping social actions is however more diverse than that of the Catholic church. The abilities to act cohesively is limited by its sectarian and ethnic diversity. In the Arab world, Islamic civilisation is advocating conservative, patrimonial, often non-democratic values, with a lower level of tolerance. In South-East Asia, where the cultural hegemony of Islam is weaker it is accomodating cultural pluralism. Islamic radicalism in its most extreme and violent forms is however not confined to the Mediterranean region.

The influence of the global spread of *democratisation brought new opportunities and problems for the churches and religious movements. It has strengthened secularism with its* diversity of governance, opening up opportunities for hundreds of millions to govern their lives, has brought political struggles within countries, along ethnic, tribal or socio-economic dividing lines. These will also surface increasingly around such issues as poverty, exclusion and income distribution.

Ethnic movements occupy a special place in the civil society. They are often fighting for statehood and may be the nucleus of future government. Ethnic problems in the new century are particularly important and dangerous sources of potential conflicts. From among the 189 members of the UN, more than 120 states are ethnically heterogeneous.[91]

There are different, often unmet demands put forward by ethnic minorities, like official acknowledgement of their distinctiveness, special cultural and political arrangements, representation in decision-making, territorial autonomy, etc., which are articulated more freely in democratic societies. The number of those, which consider armed struggle as the best instrument for strengthening identity and cohesion has been growing. From among the over 5000 ethnic minorities in the world, at the beginning of the 21st century 80 ethnic communities have been involved in major conflicts. An other 240 ethnic communities have been involved in low-intensity conflicts for national self-determination. In the post-Cold War era these conflicts became the main sources of political instability.

The future role of the civil society both in national and global level depends in many ways on the process of democratisation. The global spread of democracy, an important component of global transformations itself, opened new opportunities for the different groups in civil society to advocate their interests and values in an organised way. This process created also new challenges for governance and opened a new dialogue on democracy and on its future.

The collapse of dictatorial regimes, the systemic changes in Central and Eastern Europe and the spread of the democratic regimes in the developing world introduced such issues into the debate as the conditions, the character and sustainability of democratic regimes. Is it fundamentally a technical matter of how political power is obtained, sustained, distributed and changed? Can a system function without strong social groups committed to democra-

[91] Based on the UN University research programmes on „Problems and Prospects of Multi-ethnic States."

cy? Should certain political ideologies, which formally embrace certain institutions of democracy but using them for their goals, like neo-nazism or authoritarian regimes, qualified by various attributes such as "guided", "limited" or "protected by law and order" be tolerated by the international community? What type of democracy can be seen as appropriate in the era of globalisation, when many economic and political issues lie beyond the province of states? Is the concept of democracy of the 19th century rooted in classical Greek theory, known as direct democracy or rule of the people, satisfactory and appropriate for the early 21st century? Does the liberal concept of democracy, which allows far greater tolerance of social inequality than what is considered as morally acceptable today, offer a feasible alternative? Is populist democracy, which is hostile to globalisation a feasible model? Is the model of social democracy, with its liberal concept advocating the principle of equality in social life, including the possession of wealth a realistic alternative in the era of large corporations? There is no easy answer to these questions. In practical terms democracy in the West and the new democracies in the developing world and in the former socialist countries have many specific features, problems and limitations. However, there are some important common features and postulates as well. We examine the process of democratisation and the evolving models of the former socialist countries, which embarked on a process of democratic transformation a decade ago in order to find practical answers to some of the questions raised in the new debates on democracy.

9. THE "DEMOCRATIC PROCESS AND THE MARKET". EASTERN EUROPE AFTER A DECADE OF TRANSFORMATION: A CASE STUDY

Some political thinkers see the collapse of the communist regimes in Central and Eastern Europe as a global victory not only for constitutional democracy, particularly its liberal version, but also of capitalism over socialism. Socialism, or at least the variant practised in the former Soviet Union and Central and Eastern Europe, has indeed lost its ability to mobilise masses against the capitalist market system. Capitalism as such is however not a closed or homogeneous ideological system. It provides socio-economic foundations for a broad spectrum of ideologies, from libertarians and liberals to right-wing populists. Some of these ideologies have been unresponsive to basic global problems, while others recognised them at an early stage. Capitalism has also accommodated fanatical ideologies such as extreme nationalism and fascism, which lamentably are gaining ground again in various parts of the world. Fuelled by growing socio-economic problems and political impasses, these creeds preaching divisive doctrines such as racism, ethnic hatred and religious bigotry cannot be expected to further global solutions to the problems of poverty, environmental degradation or crime.

The changes in the former socialist countries are described either as a "transition" or a "transformation" from a centralised, totalitarian, non-market system to a modern, democratic, market-economic system. The transition concept is a narrower one, while transformation implies something more comprehensive that embraces political, economic, social, psychological, institutional, national and international changes. Many questions have been raised over the past decade. Fundamental to many of them is the historical perspective. Is political, economic, social and cultural transformation a realistic goal? Can there be a transition to an economy of a Western European standard, to a "social" market economy or some other type of modern market system? Will the process be only a transition from one form of persistent state of semi-development or under-development to another? More generally, to what extent can democracy be stabilised and sustained in the environment of semi-developed countries that have lived under totalitarian regimes for several decades? Are there sufficient guarantees for the sustainability of the democratic process? In methodological terms, does a decade of change

175

suffice to draw firm, meaningful conclusions about problems, nature and sustainability of democracy in the region? Countries may already have the formal, institutional framework of a pluralist system, but the transformation process is far from over. The outcome will also differ from country to country.

Despite these qualifications, some conclusions can be reached, even at this relatively early stage in the process, about its problems, benefits and drawbacks and the ways to manage its conflicts. Some of the dilemmas and policies may also be of interest and relevance to other countries and regions.

The 27 *transition countries*[92] are extremely diverse in size, development level, historical background, and social and political structure. The Russian Federation is still the most important power in the region, occupying 76 per cent of the territory of the former Soviet Union, with over half of its population (80 per cent Russians) and about half its natural endowments. Russia inherited about half the economic capacity and about 80 per cent of the R & D and military potential. It is a major Eurasian power of geo-strategic importance, encompassing 67 regions and 21 national republics.

There are also big differences in the origins of countries. Some were born or reborn in new forms after the First World War, on the ruins of the great Austro-Hungarian, Russian and Ottoman empires. Others gained independence after the disintegration of the Soviet Union, Czechoslovakia and Yugoslavia. After World War I, Central and Eastern Europe became a backward semi-periphery of Western Europe and a buffer against Soviet Russia. After World War II, the Soviet sphere was extended to the area, which became a buffer *for* the Soviet Union. I therefore define the broader zone as an ethnically and economically heterogeneous, geo-strategic region between Western Europe and the Pacific Ocean. It is a turbulent, strategically important zone divided by ethnic and religious diversity,[93] cultural traditions,

---

[92] Albania, Armenia, Azerbaijan, Belarus, Bosnia-Herzegovina, Bulgaria, Croatia, Czech Republic, Estonia, FR Yugoslavia, Macedonia, Georgia, Hungary, Kazakhstan, Kyrgyzstan, Latvia, Lithuania, Moldova, Poland, Romania, Russian Federation, Slovakia, Slovenia, Tajikistan, Turkmenistan, Ukraine and Uzbekistan.

[93] Cohabiting in the region, often in the same country, are Poles, Slovaks, Czechs, Moravians, Hungarians, Germans, Lithuanians, Ruthenians, Romanians, Bunevać, Sokac, Serbs, Croats, Slovenes, Bosnians, Albanians, Bulgars, Turks, Russians, Ukrainians, Gypsies etc. The cultural divide in runs between the Orthodox faith and the Western Christian denominations (Roman Catholic, Reformed, Lutheran and Unitarian). Poland, for instance, has a strong Roman Catholic identity. Other countries in the region, such as Bosnia and Bulgaria, contain Moslem minorities. Hungary is heterogeneous in its religious affiliations. There is a division between Greek Catholics and Orthodox believers running down Ukraine. A challenge is posed by the region's unresolved ethnic conflicts, which are more divisive than those elsewhere in Europe are. Majority-minority conflicts are constantly erupting, causing political unrest and carrying the potential of igniting a social explosion.

political interests and economic potentials. It is no accident that the two world wars started in the region, which also saw in the 1990s the longest post-war civil conflicts in Europe. The rivalry between great powers for control, furthered by policies of divide and rule, fuelled violent nationalism and chauvinism in some countries, bringing serious conflicts and tragedies.

The character of the systemic transformations

History has witnessed a number of systemic transitions and transformations. Some have resulted from long, organic processes of development and reform. Others have arisen out of revolutions, wars or external occupation that caused the old regime to collapse. However, seldom in human history has the challenge for the countries concerned and for the international community been so great as it was in the former socialist countries of Europe. This has been due to complex interactions between past and present, and between political, economic and social processes, cultural values, national and international factors and institutions. Another set of challenges related to the changes derives from the special role played by the region, especially the Soviet Union, in the global political, ideological and military confrontations of the 20th century.

The historical experiences of the countries in the region also show that the breakdown or serious limitation of former systems necessitates a *fundamental* transformation. Strangely, the 20th century repeated the historical pattern of several previous centuries, in a form magnified by political and ideological factors, by dividing the two areas of Europe with an Iron Curtain. The Western European or Euro-Atlantic region has undergone, in the last half-century, one of the biggest spurts of development in its history. This has yielded a modern economy with a welfare state and imbedded pluralist democracy and a constitutional system. In the global political arena, it has projected an image of developed countries with a high standard of living, democratic systems, individual freedoms and social welfare. Regional co-operation became an important instrument for the solution of many problems which had been the sources of traditional animosity between Germany and France.

Meanwhile the Soviet Union and Soviet-dominated Central and Eastern Europe experienced a *command economy* and dictatorial rule. This state of affairs initiated a modernisation process, which resulted in important structural changes in some fields. However, the region ultimately failed to achieve radical modernisation or escape from its peripheral position and its relative backwardness. On the other hand, the socialist countries had different characters. These go some way to explain why their etatist-socialist regimes collapsed in different ways, producing the present spectrum of post-communist regimes.[94] These differed in the way their markets developed and in the character of their political regimes. The diversity extended to the degree of progress they made in establishing a civil society and deepening and stabilising democracy.[95]

[94] There were different sources of strength and of fragility and weakness in the various political systems and political structures. The former etatist-socialist regimes of Central and Eastern Europe legitimised their political systems largely by promising economic advances and continual improvements in living standards. It was becoming clear by the 1970s that they could not keep their promises or even sustain the levels achieved. Stagnation and decline in living standards and intensifying domestic political conflicts resulted from the strains of the arms race, external economic difficulties, particularly the oil-price explosion, and deteriorating economic performance. Another factor was change in the Soviet Union. There had been popular uprisings in East Germany in 1953 and Hungary in 1956. The Prague Spring of 1968 was also an effort to introduce systemic changes. These attempts had been crushed by Soviet forces, at times when the domestic political structure of the Soviet Union was still relatively stable. By the end of the 1980s, a major domestic crisis had developed in the Soviet Union, which was neither willing nor able to use its earlier methods of crushing mass movements in the satellite countries. There have been substantial differences in the character of the systemic changes and their consequences. East Germany underwent the unification process. In Hungary, the replacement of the Kádár regime with a more liberal, reform-communist approach ensured a peaceful transition. In Poland, the long struggle of Solidarity culminated in the collapse of the Jaruzelski regime. Czechoslovakia underwent a "velvet revolution" of mass, peaceful protests. In Romania, a violent revolution erupted against the Ceauşescu regime. Bulgaria had a relatively peaceful transition. In Yugoslavia, the process of disintegration, beginning with the oil crisis of the 1970s, brought decades of political and economic crisis, leading to civil war and the re-emergence of deep-rooted ethnic conflicts. Disintegration and civil war have also resulted from political errors and mismanagement. In the Soviet Union, the disintegration brought major changes and various political structures.

[95] The main cause of the collapse was the historical failure of the Soviet Union and the Central and Eastern European countries to build up efficient and competitive economies. This cannot be understood in isolation from the political factors and forces: a totalitarian bureaucratic state, a one-party system, and politicisation and bureaucratisation of the economic processes. The "centrally planned" economies achieved important goals at a relatively early stage of development, later described by Soviet economists as the era of extensive growth, since it was based not on raising productivity and efficiency, but on greater factor inputs. Even then, the gains were costly. The economic issues became acute at a stage when the sources of growth should have been rapid technological change, improving productivity and efficiency, and fast, efficient structural adjustments. The need for reform was recognised at various stages in the Soviet Union and other socialist countries. While all countries introduced some measures to change the functioning of the system, they left the foundations unchanged. In the Soviet Union, reforms were "aborted" either by a bureaucracy jealous of its privileges or by a partial and irrational nature that brought economic chaos, stagnation and decline. Central and Eastern Europe had specific problems. The political landslide after World War II imposed the Soviet model regardless of historical attributes or national development levels. The political changes also iso-

The issues raised in academic discourse in the context of transformation have necessarily been broader and deeper than those in the political struggles and propaganda war. There was concentration on the democratisation process and the advantages of the market economy. An important dimension of the dialogue on democracy relates to the failure of communism as an ideology and a political movement to fulfill its promises to create a world "free from need and war". Some political thinkers saw the collapse in Central and Eastern Europe as a global victory for liberal democracy.

The ideas and preferences of different schools of thoughts also emerged in the *international dialogue* on the transition.[96] Many Western scholars tended initially to regard the transformation as a kind of ideological training ground for testing their theories – radical, orthodox, gradualist and evolutionist models alike. Others viewed the post-communist economies as a late and delayed imitation of their own social and economic conditions. In the countries themselves, two alternatives arose, mainly in academic debate, but not without influence on the political process: (1) transformation to the Euro-

---

lated countries from traditional Western trading partners and suppliers of modern technology, tying them to a less developed Soviet economy that could not provide the new technologies and managerial expertise needed for modernisation. Countries like Czechoslovakia, East Germany and Hungary were locked into their existing development level, their technological capabilities being downgraded in relative terms in an era of rapid global technological changes elsewhere. The Central and Eastern European countries became dependent on Soviet supplies of raw materials and energy and Soviet markets for their goods. This helped full employment and offered some supply and sale security, but it also furthered relatively obsolete, globally uncompetitive economic structures. Some satellites also experimented with political and economic reforms after the death of Stalin. The most important, far-reaching reforms were made in Hungary, as an indirect outcome of the 1956 Revolution, but even these proved insufficient.

[96] An interesting contribution to the debates on the character of the systemic changes in the former socialist countries was made by the well-known sociologist S. N. Eisenstadt. Analysing the character of the "velvet revolutions" in Central and Eastern Europe, he stated, "These revolutions were not oriented against 'traditional', pre-modern, or even modernising regimes. They were not rebellious protests against traditional authoritarian regimes, against a divine right of kings, made in the name of modernity and enlightenment. Rather, they constituted a rebellion and protest against what was increasingly perceived by large sectors of the Eastern European societies as a blockage or distortion of modernity, effected by totalitarian regimes." The Hungarian scholar József Bognár, on the other hand, saw in the changes in Central and Eastern Europe "a *conservative-liberal revolution*". "It constitutes a revolution because ownership, the economic 'sub-system', power relations and the social structure all undergo deep, rapid and radical changes. The revolution is conservative because it replaces the state-socialist system with a restored national-*cum*-religious value system, because it strives to establish the predominance of a class of property owners (the bourgeoisie), which already exists or needs to be formed, and because it joins conservative schools of thought on current international developments."

Atlantic system, and (2) a "third road" that evades the problems of world capitalism, while leaving the region in the global market system. In reality, there was no real choice. The domestic and international environment left insufficient leeway for countries to choose between alternatives.

There was an interesting convergence in the academic discussions. Most participants disregarded the economic, social and political realities of the world and some of them those of the region. Many did not pay enough attention to the changes over time in the socialist regimes, with some countries departing a long way from the Stalinist model. One type that emerged was a "post-Stalinist" or "post-totalitarian" regime that foreswore terror and direct dictatorial rule, but continued to suppress political opposition. The other type became more liberal and less oppressive, and tolerated some forms of opposition within one-party rule (Kádárism in Hungary, the reforms of Gorbachev in the Soviet Union, and the liberalisation in Poland). A third type sustained or even strengthened dictatorial rule and the totalitarian character of the regime, with a different degree of oppression, but without the traits of Stalinist terror (the Ceauşescu regime in Romania, and the East German and post-Dubček Czechoslovak regime.) A variety of movements fought for liberalisation and democracy, even within the ruling elites. Also disregarded by pundits was the diversity of the capitalist system, which was to serve as a model. The one projected for the transition was a liberal, free-market system.[97]

It was anticipated by many experts, politicians and members of the public in the early 1990s that reintegration into global markets and the transformation process would open historic opportunities for the former socialist countries to accelerate their economic modernisation, with positive welfare effects. It was generally believed that the richer world, along with the institutions and processes of forms of global co-operation from which they had been excluded or in which they had been marginalised, would help the transition countries to fulfill those expectations. It is not easy to gauge what actually happened. The new problems and sources of risk and instability brought about by the transformation have to be weighed against positive aspects of the changes. Such judgements are impeded by the qualitative and quantitative aspects of the process and the differences between countries.

[97] This was basically the policy of the Bretton Woods institutions in harmony with the "Washington Consensus" of the early 1980s. Most of these countries were not prepared for

Achievements and problems

The successes or failures of the transformation process are complicated to evaluate. Comparisons of countries have shown that past "success stories" in the international system depended on a number of internal and external factors, including long-term policies and short-term components, including luck and sound political and economic governance. There have been also many specific factors involved in the failures: a politically divided population, mismanagement, weak institutions, adverse external conditions, etc.

The transformation process has proved *slower and more difficult* than expected by the observers who emphasised the impact of political factors, rather than cultural traditions, past inertia and new difficulties. To establish the causes and consequences of the positive and negative outcomes and experiences would require a more detailed analysis of the interaction between the domestic and external factors of the transformation than this chapter can provide. The transition countries had to learn by their own experience that it was deceptive to expect sudden, simultaneous, favourable changes in all areas. The different processes of systemic transformation moved at different speeds. The fastest was political change. Somewhat slower went the work of building political institutions, and slower still, the building of market institutions. Despite the difficulties caused by the speed of elaboration, the lack of expertise and experience, and the compromises made to various pressure groups, the evolving legal system today approximates closely to the accepted international standards in the main areas of social and economic activity. Another factor to remember when evaluating the transformation process is that democracy has been open to various practical interpretations during the long history of human efforts to achieve it. It has been seen as an ideal political system unattainable in full, a set of political institutions for sustaining or changing the political establishment by regular elections, a system that only functions when based on a broad middle class and a developed civil society, and so on. Democracy, as an ideal and in practice, has changed over the more than 2000 years since its "invention". By the 20th century, there were important conditions to be met for the democratic process to succeed, in the sense of being able to reproduce itself, without creating situations that require or elicit non-democratic methods of governance. These include socio-economic and institutional factors and others related to the nature of the political elite. Those elected to the legislature or local or national office need to be of relatively high quality and probity, and also responsive and accountable. Democratic systems, particularly at an early stage, do not produce automatically more experienced and responsive politicians than other systems. The principles of responsiveness and accountability must be rendered operational by sustainable institutions, democratically elected parliaments, political parties, a free press, and abundant civil organisations.

Another important issue in the former socialist countries has been how to manage the tasks of the transformation process, especially the conflicts that can emerge from interactions between the democratic process and market building. Relations between market forces and the development of democracy have never been simple or straightforward. Many politicians, scholars and others have therefore assumed that the postulates of a sustainable democratic political system and a theoretically efficient "undistorted" market are conflicting, contradictory categories. The American scholar Lester C. Thurow, in his best-selling book *The Future of Capitalism*, writes, "Democracy and capitalism have very different beliefs about the proper distribution of power. One believes in a completely equal distribution of power, 'one man one vote,' while the other believes that it is the duty of the economically fit, to drive the unfit out of business and into economic extinction" (Thurow, 1996, p. 242). He adds that over the past couple of centuries, two factors have allowed these two power systems to coexist as democratic capitalism. First, it has always been possible to convert economic power into political power, or political power into economic power. Secondly, government has been actively used to alter market outcomes and generate a fairer distribution of income than the market alone would produce. Thurow also raises doubts about the sustainability of this balancing act in an era when market forces are producing much greater inequalities. The pre-Second World War patterns in Central and Eastern Europe also demonstrated that market economies could coexist with various forms of political system, dictatorial or democratic. Historical evidence also showed that market economies preceded democratic changes in governance. The progress of democracy was in most cases a long historical process. Democratic rights were progressively expanded, often after bitter social and political conflicts. However, there are no historical cases of liberal, democratic systems being established before the emergence of a market economy that has defined, transparent property rights, a fairly wide dispersion of economic power, free entry and exit, and a non-discriminatory system of competition. Democracy is not necessarily a prerequisite of the market system, nor is it indispensable to economic development. Empirical evidence suggests that authoritarian governments were often less vulnerable against powerful interest groups and popular pressures to implement major socio-economic policies.[98] Thus, they were more decisive in carrying out painful

[98] A prominent Western political scientist, Richard Lowenthal, suggested at an early stage in the debate in 1953, that "every measure of freedom is paid for with slowing down economic development" (Lowenthal, 1986, pp. 241–245).

structural reforms. Democratic methods proved particularly disadvantageous in troubled times. Non-democratic regimes were often able to create higher savings through enforced public savings and other measures. The concept of a "development dictatorship" has often been applied to the East Asian countries. Of course, a thorough cost-benefit analysis of non-democratic regimes would question not only the allocative efficiency of some totalitarian regimes, but also the preferences given to various groups in the ruling elite or the army. The political and social costs of non-democratic regimes were often extremely high, compared with their favourable influence on some economic indicators.

Here are a few major features of the regimes in the new market-economic democracies in the region:
- There is ambiguity about rejecting the collectivist past. Many people insist that the state should provide job security, price stability, full social services, free health and education, and pensions. This is not just due to the socialist past. The region's strong etatist traditions have even been reinforced by the role of the state in the transformation process.
- There are strong egalitarian and populist pressures in society, rooted in the experiences of the past few decades. These coincide with rapid divergence of incomes and economic polarisation. The presence of the two is strongly apparent in political life.
- The chosen concept of democracy lays overwhelming emphasis on majority rule. This is due to the traditional weakness of civil society, and to some extent, to ethnic diversity. The result is a low level of tolerance, opposition to the rights of various minorities, distortions and constraints in the work of democratic institutions, and frequent instances of exclusion.
- There are tendencies towards paternalism and the use of political power to build client relations for private gain. These important constraints distort the democratic process in several countries, notably, but not exclusively in Soviet successor states. This is not confined to former socialist countries, of course, the absence of strong countervailing forces may cause serious problems in the future.

Having summarised some of the main issues important to the democratic process, it is necessary to emphasise that the trends discussed in this section may vary in importance from country to country. There are also differences in the experiences of countries in dealing with the new problems. The issues selected, however, are sufficiently general and characteristic to illustrate the transformation process and democratic development, with their achievements and difficulties.

Political freedom and the rule of law

Totalitarian, one-party regimes place important limitations on individual freedom. Not unsurprisingly, the collapse of the totalitarian state was followed in several Central and Eastern European countries by *almost unrestricted freedom*, as one of the initial steps in the democratisation process. In an inevitable reaction to the past, individual freedom was seen as fundamental to building a civil society, ensuring the emergence and development of various social and political groups, and providing chances for these to articulate their interests and values. Freedom in a literal sense prevails in almost every European post-socialist country except some of the ones that emerged through the disintegration of a multi-ethnic state. Censorship has vanished and anyone with the means to do so may publish a newspaper, a leaflet or a book. There is almost unlimited freedom of association and numerous active political parties and trade unions. This process has occurred much faster than it did in the Western countries and there have been almost no moral, ethical or institutional constraints on it. The result has often been anarchic conditions. Among the major economic drawbacks have been the rapid development and spread of the black economy, the absence of tax-payment discipline and neglect of consumer interests. Looser government controls have paved the way for crime on a scale unprecedented in the history of capitalism. The crime increase corresponds with a global process, of course, but in the former socialist countries, it is compounded by impoverishment and mounting income inequalities. Crime is not just one of the social costs of the transition process, but the opening of countries and loosening of government controls created particularly favourable conditions for domestic and international organised crime, drug trafficking, prostitution and money laundering, for which states were unprepared. Other problems, particularly in the Russian Federation, Ukraine and most of the former Soviet republics include the absence of a requisite legal framework, especially in property law and legal enforcement of contracts. This provides fertile ground for organised crime. In Russia, for instance, it has brought a variety of capitalism that is one of the greediest, most lawless systems ever seen in any country. However, "gangster economics" or "klepto-capitalism" of this kind is not confined to Russia.[99]

[99] Democratisation of political systems in the post-Soviet region has been impeded by the totalitarian past more than in the Central and Eastern European countries. The collapse of the Soviet Union brought down with it the multi-tiered political system. Independence for the former Soviet republics removed one political tier – the imperial centre – and caused major domestic changes as well. The demise of the party-state system "nationalised" and in many ways simplified the structure of political power and administration. Although formal institutions of democracy were founded, an essentially authoritarian system remained: a multi-party system,

The *rule of law* has been seen as another postulate of political transformation in societies where the ruling party was above the law and arbitrary decisions and government decrees provided the bulk of the institutional framework. The law in a democratic society is an important instrument for social control within a jurisdiction. In the totalitarian one-party state, the ruling party was above the law, which gave it and its executive arm in the structure almost unlimited power. Democratic states have to rest on the rule of law, rather than the rule of police or dictators, to protect personal security and rights, safeguard personal freedom from arbitrary intervention, and regulate the ways the democratic system functions.

New constitutional guarantees were needed to establish the rule of law. One of the main new elements in the *constitutions* enacted (or in Hungary's case, radically amended) is recognition and respect for private ownership as the fundamental form of property holding. This recognition, which extends to the property rights of foreigners, is basic to the development of a capitalist market system. An important and controversial issue in the debates on limiting ownership has related to foreign ownership, especially of land. The law that developed out of the new constitutions has frequently been ill designed and formulated. Thousands of rules had to be replaced or amended. Even in countries that made rapid progress with modernising the law – Poland, Hungary and the Czech Republic – there have been major legislative shortcomings. Progress with the legal system has also been complicated by the desire of these countries to join the European Union. Several problems have remained in this field, with many grey areas in a number of countries. In Russia, Ukraine and other former Soviet republics, there is an "enforcement gap" and the degree of judicial independence is slight. The constitutions of the former socialist countries call for respect for human rights, but there are problems here. The economic, social and cultural rights considered of prime importance under the communists are less strongly established and protected. The constitutional and legislative emphasis is on political and civil

national presidential and parliamentary elections, and greater freedom of expression. Executive power in the Central Asian states, Kazakhstan, Belarus and Moldova is held by groups drawn from the upper and middle layers of the Soviet *nomenklatura*. Most CIS countries are presidential republics. Some presidents have gained the post for life or for a long term through a referendum, along with extensive powers, especially in Turkmenistan, Uzbekistan, Azerbaijan and Kazakhstan. Often the presidency went to a former first secretary of the republic's communist party. Old state institutions have remained, including the militia and state security police, in a more bureaucratic and corrupt state than ever before. A weak, rudimentary legislature is subordinate to or manipulated by the executive. The media are also controlled by the executive or by an industrial and financial oligarchy. These arrangements help to maintain law and order and regulate the course of market reforms, but they also obstruct the emergence of new policies and a market mentality.

rights. In terms of practical policy, the public is unwilling to accept the loss of full employment, reduced social security or free health and education as a trade-off for their new political and civil rights. They want both types of rights, which has proved impossible in most cases.

Institutions have been established in many countries to protect the democratic system, such as constitutional courts, ombudsmen and a state audit system. However, the rule of law is far from being fully stabilised in most cases and there are major concerns about independence of the judiciary. General standards of legal conduct and procedure are relatively low, in the bureaucracy and in society at large. There often remains a medieval bias towards retribution (at the expense of deterrence and reform) in the penal system. The institutions of democracy in most former socialist countries contain ambiguities due to vague legal definitions. Electoral systems tend to be intricate, with a tendency to oscillate between proportional representation and a majority, constituency system. The latter is supported in the seemingly misplaced hope that it will combat political fragmentation and invite a more stable two- or three-party system. Proportional representation (usually with qualifying thresholds to eliminate dwarf parties) is backed as a way to stimulate the development and consolidation of political parties. Several countries have opted for an eclectic mix of the two approaches, but the criticism, debate and tinkering continue. In general, there is a failure to grasp the lesson from Western Europe: no electoral system works well until modern political parties with solid constituencies develop.

Discussion of the rule of law is complicated by the fact that some of the social diseases in Eastern Europe are ascribed to the latitude granted by the transition process: dishonesty, vandalism, delinquency, increased drug abuse, pornography, corruption, crime and violence. There are mounting popular calls for a stronger approach to law and order, with Draconian penalties designed to act as a deterrent.

Democratic institutions and society

Since democracy, by definition, is ruled by the people, any theories or practical measures concerning democracy have to comprehend and take account of the society concerned and the changes within it. The transition process produced winners and losers. The socio-economic difficulties of the losers by the transformation process in the new democracies became major sources of problems. The shock therapies proposed and the recipes of international financial institutions largely ignored the idea that losers by the changes should be compensated somehow, or at least have their losses ameliorated in some way (Kozul-Wright and Rayment, 1995, p. 15).

In most developed countries, the progress of democracy was a lengthy process, influenced by social and economic interests and conflicts, political ideologies, ethnic problems, and external and internal factors and forces specific to each country. Democratic rights expanded progressively, often after bitter social and political conflicts. In practice, the spread of democracy followed in most cases an increase in general welfare, containment of social conflict through reform, and growing social mobility. The contradiction between declared or constitutionally guaranteed equity and substantial inequalities between rich and poor in the distribution and redistribution of the national cake remained unmanageable while the cake remained small. So an important question often asked about poorer countries is what type of democracy they can develop and sustain. The capitalist system in very poor countries has not been able to sustain democracy without major setbacks. Capitalism and democracy in the second half of the 20th century have coexisted well in places where there are no major social tensions or conflicts and significant social reforms have been made. Events in several European countries in the 20th century have shown that a democratic system can be undermined by intolerable economic problems and inequalities in society.

The experiences of the transition countries also show that economic stagnation, decline and deprivation make poor foundations for an experiment in introducing democracy and marketisation. If the public's first experiences of democracy are inflation, unemployment and increasing inequalities, accompanied by declining living standards, the result will be fear, alienation and distrust. The outgoing etatist regimes spent 40 years promising "jam tomorrow": the ostensible rewards of communism in return for sacrificing some of their present welfare. Many people saw a parallel with this in the vague promises made by the new regimes advocating market reforms and democracy. In some cases, the majority took the view that the evolving regimes were "redistributive coalitions", serving the interests of a new elite.

There is another important factor involved. The main support behind the Western concepts of democracy is a pluralistic society that displays and articulates its heterogeneity of interests. The social structures of Central and Eastern European countries today differ greatly from those of the pre-war period and the early Cold War. They are no longer "traditional" peasant societies amenable to authoritarian rule. They contain wide professional strata, a broad industrial working class and other social groups, including a small, but growing entrepreneurial middle class. Most countries in Central and Eastern Europe are increasingly divided internally, along various lines. History has shown that there has to be a degree of justice, participation and equitable distribution of wealth and welfare to sustain democracy. Democracy cannot be sustained where distribution of the national cake is a zero-sum game and there is large-scale exclusion. It cannot be treated in isolation from other social or economic processes. Unequal distribution of the inevitable human costs of the transformation, with increasing inequalities in the distribution of incomes and wealth, has made many people disappointed. Another important factor in the region has been division based on ethnic and religious differences. While democracy as a goal stands higher in the values of the population, after the decades of the dictatorial regimes, it is not necessarily enough for avoiding political apathy and extremism. The progress toward a civil society and the whole democratisation process is unequal, and in certain countries rather fragile. The conflicts of interests appear in the form of differing or contrasting political ideas, goals and policies represented by parties or other organised groups. Tolerance of organised opposition by those in power is still not strong enough in certain countries. The mechanisms of consensus building and conflict management are often absent or weak.

To begin with, there is the weakness of the political parties. After the fall of the one-party dictatorship, a host of political parties sprang up in each of the countries in the region.[100] Certain patterns can be discerned. Many united political movements that embraced the anti-communist opposition or won the first free elections rapidly split into numerous factions and found their influence waning. The most striking examples are the Hungarian Democratic Forum and the Solidarity in Poland. Most parties are effectively electoral parties for parliamentary groups. Only a few have substantial grassroots organisations. After the first free elections, turnout tended to converge on the Western European patterns (around 50 per cent) and many parties collected only a fractional percentage of the vote. The former socialist countries still lack modern, integrating parties guided by a vision of a modern society and advocating stable values, but their emergence is impeded by the absence

---

[100] Large numbers of political parties were formed in all the CEE countries. One type consists of survivals or revived parties originating from before the communist period, such as Christian democrats or various agrarian and social democratic parties. Some represent narrow, even anachronistic interests and derive their ideas mainly from experiences before the Second World War. The other survivors are successor parties to the once-ruling communist party, which in some countries split into two parties. The reformers of the old communist party come to resemble modern social democratic parties in Western Europe, while the more conventional, traditional groups remain Marxist. The third type of party grew out from groups that actively opposed the communists: Solidarity in Poland, the Free Democrats (SZDSZ) in Hungary, and several in other countries. The fourth type includes some small, peculiar and even unique political groups, such as the Liberal Democrats in Russia and various monarchist groups. Some of the new parties are "non-political" in character, such as the Greens, the Beer-lovers Party in Poland, or the Independent Erotic Initiative in the Czech Republic. Apart from the traditional Marxists and the right-wing populists, most parties accept and advocate a modern market system, if with some political or ideological qualifications. The etatist traditions in the region have left a strong mark on their ideologies, especially where a party champions a specific group, such as farmers, who were heavily subsidised under the communist regime.

of large social groups with such homogeneous interests and values. The problems are reflected in the electoral alliances put together in some countries, which often have an ethnic or religious, rather than a political basis.

The new system of governance

Two important conditions of good governance concern institutional patterns. One relates to the scope of governance by democratically elected institutions. This should be relatively limited, so that it can be handled by the mechanisms of democracy, whereas the totalitarian decision-making of many non-democratic governing structures makes the use of non-democratic instruments essential. The other is the need for a well-trained, respected, professional and competent administrative bureaucracy. This must be relatively constant, to offset the non-specialist politicians.

Governments in all the countries in the region possess democratic credentials, although the extent of their legitimacy varies and may be debated, and they have all been democratically elected. Formally, democratic institutions have advanced on a wide front in the region. The transfer of power has been based formally on free elections that withdrew legitimacy from those who held power before the change of system. This mechanism is accepted by the vast majority of society, the acceptance being linked to a degree of freedom of beliefs, opinion, association, mobility, and ultimately, to acceptance of the possibility of change. Throughout the region, the independence of the judiciary has been proclaimed and enshrined in legislation. The foundations of local government have been laid, although the powers exerted by local-government authorities vary.

One weakness of the political system and conduct of government in many post-communist countries is an ill-defined and confused distribution of power among the supreme authorities of the state and between the central and local government. This is only partly due to the hastily adopted constitutional provisions, which reflect compromises dictated by expediency. More important have been personal power struggles between those in high office.

The dispute over the character of governance – whether to have a parliamentary-cum-presidential or parliamentary-cum-cabinet pattern of government – has implications that run deeper than simple emulation of the American or French presidential system. It reflects the character of domestic political struggles between autocratic tendencies and forces that support liberal democracy. Most advocates of presidential government in the post-communist countries want greater power, especially complete freedom to hire and fire government ministers, the right to issue decrees with the force of law (bypassing the legislature), and relatively wide powers to dissolve recalcitrant parliaments. These are essentially authoritarian designs or leanings. They derive from regional traditions, both recent and communist (Yeltsin sought to rule Russia as he had ruled the oblast of Sverdlovsk) or more distant and pre-communist (Lech Wałęsa's idol, Marshal Józef Piłsudski, staged a military coup in Poland in 1926 and exercised a mild dictatorship). An important factor behind these authoritarian moves is the difficulty of transformation. Both presidential and cabinet government can and do function properly in mature democracies. There is no establishing of a universal pattern of governance more conducive to democratic transformation in such countries. However, in countries where democratic traditions, political culture and the party system are weak, a strong presidential system may well turn into an authoritarian direction, especially if there is French-style limitation of the role of parliament. Political competition for power is not confined to the central organs of the state. In Russia, for instance, struggles between federal and regional power produced instability and conflicts that ended only with the election of President Putin.[101] Even with a weak presidential system, a strong government with a big majority can limit the role and control of the parliament.

One adverse experience in the governance process during the brief history of the new system in the former socialist countries has been the increase in corruption. This is an outcome of several, interrelated factors. The choice of politicians and exercise of social control over them has not been based on an "organic", long-term process of selection. The balance between the executive and the legislature has not been well defined. The rule of law is not well established. In this environment, the possibility of converting economic power into political power and *vice versa*, along with other means of gaining special advantages, has become a major source of corruption. Political power has been used in almost all these countries on an unprecedented scale, to build up people who wield economic power. The newly rich, meanwhile, prefer political forces that do not pose a threat to their new wealth.

Public administration and the democratic process

Transformation of the *public administration system* became an important issue for governance and political democracy in all Central and Eastern

---

[101] The parliamentary and presidential elections of 1999–2000 consolidated Russia's fragmented political system. The standard division in Russian elections was overcome for the first time. Before, Russia had struggled with divided policymaking on two fronts: between the president and the Duma and between the centre and the regions. Putin has begun to strengthen the centre's authority and rein in the regional governors. However, obstacles remain on both initiatives.

European countries. Some groups among the "technocrats" and "experts" in the apparatus had tried to initiate reforms in the centrally planned economy, since they felt a stronger commitment to modernisation, but these had usually been blocked or aborted by the political system. Hungary was exceptional in many respects, but even there, the reforms remained partial and limited. Full implementation would have called for pluralism in the whole political system. The technocrats were able to assist certain efforts towards reform, but they could not assemble the social and political support needed for radical change. Development of an independent, neutral civil service is an essential component for all the main aspects of the transition: from totalitarianism to democracy, from a command economy to a market system, from (almost exclusive) state ownership to (predominantly) private ownership, and from a bloc structure to national sovereignty. The civil service also needs to help improve performance and stimulate society's commitment to these essential tasks. Professional expertise gains importance as society comes under various pressures and faces difficult tasks and challenges. Only by providing such expertise, rather than simply responding to the strongest pressures upon it, can the civil service serve the long-term interests of society.

Global trends in the second half of the 20th century displayed a seemingly irreconcilable dichotomy between *legalism* and *managerialism*. Efforts to apply the management methods of private business to governance have been coupled with efforts to reduce the scope of the welfare state. The salient trend in modern public administration is the pursuit of greater operational efficiency and effectiveness. Often the desire to achieve this tempts officials to depart from tried, legitimate processes and institutions, which threatens and even jeopardises the democratic processes. The public administration faces many pressures and challenges. Many people, for instance, are losing confidence in all kinds of public institution. The institutions, on the other hand, face pressures on their resources and budgets because their existing commitments are joined by new demands. Meanwhile there are calls for more "direct" democracy and opportunities for participation, while decreasing respect is shown for the traditional instruments of representative democracy.

The tasks in the transition countries are even more complicated. The crucial issue in the region is not to redesign, but to *establish* an independent, neutral civil service. This has to be done at the same time as democratisation continues, far-reaching changes occur in the role of government, and the market economy establishes itself. The civil service must therefore be professionally expert and simultaneously transparent and democratically accountable. Furthermore, the transition countries have several specific, often difficult and unmanageable problems with the system of public administration and its civil servants.

The role of the state in the Central and Eastern European countries became extended in the 20th century, with an accompanying growth of government bureaucracy. The etatist, socialist state took direct control over a wide area of economic and social activity that did not belong to the state's traditional function. This situation has been profoundly affected by the transition to a market system. In some areas, there is a degree of continuity, while in others, there have been important changes in response to new requirements. An example of such continuity and change is the welfare function, including education, public health, pensions, social allowances and housing. Important changes are taking place in the economic functions of the state, particularly in monetary and fiscal policy and redistributive objectives and instruments. Another area of change includes regulatory activities to limit the adverse impact of behaviour: environmental protection, consumer protection, curbs on monopolies and cartels, and so on, where the importance of the state may be increasing. All these fields require major institutional and administrative reforms, and substantial changes in the role, composition, size, working methods and quality of performance of the government bureaucracy.

The reform process in public administration is still at an early stage, so that a comprehensive evaluation cannot be given. In some countries the process is advanced, and in others little or no progress has been made.

It is also important for the bureaucracies to maintain institutional stability and predictability, while keeping up with the changes. This is a big challenge to the management and staff of government agencies. Civil servants need to acquire new technical skills, attitudes and values, while preserving their traditional strengths. The transformation process calls for civil servants who can be paternalistic or protective, but also work as a partner and efficient manager. They need personal integrity and capacity for independent action. In countries applying to join the European Union, accession will call for an efficient civil service, able to guarantee that the rules and regulations involved in membership will be implemented.

Ethnic tensions, nationalism, xenophobia and other problems

One of the most difficult and dangerous aspects of the changes in the former socialist countries relates to the region's ethnic diversity. It takes the form of violent nationalism, separatism, and xenophobia (Chechnya, Bosnia-Herzegovina and Kosovo have provided the most baneful examples of this).

The political and ethnic borders laid down after World War I and largely restored by the peace treaties after World War II, created sources of latent tension that the dictatorial regimes of the past 40 years were unable and ill-prepared to defuse. Vain efforts by the communist regimes to ignore the under-lying antagonisms by emphasising loyalty to social class only contributed to the divisions. People's movements were limited and there were few guaran-tees for the rights of minorities. Some communist countries, such as Romania, even embarked on forcible assimilation. The Soviet Union promot-ed autocratic economic regimes that were connected bilaterally with the Soviet economy and had little interest in real multilateral co-operation, which strengthened the economic foundations of nationalism.

One source of the problems is institutional accommodation of the ethnic minorities. Recent empirical findings show that no state is ethnically neutral. Each country reflects the ethnic power structure of its society, and usually, the interests, values and policies of a ruling ethnic majority. Ethnic issues will remain one of the difficult problems for the new regimes, posing a danger also to democratisation. The other problem relates to the ethnic groups and how they accept the institutions imposed on them by the majority or pro-duced by political consensus. Ethnicity, more than any other form of social identity, has a totalling potential to displace other loyalties and obligations and become the one source of identity. During the Cold War, a struggle for national identity and self-determination was seen by the West as a legitimate goal and political instrument in the fight against Soviet domination. With the demise of regional Soviet hegemony, old ethnic problems resurfaced, along with the new element of separatism in multinational states, leading, for instance, to dismemberment of Yugoslavia and Czechoslovakia. Today, Western encouragement of such goals has ceased, but nationalism remains, unconstrained by dictatorship or established traditions of democratic toler-ance.

The revival or strengthening of nationalism is not confined to Central and Eastern European countries. Nationalistic and ethnic violence blights areas as diverse as Western Europe, the Middle East, Africa,[102] India and China. Nationalism in Central and Eastern Europe, however, is particularly strident and presents great dangers to regional and international security. Historic-ally, the region has been a buffer zone between great powers and its conflicts (often exploited by those powers) were catalysts for both world wars. Mass murders, especially of Jews and Gypsies in the Holocaust, have become part of the world's historical memory of the region.

---

[102] Most African countries have been governed by dictatorial regimes. The parliamentary systems installed at independence proved unable to sustain the broad political coalitions cre-ated during the independence struggle. Wracked by ethnic tensions and unrealistically high popular expectations of rapid socio-economic development, the parliamentary systems were transformed into single-party instruments to serve privileged political elites or specific ethnic groups.

In principle, there are several ways to alleviate ethnic tensions, but each is difficult to implement in practice. An important aspect relates to electoral systems, of which several recognise ethnic interests and facilitate the accommodation of them. Ethnic groups under some systems are allowed to cast votes simultaneously along ethnic lines and within the regular voting system. Another formula is federalism and regional autonomy, whose drawbacks include regional discrimination, exclusion and the potential of secession. All these are important concerns for ruling elites in transition countries. Early membership of the EU may ease the problems of ethnicity in Central and Eastern Europe, but in the absence of appropriate democratic solutions, it may remain a big source of tension in the Soviet successor states.

External factors

The chapter would not be complete without mentioning the role of the external forces and factors in the democratisation process.

External sources of power and influence have always played an important role in the region. Before and after the Second World War, they helped to introduce and sustain dictatorial regimes. In the 20th century, both Nazi-oriented and communist regimes in the region had strong outside supporters, notably the influence of a *dominant foreign power*. There are no external dictatorial regimes in Europe to support extremists in Central and Eastern Europe at the beginning of the 21st century. The world of the 2000s is not the world of the 1920s or 1930s.

The democratisation process has also had been subject to important, strong and diverse external influences from several directions.

There has been a strong, assisted "demonstration effect" from the Western democratic market systems, greater in countries with close direct contacts with Western societies, but relatively limited in others.

The various Western institutions of civil society, including social organisations, religious groups and foundations aiming to further democratic institutions have played an important part at the grassroots, by helping and stimulating local movements. In some former socialist countries, their influence has been curbed by the absence of a well-structured civil society.

Some Western countries and their government institutions have made important contributions to the struggles for human rights, in international organisations and by direct action. They will retain a role in the future as external guarantors. The sustainability of democracy depends largely on external supports and guarantees, particularly if a society lacks strong democratic forces and an integrally developed civil society. The democratic process needs strong advocates. External forces are important in countries that have young, inexperienced democratic institutions to handle the inevitable social tensions and conflicts.

International intergovernmental organisations have importance as well. The terms of the UN Charter, the Universal Declaration of Human Rights and the various covenants, conventions and declarations give a strong mandate to the UN and its agencies to support the building of democratic societies and institutions. These factors are also important in the former socialist countries. There are important guarantees of democracy in institutions such as NATO and the EU, to which most countries in Central and Eastern Europe aspire to belong.

The *UN system* deserves credit in many areas for its support of the transformation process, which has given the UN system a range of new tasks and problems. Political and economic transitions and reforms, and changes in political regimes of the member states have occurred in the past, of course, when the UN and its specialised agencies had to support a large number of new countries, born out of the ruins of colonial empires. The UN has accumulated experiences in many countries in handling the legal problems of successor states, building institutions and conducting impartial analysis of the socio-economic and administrative processes of transformation. It has also played an advocacy role in the global system, to support new countries in solving their problems, by suggesting policies and measures for moderating the human costs of the changes. In many cases, the UN was the first to provide humanitarian aid and technical co-operation. With the former socialist countries and their transition processes, the UN also faces major new problems. (1) The dismemberment of the Soviet Union and the systemic changes in Russia were the first case of a global power, a founder of the UN system and a major force in it, facing the tasks of domestic systemic change and reintegration into the global system on a new basis. This made the role of the UN politically more delicate and economically more difficult. (2) The special role assigned to the World Bank and the IMF by the main industrial countries, in guiding and helping the transformation process, also implied important constraints on the UN. The latter has a more diverse and heterogeneous economic philosophy and more limited mandates and resources than the Bretton Woods institutions. (3) In a number of areas, notably technical and humanitarian assistance, there has been some competition for UN resources between the developing countries and some transition economies.

The UNDP and the UN Economic Commission of Europe have probably been the UN bodies to make the biggest and broadest contributions to the changes in Europe, particularly in analysing the changes, evaluating successes and failures, comparing the performance of countries, and assisting with institution building. An important role has also been played by the

European Commission in raising transition issues in an integrated European framework.

The contribution of the UN system to the transformation process as a whole has been meaningful in several areas:

- helping with conflict management and resolution in the region, which may undergo a long period of political, social and economic instability;
- offering humanitarian assistance;
- providing critical, impartial analysis of the main factors, processes and outcomes in the transition process, including the role and attitude of various players;
- co-operating technically in institution building and management of the new market organisations;
- transferring knowledge and information about country experiences and solutions in similar circumstances;
- appraising and analysing various national and international programmes related to the transition process;
- analysing the implications of the transition process for various groups of countries, particularly developing countries, with a view to strengthening global co-operation;
- helping the democratisation of former socialist countries by projecting the democratic and humanitarian values of the UN Charter and of the Universal declaration of Human Rights;
- promoting reintegration of the transition economies into the global system of co-operation, by critical analysis of their policies and practices, successes and failures, and the ways the rest of the world handles the process.

The UN has also been important in keeping the transition process on the global agenda, along with reintegration into the global market system. It has done so in a way that takes into account the interests of all parties, including the developing countries.

Some conclusions

What are the most important conclusions of this case study, which may have general importance, beyond the given region?

The post-communist region is almost as diverse as the rest of the world. There are big differences in the size of countries, level of economic development, social stratification, cultural background, and linguistic and religious structures, and in their ability to address the tasks of building a democratic market economy. Furthermore, there are unresolved ethnic, socio-political and territorial problems, which threaten the region with crises and political disruption and have the potential to create tensions and conflicts within and between countries. Still, there are many similarities. Although some general experiences of the democratic process in the former socialist countries resemble those in other parts of the world, there have been many specific features. There is no simple or easy reply to questions about how strongly or to what extent democracy can be sustained in the region. The sustainability of democracy is not an abstract notion. It cannot be considered in isolation from several other social and economic processes resulting from the interactions of domestic and external factors and changes. Modern democracy exists and survives within a band of national and international, social and economic conditions. The conditions to be fulfilled for democracy to be sustainable (able to reproduce itself without creating situations that enforce or result in non-democratic methods of governance) are strongly related to those governing other tasks, notably the building of a market system. Leadership is important in the democratic process. Persons elected to parliament or chosen for local, and still more national government posts must be of a relatively high quality – reasonably honest people who do not seek political power or office for personal gain. The new government should not become the instrument of a ruling elite intent on accumulating wealth and power.

The scope of governance by democratically elected institutions should be defined in harmony with the mechanisms of democracy. This contrasts with the etatist traditions and the totalitarian past, where the state extended to all the areas of economic and social life. It does not mean, of course, that the state has to withdraw from functions indispensable to society or that everything should be privatised.

A more open and consultative system of governance facilitates greater articulation of interests and allows compromises and consensus building. However, there must be democratic self-control and tolerance by the majority and by the minority for democratic systems to function effectively. (Ethnic hatred and conflicts are traditionally problematic in the region, as are xenophobia and violent nationalism, which pose particular dangers to the sustainability of democracy.)

The postulates for transforming dictatorial, totalitarian regimes into democratic systems cannot be confined to such processes as implanting democracy from above or enforcing it from outside. It cannot be simplified or confined to formal changes in institutions or to electoral processes. The strength and cohesion, and ultimately, the survival of societies depend on their ability to fulfill their basic promises. The democratic process must not be treated in isolation from other social or economic processes, or from external and internal realities.

Success with democratic change requires wise new leadership, good governance. There must be a well-trained, respected, professional, technically competent bureaucracy in which there is little staff turnover, as a counter-weight to the politicians, who are non-specialists. The civil service should be committed to professional excellence, while subject to democratic control aimed at ensuing administrative responsiveness to popular will.

Democratic learning by society is an important task for the sustainability of democracy, even in the countries in the region with democratic traditions. This includes a formal learning process on such issues as how to organise elections and run elected bodies, parliaments and local assemblies in a democratic way, how to apply the rule of law, etc. Also important is informal learning by society about various civil and minority rights.

The sustainability of democracy depends as much on a global economy providing acceptable conditions for development for the vast majority of the population as it does on external supports and guarantees for human rights and democracy. It is important that there continue to be no external dictatorial regimes in Europe or countries with a policy of supporting domestic extremists in Central and Eastern European countries.

During the first decade of the transformation, democracy has gained solid institutional foundations in most of the former socialist countries of Central and Eastern Europe. The process has been much weaker in the post-Soviet states. However, weakness of the underlying consciousness and culture of society, where ambivalent attitudes prevail, is fairly general. Freedom is universally cherished as an inherent value, but there remains a strong current of etatist sympathy and expectations of official intervention whenever difficulties are encountered. The demand for "law and order" appears in a number of countries as a support for majority rule, which often disregards the various minorities. Many social groups are still swayed easily by demagogy. The level of political cultivation is still low, even in the political elite and the media. This means there are still threats to democracy, especially from populists and their etatist allies. External assistance has been essential in this environment, in the form of advice, expertise in building and running institutions, help with the new organisations of civil society, and assistance with preparing and supervising elections. In some countries, where the transition crisis led to civil war and economic and social disruption, humanitarian aid was requested. Peace-making operations were needed in countries where ethnic violence broke out. Important assistance came from the World Bank, the UNDP, the UN ECE and various non-UN regional and non-governmental organisations.

Of the emerging problems, the changing relationships between the state, capital and labour will have prime importance. The issue of the bargaining power of employees and their relation to the reforms and the increasing inequalities will inevitably gain importance in future political struggles. Particularly in countries that cannot achieve faster and more equitable economic growth, pressures toward extremist solutions, in various political guises, may undermine the functioning of democracies and result in forms of command systems.

The long transitional crises in the former socialist countries pointed to a need for new alternatives. They also showed the difficulties, in an era of globalisation, of creating a market system with a human face, unless there is a clear national vision or commitment sustained by democratic coalitions and strong international support.

Several decades will pass before the fate of democracy in this region will be known. Only then can a credible answer be given to the underlying question raised in this chapter. Will the region become a democratic network of friendly states, with improving standards of living for most people, or will it become again a region of poverty, turmoil, governed by autocratic regimes helped to power by unsolved socio-economic problems, poverty, marginalisation and ethnic conflicts? The transition offered a historically unique opportunity for the people of the region and the world community to avoid the latter. What remains also an open question is the extent to which the establishment of independent nation-states in place of the Soviet Union and Yugoslavia will increase regional and global stability. The reverse is also possible, with the new entities becoming sources of long-term international instability. This question cannot be answered in abstract terms, by idealising or promoting the process of change, or regarding it merely as a successful struggle for national self-determination or against totalitarianism.

10. NEW SOURCES OF RISK AND THE MANAGEMENT OF COLLECTIVE SECURITY

The nature of international risk in the post-Cold War era

The remarks of Raymond Aron have not lost any relevance since he wrote them in the mid-1960s: "Mankind has always lived dangerously. The dangers are no longer the same, but they have not disappeared. One mankind, united under a sole rational administration … would correspond to one possible end of human adventure. The adventure is still far from its final state, conforming not to the logic of history but to a partial logic that fascinates because it at once attracts and repels" (Aron, 1966, p. 502). Elsewhere, he comments, "History has more imagination than wise men do. It has thus far refused to choose between collective suicide and the abdication of states. It has gradually brought a certain order out of the anarchy common to all international systems, an order favouring the limitation of armed conflicts" (*Ibid.*, pp. 485–486).

The end of the Cold War and the diminishing dangers of a nuclear holocaust have supported Aron's analysis. The same developments, along with the disintegration of the Soviet empire and the systemic changes as a major political force, present new opportunities for nations to improve their relations and co-operate at all levels. However, it is still unclear whether countries are ready and willing to seize those opportunities and collaborate on effective global governance.

The international agenda brims with problems, old and new, each complex and connected with many others. Some are rooted in the uncertainties of the transition process and the largely unpredictable consequences of the evolving global power structure. Others concern the globalisation of particular issues. Population growth, for example, is an acute problem that endangers the ecological, political, and economic systems of the world. Similarly, mounting social tensions, unemployment and poverty are not just domestic problems. They reach across borders in a myriad of ways, affecting the whole global system. Wars provoked by ethnic tensions and human-rights violations may engulf nations and even disrupt the political and economic stability of regions. The global economy is becoming more competitive: new challengers contend with earlier players in different segments of the world market. The world may be split into mutually hostile regional blocs by trade wars. Such problems remained manageable in the 1990s, but if not treated promptly, appropriately and jointly by the international community, they may soon threaten the future of humanity.

Anticipating, gauging, managing and trying to eliminate risk factors have always been necessary to the formulation and implementation of policies in the international political and economic systems. In recent decades, transnationals, banks, international organisations and governments have employed sophisticated scientific methodologies to assess the risks attending major decisions.[103] The social sciences, especially economics, have drawn a distinction between factors of uncertainty and factors of risk. According to John Maynard Keynes (1973, pp. 112–113), the term *risk* refers to the chance occurrence of an event determined by some objectively verifiable probability distribution. Uncertainty, on the other hand, is a chance occurrence the probability of which is not known. The two terms have often been used interchangeably in the jargon of international life.

Richard Herring defines risk as the possibility of an outcome that is less favourable than the expected outcome, or the possibility of unforeseen developments that reduce our welfare (Herring, 1983, pp. 3 and 23). This definition seems appropriate to the international political and economic system, and even more so, to the ecosystem, where the impact and interrelationship of processes and factors depend on a great number of variables. These may produce incalculable scenarios of instability, even when the causes are known. Here, let us define international risks as important, potentially disturbing and destabilising factors or acts originating with, or generated by players on different structural levels, whose consequences may spill over onto other members of the international community.

Since every human activity involves elements of risk, and one group's risks may be another's opportunities, understanding and managing risks in international life calls for specific, unambiguous cases. Apart from identifying the sources of collective risk, it is necessary to understand and make allowance for sources of risks and instability that affect individual countries. Many of these may need international assistance in their risk management.

The broad character and implications of future collective risks can be summed up in five categories:
– Risks of armed conflict, due to military intervention, war, civil war and other forms of mass violence, and national and international terrorism.

---

[103] See Haner and Ewing (1985), and from the viewpoint of international banking, Junge, Georg (1988).

- Risks from the political destabilisation of governments, whose sources may be internal (revolutions, uprisings, separatist movements, ethnic problems, or the inefficiency of national and international political institutions) or external (unforeseen and unpredictable political actions by governments, adversely affecting other states).
- Economic risks, whose sources are various. They include malfunctioning of the economic system and recessions in key countries, defaults by major debtors, adverse, unawaited results of technological change, bad economic decisions, the collapse of international cooperation regimes (especially those vital to the global economy, such as the international financial system), sudden restrictions on the availability of resources, and economic warfare.
- Risks deriving from social events, such as large population increases, mass migrations, large movements of refugees, social developments that overstretch a state's capacity to provide adequate health and educational services, and ethnic, national, cultural, and religious problems.
- Ecological risks engendered by general deterioration of the environment, sudden environmental crises, and man-made and natural catastrophes.

These five categories often interrelate and overlap. In principle, dealing with any one source of risk separately should be difficult. In practice, however, collective risk management has to be specific and deal with the principal risk or risks. These may be short-term (such as temporary unemployment problems, labour disputes, or short-lived disputes between countries) or long-term (major wars, environmental degradation or the economic or political collapse of a country). Risks can also be classed according to their susceptibility to handling by the means available. It is easier, theoretically, to assess and calculate the international political risks associated with a change of government or regime than to predict the consequences, say, of ethnic conflict, which may escalate into civil or international war. Social and economic risks are different again. In the short term, they may not directly affect the international political environment, so that governments may not consider collective action. In the longer term, social and economic risks may destabilise democratic regimes, inspire protectionist pressures and disrupt international co-operation regimes. It should be remembered that accumulating social and economic discontent in the 1920s and 1930s led to the rise of the extremist, aggressive regimes that precipitated the Second World War.

Critical issues of collective risk management

There are no agreed definitions and concepts of international risk management. Governments and other international players have a vested interest in minimising risks and avoiding risk factors altogether. Risk management, on the other hand, implies that the complex world of the 21st century will be unable to eliminate old or new risk factors. It will have to coexist with them, and in doing so, seek to reduce the potential damage they may cause by employing various measures. Some measures may include unilateral adjustments, but others may entail international co-operation within a bilateral or multilateral framework.

Although the international institutional system has retained an essentially state-oriented structure, the majority of international risks cannot be dealt with in isolation, even by the strongest countries. For instance, there is no unilateral solution, in an environment of global interdependence, to global demographic or ecological problems or to problems of international trade and capital flows.

Rhetorics in the international policy arena heard since the late 1980s suggest there is a worldwide desire to upgrade and intensify international co-operation, so that it can manage the persistent and new risks and attempt to resolve a broad range of global and regional problems. However, will the community of nations, especially those most affected by the changes since the Cold War, respond to their new needs by seizing the unprecedented opportunities to intensify co-operation, or will they be tempted, in the event, to act unilaterally? This general question encompasses five others:

What sorts of services can current forms and institutions of co-operation provide to deal with the major global political, economic, and ecological problems affecting different types and groups of countries? Would those services be best provided within a bilateral, a regional-multilateral, or a global-multilateral framework?[104]

Are there sufficient incentives for nations to engage in international co-operation in the new era? How far have the interests, values, and attitudes of different countries changed since the end of the Cold War? To what extent

---

[104] Here multilateralism is understood broadly, to mean an organisational design for collective management of international agencies and co-operation regimes, for elaborating common norms to define the rights and obligations of countries and implementing collective sanctions when necessary. To date, some multilateral organisations have been multi-purpose, while others have fulfilled limited functions. The "functional" approach to the international co-operation system can be used in different senses: functionalism may relate to such problem areas as politics or economics, or more specifically to legal problems, trade, human rights issues, or capital flows. It does not precisely define the structural nature of organisations.

have the interests of countries converged, inspiring a greater readiness to support multilateral co-operation to address the global problems brought about by the new structures of global power?

In the case of multilateral co-operation, what kind of organisational responses will be the most efficient and feasible: centralised-global, harmonised global-regional, or clustered, functional co-operation regimes? To what extent can the UN system, in its present or reformed form, provide collective responses to common problems? Are such regional organisations as the EU or NATO more effective instruments for collective risk management? Can their activities be better harmonised with global institutions? Will informal "mini-lateralist" structures like the G8 group of nations (or smaller or enlarged versions of it) be more useful than larger, more formal multilateral structures?

To what extent are non-governmental players and transnational processes (such as technology and capital flows) shaping the future of multilateral co-operation, either by influencing government policies or by establishing their own co-operation structures?

More generally, which lessons learnt from past processes and outcomes of multilateral co-operation are most valuable for the future?

The experiences of the 1990s proved that the collective response of multilateral co-operation regimes to future needs should be "omni-lateral". It should take into consideration and try to harmonise global multilateral, regional multilateral, in some cases bilateral policies and actions. The UN system, however, is not only the largest and most comprehensive and democratic intergovernmental co-operation system in existence, but the most open one for managing such structures. Were the UN and its charter to be eliminated, the international environment would be dominated by unrestrained power politics, chaos and violence. Will the UN be able to respond to the new demands of the post-Cold War era? Will it be able to harmonise the policies of states and take into account the growing role of non-state players?

New opportunities and realities

There is no shortage in the rhetorics about the search for solutions in the new era. One important common denominator is the demand to strengthen the security of the individuals and the security of humankind. This is not just an extension of the security consciousness developed during the decades of the Cold War even though its heritage is still with us. Can it be blamed for the problems and for missing some of the rare opportunity to take critical steps towards strengthening global co-operation and human security?

Every new era brings some new problems and opportunities. One of the new problems is the conflict between perceived domestic and global security concerns. There is a new relationship between domestic and international issues. In a simplified way, the Cold War period could be characterised by the dominance of international problems over domestic issues. Even the strongest countries of the world had to significantly subordinate their domestic policies to policies that would guarantee their power positions in the Cold War conflict. External efforts aimed at destabilising the socio-political life and economy of opponents were tactics of Cold War games.

In the post-Cold War period, the pendulum started swinging towards the other extreme. While domestic stability, internal peace and security, and political-economic consensus have always been important to nations, they are substantially more so today.

The role of domestic social and economic issues and factors became much greater in determining the international policies of countries. Also, competing to maximise national gains and increasing national power became a motivating factor. As the role of economic factors, economic power, and competitiveness has increased, the national foundations of economic power have also taken on more significance. Was the expected new global vision for the post-Cold War era lost in this increasingly complex and diverse world? Is it still possible to reform the present system of international organisations for the governance of the evolving world, or are more radical changes required to combine and co-ordinate global and regional co-operation structures? Could the civil society play a greater and more positive role in this process than the governments in strengthening the global institutions and other instruments for co-operation in the new century?

The United Nations has been instrumental in sustaining a global order that has evolved since 1945, one that despite a certain level of stability, nevertheless has many shortcomings, tensions, and problems. In the environment of Cold War politics, there were only very limited opportunities to create an efficient and powerful world organisation. Neither the interests nor the motivations of the main global actors stimulated an increase in the efficiency of the management or functioning of the United Nations. The United Nations was however only one of several instruments of international politics used by the main powers. The global multilateral organisations in which member states of opposing Cold War blocs were present had a rather peculiar role to play during the years of the Cold War. Not only were they the instruments for international negotiations, agreements, and co-operation, but they also served as a world forum for confrontation and competition. This was especially so in the case of the UN system. Cold War adversaries were interested not only in attacking each other, but in winning allies through a "war of words," and through voting on various confrontational issues by "bandwagoning". When the opposite side achieved a majority of allies and votes, the minority side increasingly neglected the organisation. The Cold War created an attitude that was indifferent to the operational efficiency of multilateral organisations.

Global political changes under way since the late 1980s have increased the demands for the UN to improve its efficiency and meet new needs of the international community. The strategic conferences of the 1990s and their follow-ups, with the increasing participation of academics, politicians, and international non-governmental organisations have offered an array of new ideas about the necessary changes in institutions, policies and actions like the reform of the Bretton Woods System, the democratisation of the UN, the establishment of an Economic and Social Security Council, the establishment of a People's Assembly of civil society organisations parallel to the general Assembly of the UN. The debate of the Millenium Assembly, with the participation of an unprecedented number of heads of state and governments (there were 144 heads of state or governments) offers an interesting and up-to-date picture about the views on the member states on globalisation, solidarity, poverty, human rights, democracy and the role of civil society.[105]

Globalisation was one of the most frequently used terms, being mentioned 307 times, by 130 countries. Even though peace and poverty were mentioned more often, reading all the speeches together, the dominant theme was the process of globalisation and its consequences. One of the characteristic formula was presented by the President of Chile:

...we embrace with enthusiasm and optimism the phenomenon of globalisation that makes us all part of a shared time and space. We know that this is a revolution that impacts on the economy, technology, politics and culture and which affects the daily life of people everywhere on the planet. We in the south of the world are not afraid of this great transformation. Quite on the contrary, we embrace it full of hope... We have also seen how in the name of globalisation local cultures and environments are being destroyed. Situations of violence, human rights abuses and war are also arising which the international community is powerless to prevent or resolve. And we note with dismay how the gap between the haves and the have-nots continues to grow to the point at which it has become the gravest threat to the new global society.

These seemingly contradictory views may both speak the truth, just as it is also true that industrialisation brought both positive and negative features to the human condition.

---

[105] The quotations are taken from the official press releases of the Millenium Assembly and summarised by the UN University "Millenium Project". Washinton 2001. Mimeo. There were 144 heads of state or government.

The president of France emphasised some other aspects: *a new world has emerged in the space of a single generation ... in which borders are slowly disappearing, a world steeped in the new global culture of communications technologies,* there is a need for *common rules, principles and ambitions.*

Solidarity was mentioned 66 times by 48 countries, mostly in connection with globalisation, as an impetus necessary for peace and development. The President of Poland defined solidarity as shared responsibility: *It is sensitivity to the needs and anxieties of the weaker. It is willingness to cooperate and to offer support. It is priority of concerted efforts over unilateral action. It is respect for diversity and dialogue. But, above all, I perceive solidarity as freedom, dignity and welfare of the individual which are brought into the focus of attention of all political action and global campaigns.*

The President of Cameroon warned the Millennium Summit that *if globalisation is not accompanied by a new moral order, if it doesn't include solidarity between nations and the people, it risks to put in danger the peace that is so valuable to our time* The President of Brazil added that, *globalisation should be a means for creating a world of greater solidarity and, therefore, with less asymmetry.*

The prime Minister of Denmark suggested that *we need to create a human framework for the international market economy – as has been done in national economies. We need to put people before money and the market.* Iran made a similar point: *Globalisation should not be utilised to open greater markets for a few or to assimilate national cultures into a uniform global one. Instead, what is required is the collective articulation of common interests, norms and laws towards ensuring the equitable access to advancement at the global level.*

Poverty was mentioned by 134 speakers 335 times making it a leading issue among political leaders of the world. It was given even greater attention among sub-Sahara African and Latin American leaders, even though 900 million of the 1.2 billion of the world's population, which survive on less than $1 a day live in Asia. This is a "dangerous division". According to Prime Minister Vajpayee of India, the persistence of international inequality *threatens peace among nations.* Both advanced and developing countries called for a global focus that one day would solve poverty.

Human rights was mentioned 196 times by 101 countries. Human rights as a criterion for both domestic and foreign policy has grown dramatically over the past twenty-five years. The President of Iceland reminded the leaders that *opinion surveys about worldwide attitudes towards the United Nations showed human rights, as the Secretary-General points out in his Millennium Report, to be a central issue in peoples expectations towards the United Nations. If anything, such expectations may be expected to grow stronger, and the United Nations needs to respond to them.* Many issues are now included under the human rights theme. The representative of Saudi Arabia expressed the views of many developing countries when he questioned the management of progress on human rights saying: *Such human rights exist in the roots of every human civilisation, and are not a monopoly of one culture. It is absurd to impose on an individual or a society rights that are alien to its beliefs or principles.*

Essentially all leaders spoke of democracy as the central norm of governance for the 21st century, but not all have a common vision of its political evolution. Democratic evolution has to take into consideration how different cultures consider the special status of elders and gender responsibilities. Social stability has to be considered during the process of democratisation. Electoral processes and the creation of opposition parties cannot be simultaneously applied to vastly different social conditions. Yet these conditions may not change without commitments to human rights and economic development.

Poverty itself was stressed as an obstacle to democracy. *How can one speak about Human Rights without right to development? What is democracy and what means good governance without the management of common goods?* (Cameroon)

Yet Chad's Prime Minister mentioned that democracy could exist independently of richness, giving as an example his own country: *It is admitted unanimously that democracy and poverty don't often make good household. The Republic of Chad, a State classified among poorest of the planet, holds since a decade with courage, the cape of the democracy.*

Some leaders of developing countries wanted the West to remember not only how far developing countries have come, but that each country must be able to work out its own democratic evolution, at its own time and pace, and with respect for its special needs. As with the free market, Westerners are admonished that there isn't just one right way and each country should be allowed the freedom and respect to find its own way. One must have respect for the principal of self-determination.

There was a widespread recognition that national governments and international organisations are not sufficient to deal with the world's problems.

Several speakers noted that the UN needs to reach out to the institutions of civil society, bringing together international institutions, private sector organisations, and national governments to accomplish common goals.

The Chancellor of Germany stressed that *if we are to foster economic and social progress worldwide, it is essential that the civil society and, in particular, the business community, play a greater role in the United Nations' work. Secretary-General Annan, for example, provided important impetus for this with his "Global Compact" project. Should we not enhance and consider additional forms and areas of such cooperation? I would propose that the Secretary-General convene as quickly as possible a working group of business leaders from around the world to develop concrete ideas on this.*

Civil society will demand an increasingly important role in the globalised world and that is why in Chile we consulted with civil society as we prepared for this Millennium Summit (The President of Chile).

Will all these go beyond the usual rhetoric or will the diverging interests among its member-states and their institutional and political inertia dominate the process of implementation? There are no easy answers to these questions. The agenda is broader than at any time in UN history. The diversity of the problems means that the role of the UN in enforcing those norms will have to be supported more actively by the member states and shared with various regional organisations.

The Millenium Assembly reflected also a new and positive, but still rudimentary development in the international system, namely, there is a greater international commitment to hold states more accountable for their actions than they were held in the past. This measure of accountability applies not only to cases of international violence, but to violations of human rights, and to a lesser extent, to major environmental damages. Accountability is of crucial importance to the future international order and to its institutions, which, in their work to maintain peace and increase co-operation, will have to manage the multiple competing interests, and the political, military, and economic capacities of states as they seek to implement their goals. International normative standards, and accountability to them, will enable states to pursue their interests peacefully and honourably.

Making changes in foreign policy objectives and instruments is always difficult. Transforming international organisations and co-operation regimes requires lengthy negotiations and much bargaining. In the present transitional phase, the process is especially highly complex.

As the international community will have to deal with potential military actions undertaken by a greater number of small powers, civil war situations, domestic violence, international terrorism, and other similar dangers, the conflict prevention, peacekeeping and peacemaking structures will have to learn to respond in a more decentralised way, with more permanent and readily available forces. Other types of conflicts, like those that resulted in the Gulf War, or the conflicts in the Balkans, cannot be excluded in the future international system. The management of these conflicts would require leadership and the ability to form coalitions. All such security requirements justify the examination and reform of conflict prevention programs, and of peacekeeping and peacemaking measures. What requires particular scrutiny are the logistical and financing aspects of these security measures.

The institutional capacity of countries to collectively apprehend and manage factors of risks to the environment, economic development, trade, capital flows, and of poverty is outdated and needs to be adjusted to respond to new global realities. In some particular areas, however, like in the case of environmental dangers, the complex nature of the tasks is better understood, and the interests, values, and goals more clearly articulated. Consequently, international mechanisms are being reviewed in a more realistic way for problem identification and management, with the aim of improving the odds for their solution.

The main industrial powers, because they determine the main trends in production, consumption, global trade, and capital flows, hold special responsibilities for (and interests in) the stable functioning of the world economy. Some of these countries, however, may still believe in national security maximisation and in the greater efficiency of isolated, unilateral measures. This may prove counterproductive, as the present and future conditions will demand that decisions take into account multifaceted variables in order to eliminate or moderate problems between states that obstruct constructive mutual efforts for international co-operation.

There is an increasing danger of unilateralism, in spite of the fact that no single country alone can shoulder the burdens of human and material investments in a wide range of areas. Countries have still to understand fully the positive implications of their interconnection and interdependence and the need to incorporate into policy-ethical norms such as predictability, responsibility and solidarity.

The implementation of the decisions and declarations of the strategic conferences organised by the UN in the 1990s reflected the limited readiness, unequal capabilities and selective commitments of states to collective management of new problems and global risks.

The Millennium Assembly of the UN in September 2000 was a concluding phase of the strategic conferences, while opening the door to new thinking in the 21st century. The critical issue due to dominate the early part of the 21st century, is how to constrain or discipline the behaviour of states, making them more predictable, reliable partners. Effective global governance will require strong norms, enforcing authority and established codes of conduct in a global arena of constant change, full of unsolved old problems and new challenges. International organisations will need to be better equipped to confront sources of international instability and manage risks that may otherwise result in global crises. A basic condition for effective global governance is that states demonstrate an equal degree of responsibility and accountability to the intergovernmental organisations of which they are members.

Globalisation has turned "adjustment" into a universal postulate for rich and poor countries. It is changing the pattern of development itself, shifting long-term growth paths and patterns of income distribution. Over the next decade, the main issue will be adaptation of national economies and institutions to global change, and of global change to human needs. The nature of the problem and solutions will vary from region to region, but no country or region will remain untouched. The outcomes are hard to predict.

The Millennium Report of the UN secretary-general underlined that without a strong UN, it will be much harder to meet the new challenges. The UN has to act as a catalyst, stimulating action by others, and fully exploit the new possibilities, particularly information technology. He recommended identifying the core strengths of the UN, based not on power, but on the values it represents. He stressed its role in helping to set and sustain global norms, its ability to stimulate global concern and action, and the trust inspired by its practical work to improve people's lives. He suggested expanding the UN's relationship with civil organisations, the private sector and charitable foundations, in pursuit of common goals. For consideration, he listed six shared values in the spirit of the Charter, of particular relevance to the new century: freedom, equity and solidarity, tolerance, non-violence, respect for nature, and shared responsibility (UN, 2000b).

The Millenium Assembly of the UN have offered opportunities for stock-taking and balance drawing. Its key questions have been related to the future of the population of the world and of the international system. This has happened at a period of time, when the first post-Cold War decade was over. The world did not follow the recipe book of over-optimistic expectations about peace, order, increasing prosperity in expanding markets and fast consolidation of the new democracies, but the global system has become more interdependent and more fragile.

The Statements of the Millenium Assembly have been by and large realistic in their approaches. They reflected a limited intellectual consensus in understanding that the qualitative improvement of international co-operation is a fundamental requirement for a sustainable "common future". It has been an important warning that the UN and other multilateral organisations will have to serve in the 21st century a quite different community of nations than those, which formed and shaped the United Nations during the past decades. The evolving global patterns will probably require a more decentralised, more diverse, but better harmonised system of co-operation, based on greater predictability, reliability, and accountability of policies in a complex system governed by increasingly divergent interests and divided by growing economic competition.

The balancing between the common interests in global security and the various sources of discord, differences in values and interests, uncertainty, and instability will always be difficult in the global system. Humankind will probably always live dangerously, as Aron suggested. An other important scholar, Kant, a few centuries earlier, in his Perpetual Peace drew the attention to the fact that "a perfect solution impossible" and there can be only approximations, because "Nothing straight can be constructed from such warped wood as that which man is made of".[106]

The guarded pessimism of Kant and the realism of Aron may serve as signposts, marking the natural limits of human actions. Historical experiences prove that there are many possibilities within these limits. The analysis of the changes in an interactive framework may help the better understanding of the needs, the limits and the possibilities. Transformations in a given area or in one part of the world will affect, in greater or lesser degree, other processes, regions and countries. The cumulative impact of them may unleash energies that are catapulting the world to a qualitatively new trajectory of development, with new promises and problems. The clockwork of history however moves with different speed in technology, politics, economics and culture. The trends also differ in the degree of certainty that can be attached to each of them. Political and economic decisions in bigger countries clearly impact more on smaller ones. All these make changes in a complex world more unpredictable. There are at the same time important and predictable realities. The individuals of the 21st century will have to share the globe with a much larger number of people than their predecessors in past centuries. Pressure on resources will be a more important source of new challenges but it may bring about more efficient solutions. A qualitatively more advanced information sphere in which the interactive capacities are vitally important will surround the individuals. The infosphere may serve different goals, interests and values. It may be an instrument for spreading new knowledge, for manipulation of people. It may be used by the civil society, for the improvement of governance on local and gobal level for channeling public concerns at the level of public policy-making more effectively and faster than in the 20th century. The transformations in technology may be resulting in more convergence in institutions. The social and political changes may increase diversity and making interests, values and ethics more difficult to harmonise for the purpose of global governance. On the basis of all these different global, regional and country scenarios have been adopted for the 21st century by those who tried to anticipate the cumulative consequences of the changes. "Reading" of the main messages of the ongoing transformations dealt with in this project one may arrive to rather grim conclusions. So far the countries of the globe did not utilize the rare and in many ways unprecedented opportunities offered by the relatively peaceful post-Cold War years for the improvement of international cooperation. The promised benefits and the globalization process have been distributed in a

[106] Perpetual Peace in "Kant's Political Writings". (Cambridge: Cambridge University Press, 1970), p. 130.

212

rather unequal way. The use of the historically unprecedented accumulation of knowledge remained much below its potentials.

In an increasingly undisciplined environment, the resolution of such problems as the growing inequalities, the elimination of poverty, the strengtening the life support systems of the planet, requiring the efficient collective management of different regimes could become in fact much more difficult. Old and new sources of risks and instability may overwhelm the opportunities for constructive action in the absence of significant, deliberate, and new national and collective efforts to engage in such opportunities. Progress towards a more humane, equitable and sustainable global system depends not only on the declarations or intentions of countries but on their domestic politics, and on a wide range of other independent political variables, both domestic and international. The process is especially complex and demanding in the present era of multiple transitions and transformations. False certainty, man-made errors can send the world in dangerous directions. The expectations are not for utopias, but for realistic alternatives particularly in such areas as improving the quality of life, sustainable development, and increasing security for individuals, countries and humanity.

REFERENCES

Ahrendsdorf, P. J., Pangle T. L. (1999) *Justice among Nations.* Lawrence: University Press of Kansas.

American Council for the United Nations University: "The State of the Future", Reports for 1999, 2000, 2001 in the frame of the Millenium Project, ed. by Glemm, J. C. and Gordon, T. S., Washington D. C.

Amin, T. (1991) *Nationalism and Internationalism in Liberalism.* Islamabad: *Marxism and Islam.* The International Institute of Islamic Thought.

Archibugi D., Held, D., Kohler, M. (eds) (1998) *Re-imagining Political Community: Studies in Cosmopolitan Democracy.* Stanford: Stanford University Press.

Aron, R. (1966) "The Anarchical Order of Power". *Daedelus,* Spring.

Baudot, J. (ed.) (2000) *Building a World Community.* Copenhagen: Royal Danish Ministry of Foreign Affairs.

Ben David, D. (2000) *Trade Growth and Disparity among Nations.* Geneva: WTO (Mimeo).

Berg, J., L. Taylor (2000) *External Liberalization, Economic Performance and Social Policy.* Working Paper series, New York: New School for Social Research, February.

Bertrand, M. (1989) *The Third Generation World Organization.* Dordrecht: Martinus Nijhoff Publishers.

Beveridge, Sir W. H. (1945) *Full Employment in a Free Society.* New York: Norton.

Bonser, Ch., (ed.) (2000) *Security, Trade and Environmental Policy.* Dordrecht: Kluwer.

Braudel, F. (1976) *The Mediterranean and the Mediterranean World in the Age of Philip II,* 2 vols. New York, Cambridge, etc.: Harper and Row.

Carley, M., Spapens, P. (1998) Shaning the World. Earthscan. London. 1998.

Chambers, R. (1995) "Poverty and Livelihoods. Whose Reality Counts?" In Üner Kirdar, Leonard Silk (eds), *People, from Impoverishment to Empowerment.* New York: New York University Press.

Club of Rome (1972) *The Limits to Growth. A Report for the Club of Rome.* New York: Universe Books.

Cohen, J. E. (1995) *How Many People Can the Earth Support?* New York: W. W. Norton and Co.

Daedalus Special volume: The Exit from Communism. Spring, 1992. Vol. 121 No. 2. Cambridge. Ma.

Dubiel, H. (1996), "Die Krise der liberalen Demokratie". In Gerlich, P., K. Glass, B. Serloth (eds), *Mitteleuropäische Mythen und Wirklichkeiten,* Wien-Torun: Österreichische Gesellschaft für Mitteleuropäische Studien Verlag.

Drucker, P. F. (1994) "The Age of Social Transformation". *Atlantic Monthly,* November.

Durch, W. J., B. M. Blechman (1992) *Keeping the Peace: The United Nations in the Emerging World Order.* Washington, D. C.: Stimson Center.

Erlich, P. (1968) *The Population Bomb.* New York: Ballantine.

EU (1999) *1999 Report on Employment.* Brussels: EU.

European Commission (1999) *Scenarios Europe 2010. Working Paper*. Brussels: European Commission, July.

Falk, R. (2000) "Realizing the Copenhagen Vision: The Political Imperative". In Baudot (ed.) (2000).

Fromuth, P. J. (ed.) (1988) *A Successor Vision: The United Nations of Tomorrow*. New York: United Nations Association of the United States of America.

Gerlich, P. (1996) "Democracy and Time" In Gerlich, P., K. Glass, B. Serloth (eds), *Mitteleuropäische Mythen und Wirklichkeiten*, Wien-Torun: Österreichische Gesellschaft für Mitteleuropäische Studien Verlag.

Hammer, L. et al. (1999) "Are the DAC Targets Achievable in the Year 2015?" *Journal of International Development*, Vol. 2.

Haner, F. T., J. S. Ewing (1985) *Country Risk Assessment, Theory and Worldwide Practice*. New York: Praeger Special Studies.

Hardin, Garrett (1968) "The Tragedy of the Commons" Science 162. Dec. 13. 1968, pp. 1243–1248, A.A.A.S., Washington D. C.

Held, D., Grunberg, I., Stern, M. (eds) (1999) Global Transformations:Politics, Economics and Culture. Cambridge, UK Polity Press.

Hennessey, P., A. Seldon (eds) (1989) *Ruling Performance. British Governments from Attlee to Thatcher*. Oxford: Blackwell.

Herring, Richard J. (ed.) (1983) *Managing International Risk*. Cambridge: Cambridge University Press.

Hoyningen-Huene, P., M. Weber, E. Oberheim (1999) *Science for the 21st Century*. Paris: Unesco.

Huntington, S. P. (1996) *The Clash of Civilizations and the Remaking of World Order*. New York: Simon and Schuster.

Inkeles, A. (1983) *Exploring Individual Modernity*, New York: Columbia University Press.

Inkeles, A., D. H. Smith (1974) *Becoming Modern: Individual Change in Six Developing Countries*. Cambridge, Mass.: Harvard University Press.

John Paul II, Pope (1991) "On the Hundredth Anniversary of *Rerum Novarum*: *Centesimus Annus*.' *Encyclical Letter*, May 1, Publication 436–438. Washington D. C.: Office for Publishing and Promotion Services, United·States Catholic Conference.

Junge, G. (1988) "Country Risk Assessment, Swiss Bank Corporation Approach". In Swiss Bank Corporation, *Economic and Financial Prospects Supplement*. Basle and Zurich: Swiss Bank Corporation, February–March.

Kaufman, J., Nico Schrijver (1996) "Changing Global Needs: Expanding Roles for the United Nations System". In *Reports and Papers 1990–1995*. Hanover, N. H.: The Academic Council for the United Nations System [1966].

Kavanagh, D., P. Morris (1989) *Consensus Politics from Attlee to Thatcher*. Oxford: Blackwell.

Keynes, J. M. (1973) "Part 2: Defence and Development". In *The Collected Writing of John Maynard Keynes: The General Theory and After*. (ed.) Donald Moggridge. Cambridge: Cambridge University Press, Vol. 14.

Kirdar, Ü. (ed.) (1997) *Cities Fit for People*. New York: UN.

Kissinger, H. (1995), *Diplomacy*. London, etc.: Simon and Schuster.

Kozul-Wright, R., P. Rayment (1995) Walking on Two Legs: Strengthening Democracy and Productive Entrepreneurship in the Transition Economies. Unctad Discussion Papers No. 101, August. Geneva: Unctad.

Kropotkin, P. (1910) "Anarchism". In *Encyclopedia Britannica*, 11th edition, Vol. I. Cambridge: Cambridge University Press.

Kuznets, S. (1966), *Modern Economic Growth*. New Haven: Yale University Press.

Klingemann, H.-D., D. Fuchs (eds) (1995) *Citizens and the State*. Oxford, etc.: Oxford University Press.

Löwenthal, R. [1953] (1986) "Staatfunktionen and Staatsreform in den Entwicklungslandern". In Nuscheler, Franz (ed.) *Politikalwissenschaftliche Entwicklungländerforschung*. Dartmudt.

Maddison, A. (1995) *Monitoring the World Economy 1820–1992*. Paris: OECD.

Malin, K. M. (1963) Hány embert tarthat el a Föld? Budapest: Kossuth kiadó.

Malthus, Th. R. (1798) *An Essay on the Principle of Population…* Reproduced in: *Literature of England*, Vol. II, 1936, p. 21.

Marx, K., F. Engels [1848] (1971) *Manifesto of the Communist Party* (English translation by Samuel Moore, 1888). Moscow: Progress Publishers.

Mayor, Dr. F. (1990) *Universality, Diversity, Interdependence: The Missions of the University in Higher Education and Society*. Opening speech at the 9th General Conference of the International Association of Universities, Helsinki, August 5.

Mills, C. W. (1956) *The Power Elite*. New York: Oxford University Press.

Nordic UN Project (1991) *The United Nations in Development: Reform Issues in the Economic and Social Fields – A Nordic Perspective*. Stockholm: Nordic UN Project.

OECD (1994) *Societies in Transition*. Paris: OECD.

OECD (1996) *The Knowledge Based Economy*. Paris: OECD.

OECD (1999) *Progress Report on the OECD Three-year Project on Sustainable Development*. Paris: OECD.

Panos Institute (1999) *Globalization and Employment*. Panos Institute Briefing No. 33, London: Panos Institute, May.

Pearce, M., G. Stewart (1992) *British Political History*. London–New York: Routledge.

Przeworski, A. (1991) *Democracy and the Market: Political and Economic Reforms in Eastern Europe and Latin America*. Cambridge: Cambridge University Press.

Rosenau, J. (1990) *Turbulence in World Politics: A Theory of Change and Continuity*. Princeton, NJ: Princeton University Press.

Rosenberg, N. (1976) *Perspectives on Technology*. Cambridge: Cambridge University Press.

Runnymede, Trust (1997) *Islamophobia: A Challenge for All of Us*. London: Runnymede Trust.

Sachs, J. (2000) *The Economist*, June 24, pp. 99–101.

Sakamoto, Y. (1974) *Global Transformation*. Tokyo: UNU.

Simai, M. (1981) *Interdependence and Conflicts in the World Economy*. Rockville, Maryland: Sijthoff and Noordhoff.

Simai, M. (1994) *The Future of Global Governance. Managing Risk and Change in the International System*. Washington DC: USIP Press.

Simai, M. (1996) *International Business Policy*. Budapest: Institute for World Economics of the Hungarian Academy of Sciences.

Simai, M. (ed.) (1999) *The Democratic Process and the Market*. Tokyo: UNU Press.

Smith, M. (2000) "India's Chance to Lead the World". *For a Change*, Vol. 13, No. 3, June/July.

Stavenhagen, R. (1986) *Problems and Prospects of Multi-Ethnic States*. Tokyo: United Nations University.

Stigler, S. M. (2000) *Statistics on the Table: The History of Statistical Concepts and Methods*. Cambridge, Mass.: Harvard University Press.

Thurow, L. C. (1996) *The Future of Capitalism*. London: Nicholas Brealey Publishing.

UN (1954) *Report on International Definition and Measurement of Standards and Levels of Living*. New York: United Nations.

UN (1992) Bontros Bontros-Ghali: An *Agenda for Peace: Preventive Diplomacy, Peace Making and Peace Keeping*. New York: United Nations, 1992.

UN (1995) *The Copenhagen Declaration*. New York: United Nations.

UN (1999a, 1999b and 2000c) *World Population Prospects: The 1998 Revision*, Vols I–III. New York: United Nations.

UN (2000a) *UN World Economic and Social Survey 2000*. New York: United Nations.

UN (2000b), *We The People. The Report of the Secretary General to the Millennium Assembly*. New York: UN.

UN (2000d) *The Demographic Yearbook 2000*. New York: United Nations.

UN (2000e) "World Summit for Social Development: Achieving Social Development for All in a Globalizing World". A/AC.253/L.5. New York: United Nations.

UN (2000f) Document A/AC.253/L.5. New York: United Nations.

UNCTAD (1999a) *Trade and Development Report, 1999*. Geneva: Unctad.

UNCTAD (1999b) *World Investment Report, 1999*. Geneva: Unctad.

UNDP (1991–2000) *UNDP Human Development Report*, annual volumes. New York: Oxford University Press.

UNDP (1997b) *Governance and Sustainable Development*. Policy paper. New York: UNDP.

UNDPI (1992) *The Statement of the Secretary-General of the United Nations at the Security Council Summit Meeting*. New York: United Nations Department of Public Information, January 31.

UNDPI (2000) UN Department of Public Information 2000. DPI/2117. New York.

UNICEF (1999a) *After the Fall. The Human Impacts of Ten Years of Transition*. Florence: Unicef Innocenti Research Centre, November.

UNICEF (1999b) *The Progress of Nations*. New York: Unicef.

UNICEF (2000) *The State of the World's Children 2000*. New York: Unicef.

UNPF (2000) *The State of World Population*. New York 1998: United Nations Population Fund.

UNRISD (1995), *States of Disarray*. Geneva: UNRISD.

US Department of State (1975) *A New National Partnership*. News release, January 24, Washington D. C.: US Department of State.

USGPO (1976) *Science, Technology and Diplomacy in the Age of Interdependence*. Washington D. C.: USGPO.

USGPO (2000) *Economic Report of the President, 2000. Council of Economic Advisers*. Washington D. C.: USGPO.

Walker, M. (1995) "Clinton Decides to Woo Black Workers". *Guardian Weekly*, March 5, p. 6.

Wallerstein, I. (1999) The end of the world as we know it. Minneapolis: University of Minnesota Press.

WCED (1987) *Our Common Future*. Report of the World Commission on Environment and Development (Brundtland Report). Oxford: Oxford University Press.

WHO (1988) The World Health Report. Geneva.

Wider (1989) *World Economic Summits: The Role of Representative Groups in the Governance of the World Economy*. Wider Study Group Series, No. 4. Helsinki: UNU/Wider.

Wider (1994) *Research for Development. The First Ten Years of UNU/Wider*. Helsinki: UNU/Wider.

Wiedner, H. (1991) *The Capability of the Capitalist State to "Solve" Environmental Problems*. Paper presented at the 15th World Congress of the International Political Science Association, Buenos Aires.

World Bank (1990) *1990 World Development Report*. Washington D. C.: The World Bank.